Contents

Hard Disk Recording for Musicians

by David Miles Huber

A practical guide to computer-based sound, music, and multimedia production. In-depth and easy-to-understand information on computer-based synchronization technologies, hardware and software systems, digital signal processing techniques, multimedia applications, and much more.

Hereward College

LEARNING RESOURCES
CENTRE

Amsco Publications
New York • London • Paris • New York

Reggie, (Dave's alter ego's) motto.......

To hell with rules... Let's make Music!

Cover photograph by Comstock, Inc.

Order No. AM 92228
US International Standard Book Number: 0.8256.1433.3
UK International Standard Book Number: 0.7119.4353.2

Exclusive Distributors:
Music Sales Corporation
257 Park Avenue South, New York, NY 10010 USA
Music Sales Limited
8/9 Frith Street, London W1V 5TZ England
Music Sales Pty. Limited
120 Rothschild Street, Rosebery, Sydney, NSW 2018, Australia

Printed in the United States of America by
Vicks Lithograph and Printing Corporation

Acknowledgments

I would like to thank the following individuals and companies who assisted in the preparation of this book by providing photographs, technical information, and much appreciated assistance: Steve L. Royea, Vancouver Recording Studios; David M. Hines, Trigger Recording; Bruce F. Hamerslough, Walt Wagner, Walt Wagner Productions; Ray Reynold Hillquist; Garth Heddon, Audio Images-Seattle; Dana S. Byrd, Hybrid Arts, Inc.; Mark Calice, Otari Corporation; R. William Wanamaker, Gotham Audio Corporation; Erika Lopez, Audient Marketing Services (JLCooper Electronics); William E. Amos, nVision, Inc.; Margaret Sekelsky, Solid State Logic, Inc.; David Roudebush, AKG Acoustics, Inc.; Kym McQouwn, WangDAT; Suz Howells and Paul Lego, Digidesign Inc.; Charles Conte, Siemens Audio Inc.; and David Crowell, Hyperception.

Likewise, the following people and companies have my grateful appreciation: Paul Trimble, Lester Audio Laboratories; David Kaplowitz, Opcode Systems, Inc.; Larry Daley, Radar Electric Co., Inc.; Marc C. Vernon, Tripp Lite; Nicole Taggert, Apple Computer, Inc.; Valentine Michael Cortez, Creative Labs, Inc.; Diane W. Scott, Mass Microsystems; David Goldberg and Laura Delia, Korg USA Inc.; Margaret Sekelsky, Solid State Logic Inc., Daniel Rose, Mark of the Unicorn; David Ellis, Rogers & Associates; Rick Griencewic, Gateway 2000; Sandra Hale, Studer ReVox America, Inc.; Suz Howells, Grey Matter Resonse; Bill Snow, E-Mu Systems, Inc.; N. Tokutake, Denon America, Inc.; David Kaplowitz, Opcode Systems, Inc.; Scott Blum, Pinnacle Micro; Mark Doenges, Spectral Synthesis; Deborah Bryce, Otari Corporation; and Ron Koliha, Mackie Designs Inc.

Trademark Acknowledgments

Chapter 1

Introduction to Random Access Technology

I remember vividly, as a teenager, sitting in my bedroom back in Indiana in front of my pride and joy, a 7-inch quarter-track reel-to reel stereo recorder (this was before cassettes were anything but a toy), and thinking to myself, "One of these days the reel is going to go by the wayside, and this machine will be a dinosaur."

After twenty years, this premonition is coming true. Am I sad? Nope! I'm excited about the advent of digital audio and MIDI production. The primary motivator that has ushered in this new era in music technology is, of course, the personal computer.

During the 1990s, the technologies of musical performance, digital audio, and the personal computer have continued to merge into a medium that's able to record, manipulate, and reproduce digital audio. By placing audio data into some form of digital memory, all or parts of a signal or audio program can be accessed and manipulated in any order and at any time. In other words, audio or performance-related data can be accessed, copied, moved, edited, and replaced in much the same way that a writer can manipulate words and graphics on a word processor.

To me, random access audio has opened up a whole new world of sonic possibilities. This technology makes it possible to edit, resynthesize, and organize short samples of sound and then transmit these sounds to devices so that they can be musically played in a performance setting.

It's also possible to capture performances of practically any length into computer memory, so that they can be played along with other sampled or synthesized sounds in a song (hey, wanna lay down a sax solo now?). Even the final recorded mix can be placed into computer memory, where it can be edited, faded, and processed in any number of ways . . . all in the digital domain.

Before we look at how this new technology is being applied in almost every facet of audio production, let's take a brief excursion into the past to see how the audio industry has evolved into its present state.

A Brief History

During the 1920s and early 1930s, the newly emerging music industry was truly ripe with potential. At that time, an artist would sing or play into a "sound horn" that was acoustically coupled to a needle. The needle would etch the recorded performance directly onto a lacquer disc. After the process of record pressing had been invented, these performances could be duplicated and distributed. The buyer could place the record on his or her gramophone and dance the night away.

By the late 1930s, tube amplifiers had become available to professionals and consumers alike. This development brought the acoustic recording era to a close and ushered in the age of electrical recording and reproduction. At last, the recording "engineer" was able to electrically record a performance directly onto a lacquer disc, with the aid of an electrically driven stylus. Since microphones were used instead of the insensitive acoustic horns, the engineer could even mix a few microphones together, achieving a sound balance and recorded clarity heretofore unheard of.

The year 1947 heralded the end of the "all in one take" era. The reason was the introduction of magnetic tape. It was now possible to alter program material after it had been recorded. This breakthrough was followed more than a decade later with the introduction of multitrack recording technology. During the 1960s and 1970s, the age of rock 'n' roll brought about advances in recording technology that gave music production an unprecedented amount of flexibility.

Over the course of the 1980s, another technological development introduced the next new era in audio production. This leap forward was, of course, the advent of digital audio. Its impressive capabilities, including wide dynamic range, practically noiseless reproduction, and cloned copies identical to the original, sent chills down our technological backs sending many a precious record collection the way of the Model T in favor of the digital compact disc.

Although digital audio is responsible for advances in recorded quality, its chief contribution lies elsewhere. From a design and production standpoint, a more important aspect of digital audio is the fact that it speaks the binary language of on (1) and off (0). This fact brings up two fundamental points that have helped to shape the production industry as it enters the 21st century:

- Many digital audio systems can be interfaced with, and speak the same language as, the personal computer.

- Digital audio can be integrated into devices that are random access in nature.

What Is Random Access Technology?

To understand hard disk recording and computer-based audio technology, let's take a short journey into an imaginary past. In this past, pretend that an event has just occurred that will affect the way our brains store information. The course of human evolution will forever be changed. From now on, our brains will store all our personal experiences as a series of consecutive events (one following the other). The only way that we can retrieve an event will be to search each and every memory until we find the particular one we want.

If this scenario were true, it might take hours or even days for us to search our brains just to remember our partner's name or a phone number that had been memorized two days ago or even an hour ago. Scary thought, huh? No doubt, such a retrieval system would soon have us swinging from trees. This kind of retrieval system is an example of linear-access memory (Fig. 1.1) because each event can be stored or retrieved only in a linear fashion.

Fortunately, the human brain functions very differently on a day-to-day basis. For the most part, all of our senses and our memories of past experiences are directly available to our conscious memory on demand. For example, if I were to ask you for your phone number, your favorite color, or least-favorite food, you'd probably be able to answer without much delay. It's a simple matter of accessing the information, processing it, and spitting it out.

This method of information access is known as random-access memory (Fig. 1.2). That is, all the information stored in your conscious memory can be accessed with a reasonable degree of speed, without regard to the chronological order in which it was originally stored (within human limits, of course).

Fig. 1.1: Example of a brain that uses linear-access memory.

Rainbow Crystal

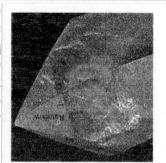

A gentle crystal that gives out light and protection to everyone. Warding off evil and promoting goodness in everything, they are able to help us relax and dream. Some think that they have the ability to make our dreams come true. Refraction in the crystal causes the rainbow to appear, but they defy scientific analysis, owing to the fact that the rainbows appear and disappear. This is due to temperature and light changes that can occur all the time.

Merlin Crystals

A generator crystal with six evenly spaced sides and six approximately equal faces that center at the tip. The base is usually cut flat when removed from the matrix to enhance the stance. They can be clear to milky with or without inclusions and they occur in other forms like Rose Quartz etc. The size of Merlins range from very small to very large and the energy and flow is not related to the size at all. Used in meditation and healing to direct the energy like a wand. Merlins are a favorite of groups, placed at the center of a circle they can help to direct group consciousness towards a target, such as a sick person or someone in need of support.

Phantom Crystal

Ghosts and inclusions can be white, green, brown, gold and black but other colours do appear from time to time. When present in the Master Crystals it seems to increase the energy. More in tune with the past, due to the evolution of the inclusions, frozen in time.

This type of crystal is also known as Nature's Garden in some parts of the world and The Garden of Eden in other parts. It is thought to promote the love of Nature and Animals in those who come into contact with it. It is a fully fledged member f the Mineral Kingdom and will not allow us to overlook the beauty of both.

Double Terminated

These are crystals which have been fortunate enough to have developed termination's at both ends. They can receive or transmit energy from both ends. They are protective, healing crystals and bring calmness and relaxation. Having the ability to re-energise the Chakras and help with awareness of the spiritual. They are used mainly by healers to direct energy from one person to another.

Now let's bring these examples a little closer to home by applying them directly to audio production. Tape based analog and digital recorders both operate by physically recording audio data onto a continuous band of tape. To play back the audio data, the tape must be transported across a playback head at the same speed at which it was recorded, in a linear-access fashion.

To access a recorded section that's either before or after the present location, you must rewind or fast-forward the tape to a new position and then play the signal (Fig. 1.3). Although this memory media is still serving us well in production worldwide, it places restrictions on the speed and methods by which the recorded information can be accessed and manipulated.

Fig. 1.2: *Example of a brain that uses random-access memory.*

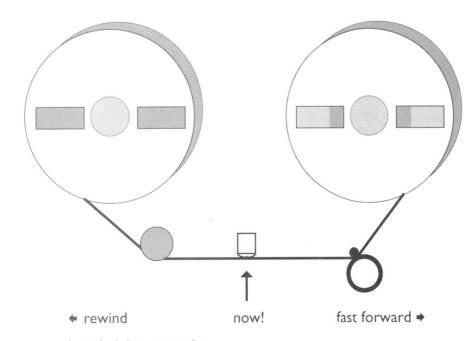

◄ rewind   now!   fast forward ➤

Fig. 1.3: *A tape transport is a good example of a linear-access medium.*

One way around the problem of access is to add extra tracks. A number of simultaneous signals can then be accessed at the same time. However, these tracks must be recorded onto the same physical piece of tape and thus are subject to the same linear restrictions.

Systems using random access technology differ extensively from their linear predecessors. This is due to the fact that audio isn't recorded onto a linear-access medium (such as magnetic tape), but instead exists as blocks of stored data that can be addressed at any time and in any order, with instant or near-instant access data response.

This speed and ease is precisely what the digital medium of random access audio is all about. In such a computer-based environment, you can gain access to audio and related data that are stored within various types of memory media (Fig. 1.4). The advantages of random accessibility can then be designed into a system so that audio data can be retrieved, organized, and reproduced in a way that best suits the task at hand.

The Digital Chameleon

Tackling a production job or any job brings up an interesting bonus that's unique to random access technology. I'm speaking of the medium's inherent ability to change its "form and function" to fit the needs of a particular application. My favorite analogy is to compare a random access device to a chameleon. Just as a chameleon can change its color to match its environment, many computer-based systems can change their form and function to match their particular production environment.

Unlike an analog device that has been designed to serve a single purpose, a computer processor-based system can be reprogrammed in such a way that it can perform a number of individual or simultaneous tasks, depending on what the applications are. For example, an analog compressor for limiting a signal's dynamic range is just that: a compressor, period. On the other hand, at the push of a few buttons a single multifunction digital signal processor can easily be programmed to provide digital compression, delay, chorus, reverb, basic sampling, pitch shifting . . . the list goes on.

To better explain how such a computer-based system might jump through these hoops, let's look at the life of "The Dead Mickeys," a fictitious alternative rock group that's been at the top of the charts for a few months now. This morning (well, the group thinks it's morning), Ray, the lead singer, gets a call from the group's manager saying that a record company wants to hear a demo of the new song they've been working on. And they want it ASAP.

Being under the gun, The Dead Mickeys decide to buy a full-blown computer system capable of producing music in their rehearsal studio. The system is loaded with a four channel hard disk recording system, lots of disk and RAM memory, MIDI (musical instrument digital interface), and sequencing software for controlling all of the obligatory synths, samplers, drum machines, and various other toys.

First on the drummer's list is the task of editing a few samples that she captured onto tape from a jam session a couple of nights ago. The rowdy sounds from the jam session are perfect for the new song's mood. The drummer can then go about

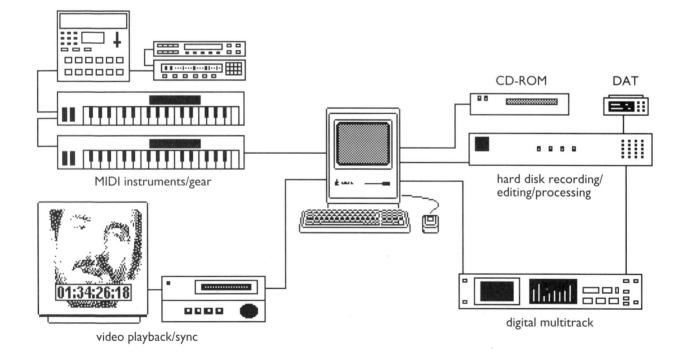

MIDI instruments/gear

CD-ROM DAT

hard disk recording/
editing/processing

video playback/sync

digital multitrack

Fig. 1.4: Instant or near-instant data access times are possible in a random access computer-based environment.

making the edits by transferring segments of the tape onto hard disk. From there, the sampled sounds can be edited, saved to disk for future use, and then transferred to a performance sampler where they can be triggered from a musical keyboard (Fig. 1.5).

Today's technology has made it commonplace for MIDI sequencing programs and interface hardware to be installed into a single computer. Thus, it isn't that difficult for the group to record the basic rhythm and keyboard parts as a set of sequenced MIDI tracks. After all the kinks have been removed from the sequence, the group records the guitar and vocal tracks directly onto the four available hard disk channels (Fig. 1.6).

Once the tracks are finished, the group adds effects processing to the song and mixes the final results onto a digital medium (like DAT). After finishing the mix (which is fully automated under MIDI and direct level control), the lead singer has a new idea. He wants to dump the song back to two tracks of the hard disk recorder so that he can overlay a 20-second segment edited from the original wild jam session onto the beginning of the song (Fig. 1.7).

The hard disk editor is then used to create a fade-in and fade-out (the group gave up using the mixer to do manual fades long ago), and then the brawl samples are "flown in" before the song's intro. It worked! It spiced the song up perfectly for their purposes, and the final results are transferred to tape for shipping to the record company.

Although the scenario just described was fictitious, it does show how in real life a computer system can change from being a device that edits, stores, and transmits sounds to being a sampler, to being an integrated MIDI/hard disk audio system that acts as a random access platform for capturing an artist's creative juices, and finally to being a two-channel hard disk editor for putting together a finished product.

Of course, such a multifaceted system doesn't need to stop here. After finishing the recording, this computerized chameleon in digital clothing could be used to draw graphic ideas for the CD's front cover and then for writing an accompanying cover letter. Quite simply, never before in the history of audio production has such flexibility and power been available to the user at prices that are becoming increasingly affordable.

Fig. 1.5: One example of how audio can be transferred and edited in a random access environment.

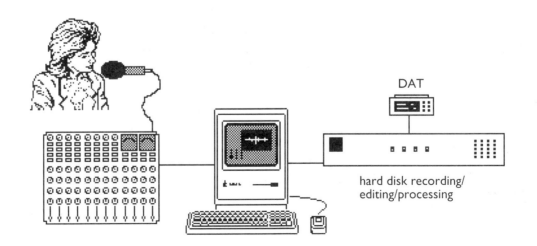

Fig. 1.6 A: "Dead Mickey" recording session

Fig. 1.7: The OmniMix hard disk-based audio-for-video system. (Courtesy of Solid State Logic and The Tape Gallery, London.)

An example of a few of the tasks that can be performed in a computer or microprocessor-based environment include (but are not limited to):

- Sequencing for recording, editing, and reproducing MIDI performance data
- Sequencing triggered event and controller data for the automation of external equipment such as MIDI or digitally controlled mixers, digital effects devices, CD players, and tape machines
- Communicating MIDI system exclusive data for the purpose of transmitting sampled data or configuring sound patches and/or MIDI effects devices
- Receiving and/or transmitting sampled data via a MIDI sample dump format
- Categorizing samples, sounds, and patch data into organized libraries
- Transferring digital audio to and from a disk-based memory medium
- Multichannel production
- Sound editing

The preceding list demonstrates that random access technology has the potential for being a flexible audio medium. And, for the first time in production history, most devices within such a connected system speak the same language digital. This makes it possible for devices to easily communicate with each other without being converted back into analog. This ability brings the realization that a random access system isn't so much a device but an overall concept for accessing digital information in a "global" or system-wide fashion.

Such a system offers many advantages:

- Improved Performance. The speed, reliability, and repeatability displayed by such systems make them a time- and cost effective production tool. An additional strong point of random access systems is their ability to quickly and effectively manipulate digital audio data in a standard computer "cut and paste" environment.
- Improved Quality. Although the digital audio chain isn't perfect, it has distinct advantages and characteristics. For example, a performance might be digitally recorded and reproduced with noise figures that are commonly greater than 90 dB (10 30 dB better than the average analog recording), with none of the sideband noises and hiss commonly associated with analog tape.
- Digital Signal Processing (DSP) Capabilities. Digital processors allow audio data to be directly manipulated through the use of computer-based algorithms (programs that perform complex calculations according to a set of controlled parameters in order to affect the original soundfile data). This use of algorithms makes it possible for the digital

audio data to be numerically "reshaped," changing the characteristics of the original waveform.

- Direct Digital Transfer. It's my own experience, and most other peoples', that digital audio can be copied numerous times without degrading in quality. This characteristic is one of the strongest aspects of a digital system. It means that audio can be copied from one digital format to another, placed into a sound library, or processed without noticeable signal deterioration.
- Systemwide Communication. With the aid of hardware interface systems, most computer-based production systems can speak directly to, and provide links between, various connected subsystems. Data links within the system can be used to distribute digital audio, MIDI data, synchronization data (such as SMPTE and MIDI time code), and control-related data.
- Automation. In a digital, computer-based environment, it's often a simple matter to automate program-, soundfile-, DSP-, and effects-related parameters. Such a capability can greatly simplify the process of setting up a system because these automation functions can be saved to, or recalled from, disk.
- Flexibility. When speaking of random access performance, flexibility is a characteristic that comes to mind because such systems are often capable of performing a wide range of tasks. This also implies that such systems can be designed to operate in a number of ways and environments, according to the user's creative and production needs.

Music Production

To the artist, producer, and engineer in many of us, random access technology easily translates into increased speed, power, and signal-processing capabilities. It allows digital hardware and software systems to be brought together under computer control for performing a wide range of production-related functions.

Hard disk-based audio systems are gaining wide acceptance within today's professional and project-oriented music studio facilities (Fig. 1.8). Through the use of MIDI, electronic instruments are able to communicate performance- and control-related data. The data can thus be transmitted, received, and recorded in a random access nature. MIDI sequencers and sequencing programs allow entire musical productions to be composed and played with complete automation and programming capabilities.

In addition to music-related information, MIDI can transmit device-specific data through the use of system exclusive messages. This digital protocol can be used to transfer data between electronic

Fig. 1.8: Producer, engineer, songwriter and arranger Gary Henry using a Roland DM-80 hard disk recording system at Hide-Out Studios in Hillside, NJ. A few of his credits include: George Benson, Pheobe Snow and Boyz II Men. (Courtesy of Roland Corporation US, Pro Audio Division.)

instruments, MIDI-capable effects devices, and a personal computer. Such data could include sample-related data, patch data (system settings relating to the sounds generated by an electronic instrument), and program change data.

For example, a set of system exclusive messages could be used to transmit sampled audio data from a computer into a sampler or, alternatively, these messages could be used for receiving, transmitting, and/or editing patch data.

Time-related data can also be transmitted through MIDI data lines, using the MIDI-time code (MTC) standard. Just as SMPTE time code is used to synchronize multiple transports within professional audio or audio-for-video production, MTC can be used to synchronize ATRs (audio tape recorders), VTRs (video tape recorders), triggered SFX (sound effects), and digital audio workstations within a MIDI digital production environment.

The power that MIDI and sequencing technology bring to music synthesis can be heightened through the use of sampling technology. Keyboard-based samplers combine the expression of polyphonic music production with the speed and expanded capabilities of digital audio. Once loaded with sampled sounds, these flexible devices can be used to add to a composition such digitally recorded sounds as drums, horn shots, piano sounds, James Brown screams, and Pee-Wee Herman chuckles.

The ability to receive and transmit samples from a user created, hard-disk based samplefile library is greatly expanded through the addition of a software program known as a sample editor. Such programs use available sample dump standards for transmitting samples to any MIDI-capable sample playback device.

After a sample is loaded into a sample edit program, these samples can be processed by using such standard edit functions as cut, copy, paste, adjust volume, draw wave, draw envelope, invert, reverse, stretch, and squeeze.

The edited sample can be copied to a hard disk library or routed to any sampler in the system. In conjunction with sample editors, programs can be used to analyze and resynthesize a sample, giving it a different waveshape and timbral characteristic.

Hard disk recording capabilities can be added to this list. Magnetic and optical recording technologies make it possible for longer samplefiles to be an integral part of random access music production. A hard disk recorder makes use of a dedicated processing system and/or personal computer, RAM and hard disk memory, and various digital audio and synchronization signal ports.

Extensive soundfile editing capabilities are thus available to the user, including cut, copy, and paste-style editing, along with features such as reverse, invert, fade-in/fade-out, crossfade, looping, adjust gain, and envelope drawing.

Digital signal processing (DSP) functions offer features such as digital equalization, time compression/expansion, digital sample mixing, and digital crossfading.

Almost every random access system offers non-destructive editing capabilities. This feature lets the user access any region of a data file, arrange these defined regions into a playlist, and output the regions sequentially and/or at a specified time-code address. This process is carried out without altering the soundfile data that was originally recorded onto hard or optical disk.

When all of these powerful features are combined with the capability of recording longer samplefiles (which are limited only by the memory capacity of a hard disk and your imagination), the result is an audio tool that offers extensive edit and processing capabilities in a package that is often both fast and cost effective.

Although two-channel hard disk systems are currently available, most hard disk recording systems and digital audio workstations are capable of sustaining four discrete channels of audio information to and from a single hard disk or optical disk drive. This ability is the result of the technological increase in speed and efficiency that has occurred on both the processing and the disk access fronts.

Besides four-channel hard disk systems, multi-channel systems are available, which can provide eight, sixteen, or more channels. They differ from two- and four-channel systems, for they typically make use of multiple hard disk systems that are synchronized to combine the power of random access editing with the increased mixing and signal-processing capabilities of multichannel sound.

Audio-for-Video Post-production

As a production medium, random access audio is almost tailor made for the audio-for-video market. Within the fast paced field of video post-production, the two most important words are speed and flexibility. These words are practically textbook definitions of a well-designed random access system.

When you are dealing with such media as video and film, it's important that the music be precisely matched to the picture in order to get the most impact out of a scene. Random access systems are ideally suited to this task. Original or prerecorded music can be transferred to hard disk, edited, and played back with frame-accurate synchronization.

Should the music be placed too early or too late within a cue, each channel can be independently "slipped" with regard to time. This is done by entering a desired time-code offset or trigger address, thereby nudging the sound either forward or backward to correct any discrepancies in time.

In addition to matching music to video or film, random access can bring speed and flexibility to sound effects (SFX), Foley (the replacement of on-screen effects, such as shattered glass, pig squeals, etc.), and dialogue replacement. One of the first phases of SFX and Foley is the process of searching for and finding the right sound to match to a scene. This process, known as spotting, is very fast and relatively painless when using a disk-based system such as a digital audio workstation.

Since the effects can be cataloged on either hard or optical disk or CD, the user need only request a category and home in on the target. For example, let's call up a category list called "animal sounds" and select it. There are lots of sounds, but at last we see it . . . pig squeal. We select it with the cursor, call it up, and play it. SCREEEEE!

Yes, it can be that easy. If you don't see what you want, you could search through a CD SFX library or create your own screeches and copy them to a personal effects library. Once found, the effect(s) can be placed into current memory or hard disk and triggered at the appropriate time-code address.

Broadcast Production

Aside from the obvious advantages offered by random access audio for the production of jingle and TV/radio spots, this technology has advantages for use in both off- and on-the-air broadcast production. More and more, radio stations are making use of the compact disc medium for airplay. Random access systems are being applied to this technology through the use of computer-based hardware/software systems. These systems allow CDs to be entered into a database by music type, artist, and title. With such an automation system, the user can create a playlist that can be used to automate the station.

Hard disk and optical recording systems can also be integrated into on-the-air production in the form of a digital cartridge (cart) machine. The system can be easily programmed to trigger broadcast spots, public announcements, etc., at a precise time cue and/or in a specific playlist order.

Multimedia Desktop Computer Publishing

Although professional music and broadcast production have been profoundly affected by random access technology, it's highly possible that one of its strongest presences will be felt in the multimedia computer publishing markets.

What is multimedia and why is it so special? Well, in a nutshell, this environment can be thought of as a conduit for simultaneously passing text, graphics, MIDI, digital audio, and even full or limited motion video to any program that can respond to these media.

Although the multimedia industry is still in its infancy, this powerful environment has already created a high-growth technology that is transforming the way we communicate, as well as entertained and educated. Such an environment

and its related hardware will almost assuredly become as familiar to us in the future as the TV, the PC, and the phone are now.

Besides being able to simultaneously offer graphics, digital audio, MIDI, text, and other media, another strong benefit of multimedia is its ability to interact with the user. For example, assume that you have just bought a computer system that is multimedia compatible (complete with CD-ROM, sound generators, MIDI interface, and digital audio playback capabilities). One of the CD-ROM discs that comes with the system is an encyclopedia of animals for kids, so you slip it in and boot it up.

Once the disc's loading sequence has finished, you begin hearing a MIDI sequence of the main page theme song. At the same time, a brief listing of the manufacturer's credits scrolls across the screen. Then you see a list of animal species from which you can select. Using your mouse or other type of cursor movement system, you select "reptiles" and then "turtles."

You narrow your selection to "endangered turtles." The system's sound generators begin outputting a short little MIDI music file as you see pictures of, and read text about, the types that are on the endangered list. A prompt asks if you'd like to hear some turtle sounds. You say yes, and the system begins outputting samples of various turtles over the speakers or headphones. You are surprised that a rare French species sounds just like a kitten meowing.

This scenario is just one example of thousands showing how multimedia could have a direct impact on education, business, or plain ol' fun.

On a Personal Note

From the preceding sections, it should be clear that hard disk-based recording is being accepted into almost every audio production and communications environment. This is due to its ability to edit, manipulate, categorize, and reproduce audio in an environment that offers fast access times, repeatability, and often, full systems automation.

As these systems continue to grow, both in power and in cost-effectiveness, this "digital chameleon" will continue to expand the horizons of our technological and creative expression in the home and in the studio. Computer-based audio production has ushered in an era that provides us with new and powerful tools that can be combined with existing technologies while offering increased power, flexibility, and automation.

I'd like to close this chapter (and begin the book) by offering a slightly off-the-wall Confusionist proverb:

> Music and its emotion doesn't exist in chips but can be found only in the expression and creativity of the human mind.

> Dive off the deep end and have fun!

Chapter 2
The Basics of Digital Audio

It's always been my belief that understanding how something works arms you with the knowledge of how best to use it. A more radical way of stating this idea is: If you want to break the rules of the game, you have to first know what those rules are.

Let me give you an example based on personal experience. When I first encountered digital audio, I saw it as this mysterious thing that just happened. The ability to record soundfile data to hard disk was almost magical. After years of study and hands-on work, that magic gave way to understanding. "Oh, I get it! You mean that's all there is to it?"

Often, this understanding produced sheer amazement at the functional hoops that these systems could jump through, given proper design and programming. This chapter is expressly dedicated to shedding light upon two of the most important building blocks to be found in random-access audio production: digital audio and MIDI.

Some Basics of Binary Data

Over the millennia of human existence, the development of language has enabled humans to convey information from one person to another or to store written accounts for future reference. The English language, for example, is based on 26 letters that are grouped together in special orders to create words, which carry a culturally agreed-upon significance. Individual words can then be joined into sentences to convey greater detail.

The language of common mathematics, on the other hand, has its foundation firmly rooted in base 10. This is due to the fact that we have ten fingers and can grasp the concept of multiples of ten with relative ease. A computer, of course, doesn't have ten fingers, nor does it directly understand the basic concepts of the alphabet.

However, these and other forms of information can be translated into a language that is easily used by computer-based systems the digital base-2 language of binary data.

In its simplest form, binary data exists as two possible electrical states: on or off, signal or no signal. In essence, instead of having 26 possible letters from which to choose, the computer is limited to only two. However, by grouping together these individual on/off states (known as bits), it is possible to create a digital word, which to the computer (and other computers that can speak the same operating language) carries a significance that is defined by a digital standard. By grouping these words together into a file or a data stream, meaning can be conveyed in the form of a computer program, text, graphics, and video or digital audio information.

Although a computer speaks its own unique language and processes information in such a way as to perform a specific task, it is common for computers to translate the final results into a form that can be understood by those notoriously nonbinary beings us. Binary data is often translated into final results that are either graphical, alphabetical, or numerical in nature.

For example, in ASCII (American Standard Code for Information Interchange), the following 8-bit "words" are equal to the letters B, A, and T:

[0100 0010] [0100 0001] [0101 0100]

In hexadecimal notation (a form of programming shorthand), these letters are equal to:

[42][41][54]

However, to humans, these grouped letters equal either a standard piece of baseball equipment or a much-maligned flying mammal.

In addition to graphics and text, other forms of communication can be translated into binary, stored to a computer, manipulated, and converted back into their original form. Two important examples are audio data and motion video data. This book deals primarily with audio data or, more specifically, with the production of computer-based digital audio.

Fundamentals of Audio Signals

Sound, whether naturally occurring or electronically generated, can be broken down into two fundamental components:

- Amplitude
- Frequency

The distance above or below the centerline of a waveform, as shown in Fig. 2.1A, represents the amplitude level of a signal. The greater the distance or amplitude displacement from the centerline, the more intense the pressure variation, electrical signal, or physical displacement within a medium, and of course the louder the sound.

The rate at which an acoustic generator, electrical signal, or vibrating mass will repeat a cycle of positive and negative amplitude is known as the frequency of that signal (Fig. 2.1B). One completed excursion of a wave, plotted over the 360Ø axis of a circle, is known as a cycle. The number of cycles occurring over the period of 1 second is measured in hertz (Hz).

Any sound, no matter how complex, can be broken down into these two components. In fact, a complex sound can be described as the combined sum of a number of simple waveforms (known as sine waves), each of which has its own individual amplitude and frequency characteristics.

Fundamentals of Digital Audio

The role of a properly designed digital audio system is to accurately translate a continuous flow of analog information into a corresponding stream of discrete digital words (sometimes referred to as a bitstream). The value of each word is equal to the instantaneous level of an analog signal at the time of sampling. When taken at short intervals, the successive sampling of an analog signal can encode this data into a bitstream that is an accurate digital representation of the original analog signal.

As you have seen, sound can be broken down into two main characteristics: amplitude, which provides the overall level component, and frequency, which provides the component of time. Similarly, digital audio can be broken down into two components:

- Quantization (level)
- Sampling (time)

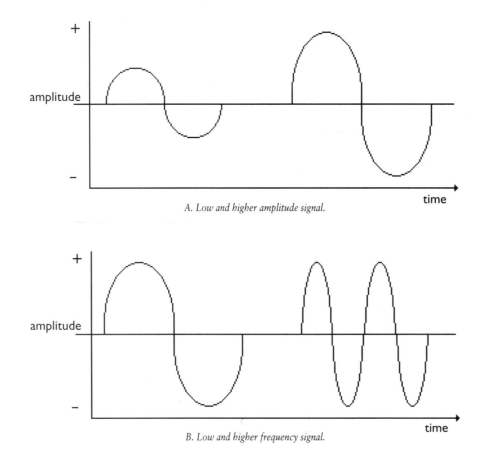

A. Low and higher amplitude signal.

B. Low and higher frequency signal.

Fig. 2.1: Naturally occurring or electronically generated sound can be broken down into two fundamental components: amplitude and frequency.

Quantization

Quantization represents the amplitude component of the digital sampling process. It is the technique of incrementing a continuous analog event into a discrete set of BInary digiTS, or bits, for storage or manipulation. In this process, the amplitude of the incoming analog signal is broken down into a series of discrete voltage steps. Each step is assigned a binary word that digitally encodes the signal level with as much accuracy as can be permitted by word length and system design.

At present, binary word lengths for game and voice applications are usually 8 bits (for example, 10101101) and 12 bits (111010010110). Professional audio makes use of a 16-bit word length, with a few systems using 10- or 20-bit resolution.

Digital signal processors that are capable of performing tasks such as reverb, time/level compression, and sample rate conversion will commonly operate using an internal 24- and 32-bit processing structure. These larger word lengths provide greater headroom, which allows for greater error margins.

The number of discrete voltage steps that are possible with digital words of 8-, 16-, and 20-bit lengths are as follows:

8-bit word	= 256 steps
16-bit word	= 65,536 steps
20-bit word	= 1,048,576 steps

From the preceding list, you can conclude that greater word lengths translate directly into increased resolution. This is partly due to the greater number of finite steps that can be encoded into larger digital word lengths.

Signal-to-Error Ratio

Although an analog signal is continuous in nature, the process of quantizing a signal into an equivalent digital word is not. Because the number of steps that can be encoded within a digital word of n bits is limited, this representative number can be only a close approximation of the original analog signal.

This degree of approximation is known as the signal-to-error ratio (S/E). Signal-to-error is closely akin, though not identical to, the signal-to-noise of an analog system. It represents the degree of accuracy in which an audio signal is encoded, due to the effects of stepped quantization. From the list in the preceding section, you can see that larger word lengths will increase the number of possible stepped voltage intervals, allowing a signal to be more accurately encoded.

Although quantization error can't be eliminated, it can be reduced to more than acceptable levels through the use of 16-bit, or greater, word lengths. With a properly designed system, the signal-to-error ratio for a signal coded with n bits is given by:

$$S/E = 6n + 1.8 \text{ (dB)}$$

For a 16-bit system, this would yield a noise figure of 97.8 decibels (dB).

Dither

Ironically, through the addition of small amounts of analog white noise, it's possible to reduce signal distortion and improve the signal-to-error figure of a digital system. This added noise (known as dither) allows signals that are lower in level than the least significant bit to be encoded (and thus heard) within a digital audio signal.

Adding dither also minimizes distortion caused by quantization. Although dithering will introduce a small amount of noise into the signal path, the noise is far preferable to the odd-harmonic (square wave) signal distortion that would otherwise occur.

Sampling

The recording of sound by means of analog technology implies the recording, storage, and reproduction of changes in signal level that are continuous in nature (Fig. 2.2). Digital technology does not operate in such a continuous manner. Instead, it takes periodic samples of a changing audio waveform and transforms these sampled signal levels into a representative set of stepped binary data.

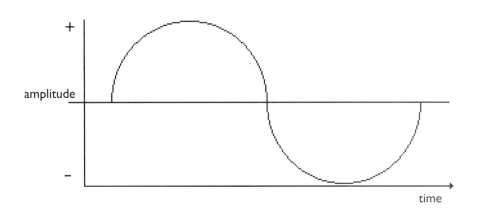

Fig. 2.2: An analog signal is continuous in nature.

In a digital audio system, the sampling rate is defined as the number of samples that are taken of an analog signal in a second's time. Its reciprocal, sampling time, is the time taken between each sample period. For example, a sample rate of 44.1 kHz (44,100 samples per second) corresponds to a sample period of 1/44,100 of a second. Since sampling is tied directly to the component of time, the sampling rate of a system will determine a system's upper frequency limits, with higher sampling rates yielding a greater frequency range.

During the sampling process (Fig. 2.3), an incoming analog signal is sampled at discrete time intervals (determined by the sample rate). At each interval, this analog signal is momentarily "held" for observation and thus represents a specific, measurable voltage level.

A mathematical conversion process is then used to generate a digital series of numbers that represents this signal level at the precise instant of sampling. Once this conversion has been made, it can be digitally stored or processed, and the system readies itself for the next sample period and repeats the process.

The Nyquist Theorem

By placing a low-pass filter before the sampling circuitry of an analog-to-digital (A/D) converter, it is possible to sample an analog signal so that the original waveform will be reproduced without any appreciable signal error.

According to the Nyquist theorem, this lossless process can be achieved by sampling a signal at a rate that is at least twice as high as the highest frequency that is to be recorded (sample rate ≥ the highest frequency). Thus, an audio signal with a bandwidth of 20 kHz would require a sampling rate of at least 40,000 samples/second. It is very important that no audio signal greater than the Nyquist limit enter into the digitizing process.

Aliasing

Should frequencies that are greater than the Nyquist limit (greater than one-half the sample rate) be introduced into the digitization process, an unwanted condition known as aliasing (Fig. 2.4) will occur. Aliasing happens when frequencies above the Nyquist limit are introduced into the

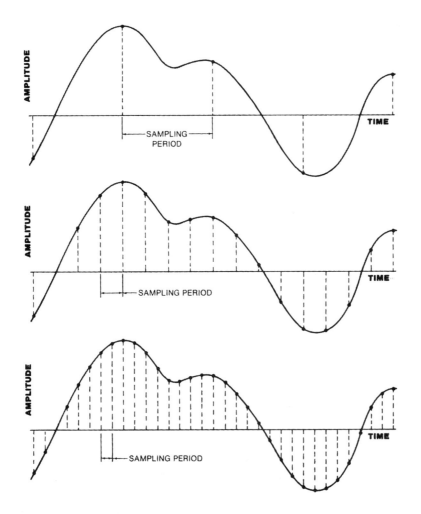

Fig. 2.3: Discrete time sampling.

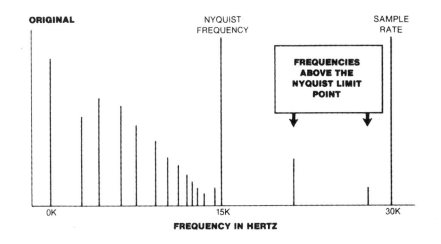

A. Sampled frequencies above the Nyquist half-sample frequency limit.

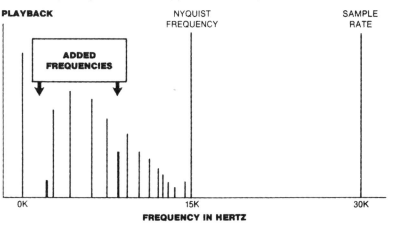

B. False alias frequencies are introduced into the audio band.

Fig. 2.4: Alias frequencies introduced into the digital audio chain.

digital path and are encoded as erroneous or false frequencies.

In practice, aliasing is not a serious problem since its effects are eliminated by a low-pass filter. This filter precedes the analog-to-digital conversion process and acts to remove frequencies above the Nyquist half-sampling frequency limit.

Such a filter requires the use of a gradual high-frequency roll-off (Fig. 2.5). An immediate or "brickwall" filter would cause severe signal distortion and phase shifts. In taking this roll-off into account, a sampling rate of higher than twice the highest frequency is often chosen to include a range of frequencies that are above the Nyquist point. For example, a system with a bandwidth reaching up to 20 kHz is often sampled at a rate of 44.1K or 48K samples/second.

Oversampling

Introducing a sharp low-pass filter into a circuit

can cause side effects. One method of reducing possible side effects, while also improving the noise characteristics of an A/D converter, is to make use of modern oversampling techniques. Basically, oversampling is a digital signal-processing function that raises the sample rate of a digitally encoded signal. Consumer and professional 16-bit converters commonly employ up to 8- and 12-times oversampling circuitry, meaning that the rates are multiplied by these factors. For example, such techniques would raise the effective sample rate of a 44.1-kHz signal to 352.8 kHz and 529.2 kHz, respectively.

By raising the effective sample rate to such a high frequency, the frequency bandwidth is raised enough that a simple single-order filter can be used to limit frequencies at the higher Nyquist limit. In addition, by altering the signal's noise characteristics, it's possible to shift much of the overall bandwidth noise out of the range of human hearing, thereby reducing its audible effects.

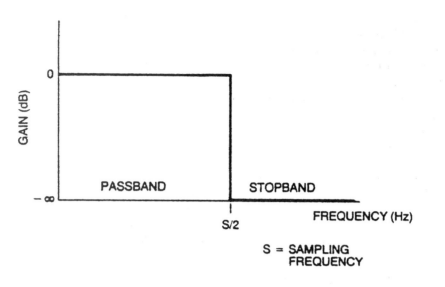

Fig. 2.5: A stop band or low-pass filter is used to keep frequencies above the Nyquist frequency limit from being sampled.

The Digital Recording/Reproduction Process

The following sections provide a basic introduction to the various stages that are encountered in the process of converting analog to digital and back again.

The Recording Process

The digital recording or sampling chain (Fig. 2.6) is made up of these elements:

- Low-pass filter
- Sample and hold (S/H) circuit
- Analog-to-digital (A/D) converter
- Signal coding

At the input of a digital sampling system, the analog signal's bandwidth (range of included frequencies) must be limited by a roll-off filter in order to avoid passing frequencies above half the sample-rate frequency. This is accomplished through the use of a sharp low-pass filter or through oversampling techniques.

Following the low-pass filter, a sample and hold (S/H) circuit is used to temporarily hold the analog voltage level for the duration of a single sample period. This important process allows the analog-to-digital converter enough time to generate a digital word that corresponds to the sampled voltage. The circuit's timing information, which is determined by the sample-rate frequency, is generated by an internal or external crystal reference clock.

It is during this sample period that the analog-to-digital (A/D) conversion process begins. A/D conversion is the most critical component of the digitization process. It's here that the DC voltage level (which was frozen at the onset of the sample and hold process) must be translated into an equivalent binary word.

One popular method for translating an analog signal into an equivalent digital word is through the use of a successive approximation register (SAR). This system operates by comparing the sample's voltage with a series of reference signal levels. In essence, the system performs a series of tests upon the signal that is not unlike the game 20 questions although this game could be called n-bit questions.

For example, during a sample period, an 8-bit register with a full scale of 5 volts would first detect if the signal were greater or less than 2.5 volts (one-half of full scale). If so, the register would set the most significant bit (MSB) as a logical 1 and continue on to see if it were greater than 3.75 volts. If not, it would register the next bit as a logical 0 and would move on to determine the next resolution value.

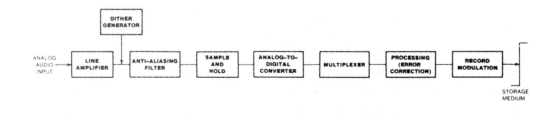

Fig. 2.6: The digital recording chain.

This process would then continue n-bit number of times, until the final least-significant bit value had been determined. The resulting values would be grouped into a single digital word that would be equal to the most accurate encoded representation of the sample value that was possible by a system of n-bit length.

It seems an amazing feat of technology, but a 16-bit system that is sampling at a rate of 48 kHz must sample and hold a signal and then perform 16 successive approximations, all within a period of less than 1/48,000 of a second.

Signal Coding

Once the signal has been converted into digital form, the data must be conditioned for further processing and storage. This process includes the use of

- Data coding

- Error correction

- Data modulation

In order for a digital word to be processed properly by a digital audio system, the individual bits (which exist in parallel form at the output of the converter) must first be encoded into a single stream of information (known as serial data). This allows the data to be consecutively transmitted over a single line and then stored within a recording medium.

Following this, data coding is performed. Such coding makes it easier for a system to identify the data and bit structure of a digital audio bitstream. For example, frame synchronization is used to group digital words into blocks that are easily recognizable by the system. This form of processing allows a system to recognize words within a bitstream, in much the same way that we use a space to separate words so that we can read them more easily.

In addition to identifying digital words through the use of synchronization, data coding can also include other status information, such as absolute time, time code, sample rate, copy-protect flags, etc.

From the number of calculations that must be performed and conveyed by a digital audio system, it can be imagined that the density of this data is extremely high. In order to ensure a minimum number of errors during the storage process, error correction is commonly used.

Generally, the data error rate for most hard disks and optical disks is quite low. However, when dealing with mediums such as digital tape recorders, DAT, and CD formats, the signal's quality and integrity would be severely compromised without the use of error correction.

One method of error correction makes use of redundant data in the form of parity bits and check codes. These serve to detect and correct for errors. A second error correction system involves interleaving techniques, whereby data is scattered across the digital bit stream so as to reduce the effects of dropouts (Fig. 2.7).

The concept behind this encoding strategy is to spread data over a wide area so that only a fraction of the encoded word will be affected when a short burst dropout occurs. When reassembled back into its original order, enough data will remain intact so that error correction can then reconstruct and recover the lost data.

When digital audio is stored to tape or disk, the binary digits are not directly stored in their original states of 0 and 1 (pulse/no pulse) because this would be an inefficient means of storing data. Rather, most systems use modulation (a method of encoding digital data as pulses of magnetic energy) in order to most efficiently use a storage medium and increase its data density. In professional audio applications, the most widely accepted form of digital modulation is pulse code modulation (PCM), shown in Fig. 2.8.

Once the preceding processes have been performed, the processed digital audio bitstream is ready to be stored onto a recording medium for later retrieval.

The Reproduction Process

The digital reproduction chain works in a manner that is essentially complementary to the way that a signal is digitally encoded. These processes include:

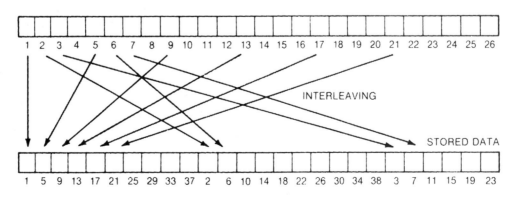

Fig. 2.7: An example of interleaved error correction.

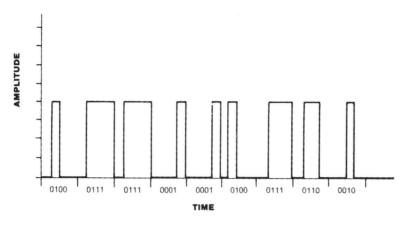

Fig. 2.8: Pulse code modulation.

- Demodulation
- Data processing
- D/A conversion
- Sample/hold
- Output low-pass filtering

When modulated data is recorded to a digital storage medium, some waveform distortion is expected. Therefore, following amplification, a reconditioning process is used to reshape the distorted signals into their original modulated transition states. Once completed, the signal bitstream can then be demodulated into its original binary data state of 1s and 0s.

Following the reconditioning stage, the interleaved data is reassembled into its original PCM form. After that, error correction is performed on the signal to compensate for any errors introduced during the storage process.

Once the appropriate playback processing has been performed, the serial PCM data will be ready for digital-to-analog (D/A) conversion. As with A/D conversion, proper design within the D/A process is an important factor in maintaining the overall quality of a digital audio signal.

This process begins by changing the incoming serial bitstream into parallel form. Once done, it is the converter's job to accept a digital word and generate an analog voltage that is analogous to the voltage level at the original time of sampling.

One common way of accomplishing D/A conversion is through the use of a stepped resistance network (Fig. 2.9). Each bit in a digital word is assigned to a leg in this network, with each step being designed to pass one-half of the voltage level passed by the previous step. The presence or absence of a logical bit at each step will determine how much of the overall reference voltage will be

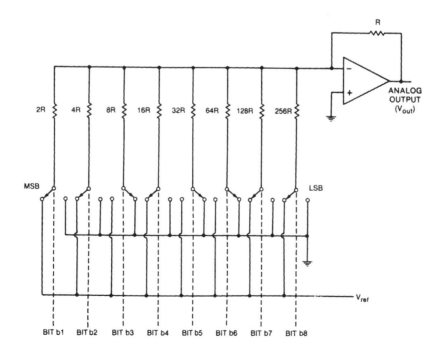

Fig. 2.9: A stepped resistance network accomplishes D/A conversion by assigning each bit to a series of resistors that are scaled by a factor of two.

allowed to pass. The combined outputs of each voltage leg are then summed together during a calculation cycle as a single, discrete voltage level.

To minimize spurious signal glitches while the D/A converters are calculating an analogous voltage signal, an output sample and hold circuit is used. Quite simply, this circuit latches and holds the previous sample's analog level until the converter has had time to calculate the present signal. At the next sample clock time, the hold circuit releases the previous signal level and then latches onto the one that was just calculated so that the next signal calculations can be performed.

Following this stage, a final low-pass filter is inserted into the path. The filter's slope characteristic corresponds to that of the input filter and has the same purpose: filtering out existing signals that are equal to or greater than one-half of the sampling rate (Nyquist limit).

Instead of guarding against the reproduction of fundamental frequencies that are above the Nyquist limit, the purpose of an output low-pass filter is to smooth out the nonlinear steps that have been introduced by the digital sampling process itself (Fig. 2.10). Since the components of these steps exist at or near the sampling frequency, the use of such a filter will result in a smoothed, linear waveform that represents the originally recorded analog waveform. The output of this stage can then be sent to any number of analog devices for mixing, processing, or just plain listening.

MIDI

Now that you've delved into the language of digital audio, you're ready for another important language that is central to modern production: MIDI. It's almost impossible to talk about random access technology without bringing up the musical instrument digital interface, or MIDI as it's better known.

MIDI is a standardized control language and hardware specification that allows suitably equipped electronic musical instruments and devices to communicate real-time and non real-time performance and control data. As a data format, it must be strictly adhered to by those who design and manufacture MIDI equipment, so that performance and task-related functions can be communicated with relative transparency, speed, and ease.

The MIDI Message

MIDI data is communicated digitally throughout a production system as a string of MIDI messages. The messages are transmitted (in a serial fashion) through a single MIDI line at a speed of 31.25 Kbaud (31,250 bits per second). This data can travel in only one direction, from a single source to a destination (Fig. 2.11). To make two-way communication possible, a second data line must be connected from the external source back to the original destination device.

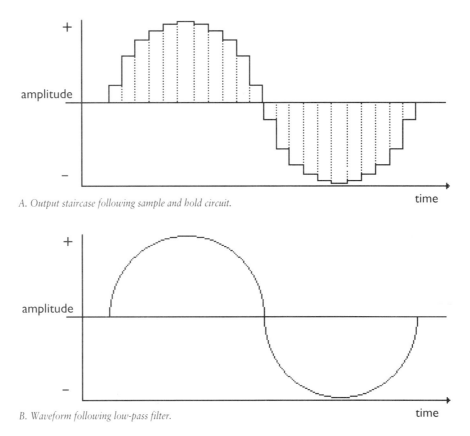

A. Output staircase following sample and hold circuit.

B. Waveform following low-pass filter.

Fig. 2.10: Effect of an output low-pass filter on a sampled signal.

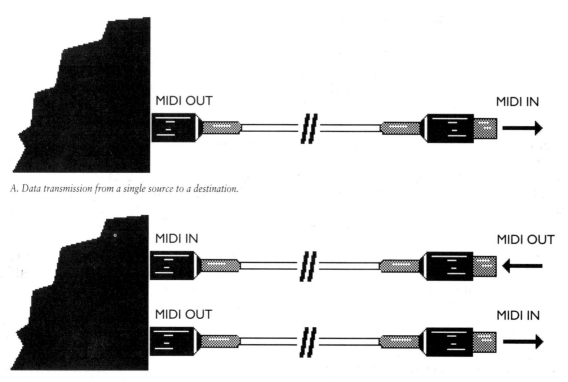

A. Data transmission from a single source to a destination.

B. Two-way communication using two MIDI cables.

Fig. 2.11: MIDI data can travel in only one direction through a single MIDI cable.

Alternatively (and more commonly), MIDI instruments and devices can be linked together in a daisy-chain fashion, so that the data can be easily distributed throughout a system with minimal wiring muss and fuss (Fig. 2.12).

MIDI messages are themselves made up of a group of related 8 bit words (bytes) that are used to convey a series of instructions to one or all MIDI devices within the system.

MIDI messages are divided by the MIDI specification into two types:

• Channel messages are messages assigned to a specific MIDI channel)

• System messages address all devices within a system without regard to channel assignment

For example, Table 2.1 shows the instructions contained by the following 3-byte MIDI Note On message in binary form (a Note On message is used to signal the beginning of a MIDI note):

(1001 0100) (0100 0000) (0101 1001)

As Table 2.1 shows, the instructions in the 3-byte Note On message can be translated as: transmitting a Note On message over MIDI channel 5, for note #64, with an attack velocity (volume level of a note) of 90.

The MIDI specification defines only two byte types:

• Status byte

• Data byte

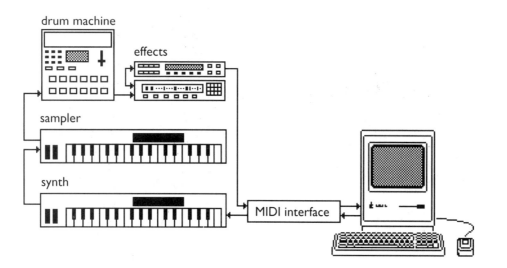

Fig. 2.12: MIDI devices can be linked together to communicate data throughout a connected system.

Table 2.1: A 3-byte Note On message.

	Status Byte	Data Byte 1	Data Byte 2
Description	Status/channel #	Note #	Attack velocity
Binary Data	(1001 0101)	(0100 0000)	(0101 1010)
Numeric Value	(Note On/Ch. #5)	(64)	(90)

The status byte tells the receiving device which particular MIDI function and channel are being addressed. The data byte encodes the actual numeric value that will be attached to the accompanying status byte.

Although a byte is made up of 8 bits, the most significant bit, or MSB (the left-most binary bit within a digital word), is used solely to identify the byte type. The MSB of a status byte is always 1, while the MSB of a data byte is always 0 (Fig. 2.13).

MIDI Channels

Just as a public speaker can single out and communicate a message to an individual within a crowd, MIDI is able to communicate messages to a specific device or range of devices. This is done by encoding a nibble (four bits) within the status/channel number byte. The nibble relays channel information to MIDI devices within a connected chain. Since the channel nibble is four bits wide, up to 16 channels can be transmitted through a single MIDI cable (Fig. 2.14).

Whenever a MIDI device is instructed to respond to a specific channel number, it will ignore channel messages transmitted on any other channel. Likewise, any device that is selected to respond to a specific MIDI channel will respond only to messages that are transmitted on that channel (within the capability limits of the device).

For example, assume that you have a single MIDI keyboard controller that is set to output MIDI data to two synthesizer modules. Just for the fun of it, you've set up your keyboard so that the bottom two octaves will transmit MIDI data on Channel 4 and the upper octaves will transmit on Channel 5 (Fig. 2.15). Even though the devices are connected by a single data chain, each module will respond only to its assigned channel or set of channels.

Electronic instruments often vary in the number

MSB of a Status byte is always "1"

MSB of a Data Byte is always "0"

Final 4-bits "nibble" of a Status byte is used to encode the MIDI channel number

[1SSS SSSS]   **[0DDD DDDD]**   **[1SSS CCCC]**

Fig. 2.13: *In a MIDI data byte, the most significant bit identifies the byte type: a status byte 1 or a data byte 0. The final four bits of a status byte encode the MIDI channel number.*

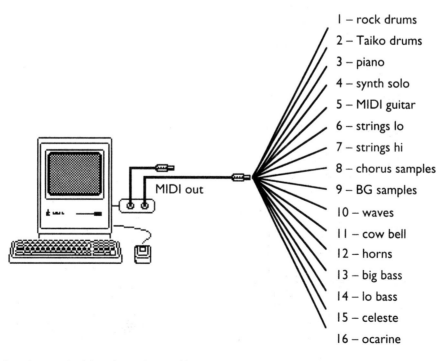

1 – rock drums
2 – Taiko drums
3 – piano
4 – synth solo
5 – MIDI guitar
6 – strings lo
7 – strings hi
8 – chorus samples
9 – BG samples
10 – waves
11 – cow bell
12 – horns
13 – big bass
14 – lo bass
15 – celeste
16 – ocarine

MIDI out

Fig. 2.14: *Up to 16 channels can be transmitted through a single MIDI cable.*

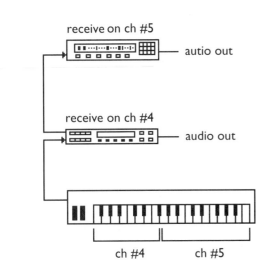

Fig. 2.15: An example showing how sound modules will respond only to data that is being transmitted over their respective channels.

of individual characteristic sounds that they can produce at a time. For example, certain instruments can produce only one note at a time, while others (known as polyphonic instruments) can simultaneously generate a number of sounds and/or notes. The latter type gives the artist a chance to play chords and more than one musical line on a single instrument.

It's also possible for a music device to output only a single characteristic sound patch at a time (for example, electric piano, synth bass, etc.). The word patch refers to the use by earlier analog synthesizers of "patch cords" for connecting one sound generator or processor to another. Likewise, an instrument can be multitimbral in nature, meaning that it can generate more than one sound patch at a time.

Channel Voice Messages

Channel voice messages are used to transmit real-time performance data throughout a connected MIDI system. They are generated whenever the controller of a MIDI instrument is played, selected, or varied by the performer. Examples of such control changes are the playing of a keyboard, program selection buttons, or movement of modulation or pitch wheels.

Each channel voice message, like all channel voice messages, contains a MIDI channel number within its status byte and thus only devices that are assigned to the same channel number will respond

to this data. There are seven types of channel voice messages:

- Note On
- Note Off
- Polyphonic Key Pressure
- Channel Pressure
- Program Change
- Control Change
- Pitch Bend Change

Note On

A Note On message indicates the beginning of a MIDI note. It is generated each time that a note is triggered on a keyboard, drum machine, or other MIDI instrument (by pressing a key, drum pad, etc.). A Note On message consists of three bytes of information (Fig. 2.16):

- MIDI channel number
- MIDI note number
- Attack velocity value

The first byte in the message specifies a Note On event and a MIDI channel (1 16). The second byte specifies which of the possible 128 pitches (numbered from 0 127) will be sounded by a MIDI instrument. In general, MIDI note 60 is assigned to the middle C key of an equal tempered keyboard, and notes 21 108 correspond to the 88 keys of an extended keyboard controller.

The final byte indicates the velocity or speed at which the key was pressed. This value (which ranges from 1 127) denotes the loudness of a sounding note. That is, the harder you play the keys, hit the pads, or blow into a wind controller, the louder the sound will be (Fig. 2.17).

Not all instruments are designed to interpret the entire range of velocity values (for example, certain drum machines), and others do not respond dynamically at all. Instruments that don't support velocity information will generally transmit an attack velocity value of 64 for every note played, regardless of the velocity that is actually being played. Similarly, these instruments will interpret all MIDI velocities as having a value of 64.

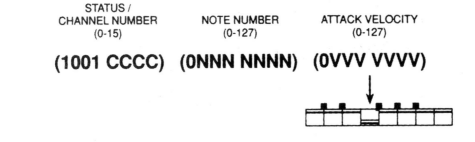

Fig. 2.16: Byte structure of a MIDI Note On message.

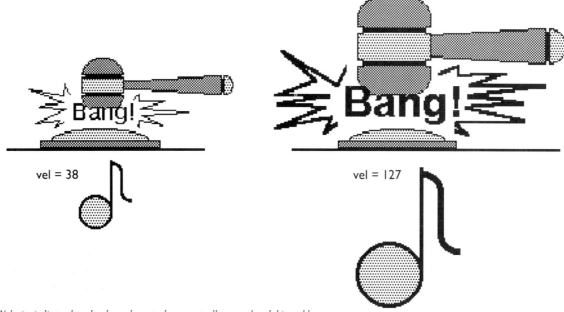

Fig. 2.17: Velocity indicates how hard MIDI *keys, pads, or controllers are played, hit, or blown.*

Note Off

A Note Off message indicates the release (end) of a MIDI note. Each note that has been played via a Note On message is sustained until a corresponding Note Off message is received. In this way, a musical performance can be encoded as a series of MIDI Note On and Note Off messages, indicating the beginning and ending times that each note is to be sounded within a performance or recorded sequence.

It should also be pointed out that a Note Off message will not "cut off" a sound; it will merely stop playing it. If the patch being played has a release (or final decay) stage, it will begin that stage upon receiving this message. Many instruments, however, do not generate a Note Off when the key is released; they generate a Note On with a velocity of zero, which cuts the note off.

In contrast with the dynamics of attack velocity, the release velocity value (0 127) indicates the velocity or speed at which the key was released. A low value indicates that the key was released very slowly, while a high value shows that the key was released quickly. Although few instruments generate or respond to MIDI release velocity, instruments that do respond can be programmed so that a note's speed of decay will vary, often reducing the signal's decay time as the release velocity value is increased.

Polyphonic Key Pressure

Polyphonic Key Pressure messages are commonly transmitted by instruments that are capable of responding to the pressure changes applied to the individual keys of a keyboard. Such an instrument can be used to transmit individual pressure messages for each key that is depressed. A Polyphonic Key Pressure message consists of three bytes of information (Fig. 2.18):

- MIDI channel number
- MIDI note number
- Pressure value

The means by which a device will respond to these messages can vary between manufacturers and instrument patches. However, pressure values can commonly be assigned to such performance parameters as vibrato, loudness, timbre, and pitch. Although controllers that are capable of producing polyphonic pressure are few and generally more expensive, it is not unusual for an instrument to respond to these messages.

Channel Pressure (After Touch)

Channel Pressure messages (often referred to as After Touch) are commonly transmitted by instruments that will respond only to a single, overall

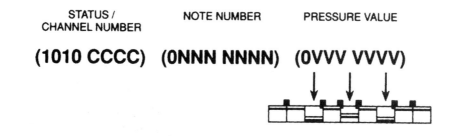

Fig. 2.18: Byte structure of a MIDI *Polyphonic Key Pressure message.*

pressure applied to their controllers, regardless of the number of keys being played at one time. For example, if six notes are played on a keyboard controller and additional pressure is applied to only one key, all six notes would be affected. A Channel Pressure message consists of three bytes of information (Fig. 2.19):

- MIDI channel number (as part of the status byte)
- MIDI note number
- Pressure value

As with polyphonic pressure changes, an instrument can often be programmed to respond to Channel Pressure messages in many ways. For example, Channel Pressure values are commonly assigned to such performance parameters as vibrato, loudness, timbre, and pitch.

Program Change

The Program Change message changes the program or preset number that is active within a MIDI instrument or device. A preset number is a user- or factory-defined number that will activate a specific sound patch or system setup. Up to 128 presets can be selected via MIDI by using this message format. A Program Change message (Fig. 2.20) consists of two bytes of information:

- MIDI channel number (1–16)
- Program ID number (0–127)

From a remote keyboard instrument, for example, a Program Change message can be used to switch between the various sound patches of a synthesizer (Fig. 2.21). It can also be used to select rhythm patterns and/or setups within a drum machine, to call up specific effects patches within an effects device or a multitude of other controller and system setups that can be recalled as a program preset. Many MIDI devices allow the user to manually disable and enable the recognition of these messages.

Control Change

The Control Change message transmits information that relates to real-time control over the performance parameters of a MIDI instrument. There are three types of real-time controllers that are communicated via Control Change messages:

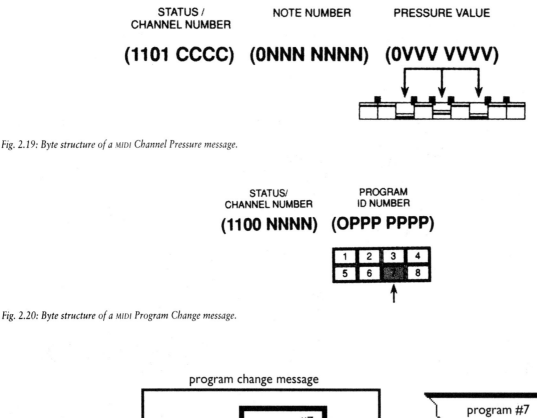

Fig. 2.19: *Byte structure of a* MIDI *Channel Pressure message.*

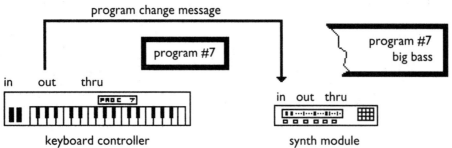

Fig. 2.20: *Byte structure of a* MIDI *Program Change message.*

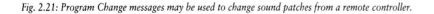

Fig. 2.21: *Program Change messages may be used to change sound patches from a remote controller.*

- Continuous controllers relay a range of possible control settings from 0 127. However, two controller messages can be combined in tandem to achieve a greater resolution.

- Switches are controllers that are either "On" or "Off," with no intermediate settings.

- Data controllers enter data either by means of a numerical keypad or stepped up and down through the use of data-entry buttons.

A single Control Change message or a stream of such messages is transmitted whenever controllers such as foot switches, foot pedals, pitch bend wheels, modulation wheels, breath controllers, etc., are varied in real time. In this way, a controller can be used to correspondingly vary a wide range of possible parameters within an instrument or device in accordance with the controller's movements or commands.

Controller ID Numbers

The second byte of the Control Change message denotes the controller ID number. This number specifies which of a device's program or performance parameters are to be addressed.

Many manufacturers follow the MIDI protocol for assigning controller numbers to associated parameters. However, manufacturers are free to assign these parameters as they wish, provided that the defined format in the MIDI specification is followed.

Controller Values

The third byte of the Control Change message denotes the controller's actual data value. This value specifies the position, depth, or level of effect that the controller will have upon the parameter. In most cases, the value range of a 7 bit continuous controller will fall between 0 (minimum value) and 127 (maximum value) (Fig. 2.22).

The value range of a switch controller is often 0 (Off) and 127 (On) (Fig. 2.23). However, switch functions are also capable of responding to continuous controller messages by recognizing the values of 0 63 as Off and 64 127 as On.

The practice of using the values of 0 127 to represent an effect depth or signal level does not pertain to the control parameters of balance, panning, and expression. Instead, these data values are used to vary the intended effect parameters themselves.

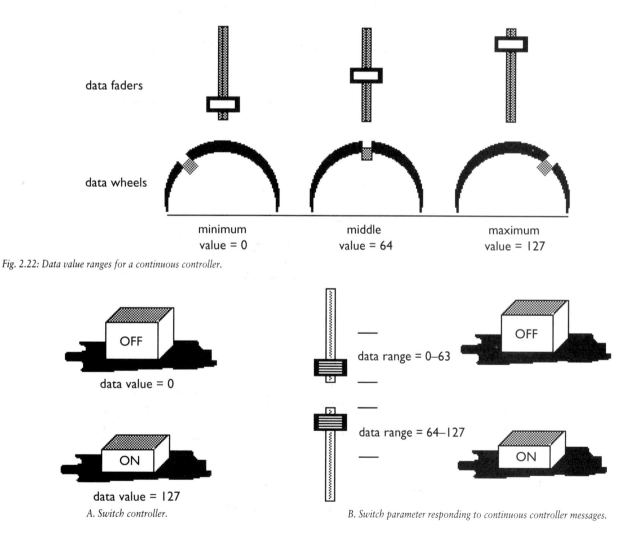

data faders

data wheels

| minimum | middle | maximum |
| value = 0 | value = 64 | value = 127 |

Fig. 2.22: Data value ranges for a continuous controller.

OFF

data value = 0

ON

data value = 127

A. Switch controller.

data range = 0–63

OFF

data range = 64–127

ON

B. Switch parameter responding to continuous controller messages.

Fig. 2.23: Data value ranges for a switch controller.

A balance controller is used to vary the relative levels between two independent sound sources (Fig. 2.24). Like the balance control on a stereo preamplifier, this controller is used to set the relative left/right balance of a stereo sound source. The value range of this controller falls between 0 (full left sound source) and 127 (full right sound source), with a value of 64 representing a balanced stereo left/right field.

A pan controller is used to position the relative balance of a single sound source between the left and right channels of a stereo sound field (Fig. 2.25). The value range of this controller falls between 0 (hard left positioning) and 127 (hard right positioning), with a value of 64 representing a balanced center field.

An expression controller is used to accent the existing level settings of a MIDI instrument or device. This control can increase the channel volume level of an instrument but cannot reduce this level below its programmed volume setting. The value range of this controller falls between 0 (current programmed volume setting) and 127 (full volume accent).

Pitch Bend Change

Pitch Bend Change messages are transmitted by an instrument whenever its pitch bend wheel (Fig. 2.26) is moved either in the positive (raise pitch) or in the negative (lower pitch) position from its central (no pitch bend) point.

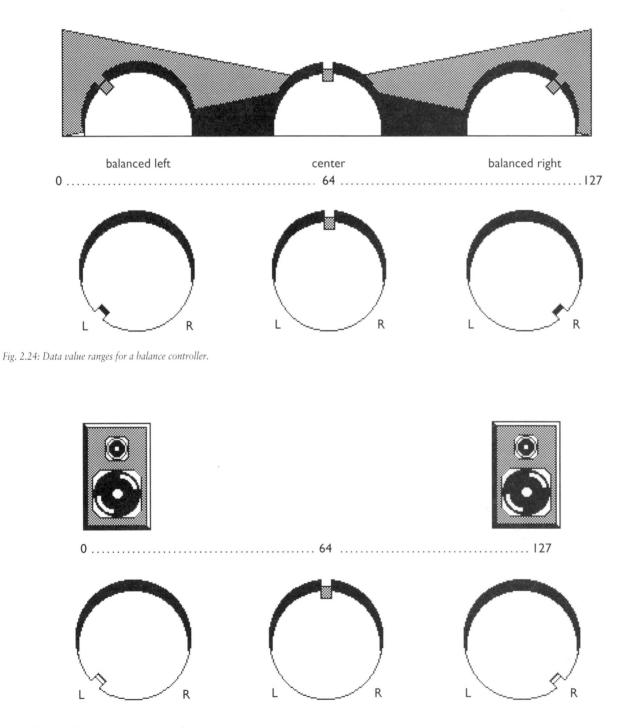

Fig. 2.24: Data value ranges for a balance controller.

Fig. 2.25: Data value ranges for a pan controller.

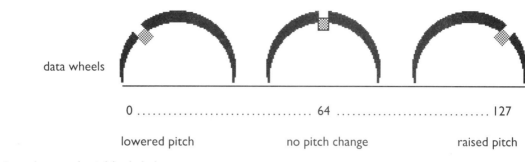

data wheels

0 .... 64 127

lowered pitch   no pitch change   raised pitch

Fig. 2.26: Data value ranges for pitch bend wheel.

Channel Mode Messages

Controller numbers 121–127 are reserved for Channel Mode messages. These include:

- Reset All Controllers
- Local Control
- All Notes Off
- MIDI Mode messages

Reset All Controllers

The Reset All Controllers message re-initializes all of the controllers (continuous, switch, and incremental) to a standard power-up default state.

Local Control

The Local Control message disconnects the controller of a MIDI instrument from its own voices (Fig. 2.27). This feature is handy for making use of a keyboard instrument as a master performance controller within a MIDI system.

Although an instrument's sound circuitry can be disconnected from its internal controller (when an instrument's Local Control is switched off), it is still capable of responding to MIDI performance and control messages from an external controller or sequencer. A Local Control message consists of two bytes of information:

- MIDI channel number (1–16)
- Local Control on/off status byte

All Notes Off

Occasionally, a Note On message will be received by a MIDI instrument, and the following Note Off message will somehow be ignored or not received. This unfortunate event often results in a "stuck" note, which will continue to sound until a Note Off message is received for that pitch.

As an alternative to searching for this note, an All Notes Off message can be transmitted. This message effectively turns off all of the 128 notes. Not all MIDI instruments are capable of responding to this panic button message, so it should be transmitted if nothing else works.

Omni Mode Off

Upon receiving an Omni Mode Off message, a MIDI instrument or device will switch modes (or remain in the Omni Off mode), causing it to respond to individually assigned MIDI channels instead of responding to all MIDI channels at once.

Omni Mode On

Upon receiving an Omni Mode On message, a MIDI instrument or device will switch modes (or remain in the Omni On mode), causing it to respond to all MIDI channel messages, regardless of on which channels these messages are being transmitted.

Mono Mode On

Upon receiving a Mono Mode On message, a MIDI instrument will assign individual voices to

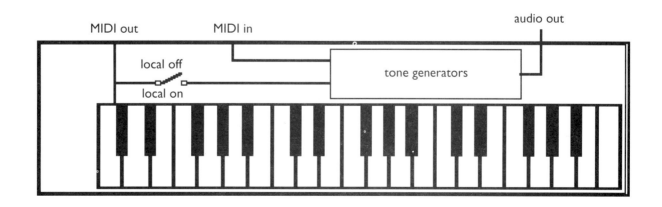

MIDI out   MIDI in   audio out

local off

local on

tone generators

Fig. 2.27: Local Control on/off function.

consecutive MIDI channels, starting from the lowest currently assigned or "basic" channel. That is, the instrument can play only one note per MIDI channel. However, it is capable of playing more than one monophonic channel at a time.

Poly Mode On

The reception of a Poly Mode On message causes a MIDI instrument or device to switch modes (or remain in the Poly On mode). This message allows an instrument to respond to MIDI channels polyphonically. In this way, a device is able to play more than one note at a time over a given channel or number of channels.

System Messages

As their name implies, System messages are globally transmitted to every MIDI device in the MIDI chain. This happens because MIDI channel numbers are not addressed in the byte structure of a System message. This fact means that any device will respond to these messages, regardless of which MIDI channel or channels the device is assigned to. There are three System message types:

- System Common messages
- System Real-time messages
- System Exclusive messages

System Common Messages

System Common messages transmit MIDI Time Code (MTC), Song Position Pointer, Song Select, Tune Request, and End of Exclusive data throughout the MIDI system or the 16 channels of a specified MIDI port.

MTC "MIDI Time Code" Quarter-Frame provides a cost-effective and easily implemented way to translate SMPTE time code into an equivalent code that conforms to the MIDI 1.0 specification. It allows time-based code and commands to be distributed throughout the MIDI chain. MTC quarter-frame messages are transmitted and recognized by MIDI devices that are capable of understanding and executing MTC commands.

A grouping of eight quarter frames is required to denote a complete time-code address (in hours, minutes, seconds, and frames). For this reason, SMPTE time is updated every two frames. Each quarter-frame message contains two bytes. The first is a quarter-frame common header. The second byte contains a nibble (four bits), which represents the message number (0 7), and a final nibble for each of the digits of a time field (hours, minutes, seconds, or frames). Chapter 7 has more in-depth coverage of MIDI time code.

Song Position Pointer (SPP) permits a sequencer or drum machine to be synchronized to an external source (such as a tape machine) from any measure position within a song. The Song Position Pointer message is used to reference a location point within a MIDI sequence (in measures) to a matching location on an external device (such as a drum machine or tape recorder). This message provides a timing reference that increments once for every six MIDI clock messages, with respect to the beginning of a composition.

A Song Select message is used to request a specific song from the internal sequence memory of a drum machine or sequencer (as identified by its song ID number). Upon being selected, the song will respond to MIDI Start, Stop, and Continue messages.

A Tune Request message is used to request that a MIDI instrument initiate its internal tuning routine (if so equipped).

System Exclusive Messages

The System Exclusive (Sys-Ex) message provides a way for MIDI manufacturers, programmers, and designers to communicate customized MIDI messages between MIDI devices. These messages give manufacturers, programmers, and designers the freedom to communicate any device-specific data of virtually any length, as they see fit. Commonly, Sys-Ex data is used for the bulk transmission and reception of program data, sample data, and real-time control over a device's parameters (as with editor/librarian programs).

The transmission format for System Exclusive messages (Fig. 2.28) as defined by the MIDI standard includes a Sys-Ex status header, manufacturer's ID number, any number of Sys-Ex data bytes, and an End of Exclusive (EOX) byte. Upon receiving a System Exclusive message, the MIDI device reads the identification number to determine whether the following messages are relevant.

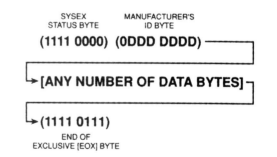

Fig. 2.28: System Exclusive data (one-byte ID format).

Determining the ID number is easily accomplished, since a unique one- or three-byte ID number is assigned to each registered MIDI manufacturer. If this number does not match that of the receiving MIDI device, the ensuing data bytes will be ignored. Once a valid stream of Sys-Ex data is transmitted, a final EOX message is sent, after which the device will again respond to incoming MIDI performance messages.

MIDI Filtering

A MIDI filter is a dedicated digital device, an onboard processor, or a computer program that allows specific MIDI messages or a range of messages within a data stream to be either recognized or ignored. A MIDI data filter can be thought of as a pass/no pass digital switch that can be programmed to block the transmission of specific MIDI messages (Fig. 2.29), such as Velocity on/off, Program Change on/off, Modulation on/off, SysEx on/off, etc.

An instrument or device may be capable of filtering incoming MIDI data, or of filtering data at its MIDI out or thru ports. In the latter case, the device itself will not be affected. However all devices that follow in the chain may contain selectively filtered data. In addition, it is possible to filter messages that are transmitted over specific MIDI channels (thus only affecting a specific device or instrument patch within the system).

MIDI Mapping

A MIDI mapper is a dedicated digital system, an on-board processor, or a computer program that can be used to reassign the value of a MIDI message to another value or range of values. Mapping can be applied within the MIDI chain to reassign channel numbers, program numbers, note numbers (for transposing notes or creating chords), controller numbers and values, etc. As with MIDI filtering, it is also possible to map specific message bytes that are transmitted over individual MIDI channels.

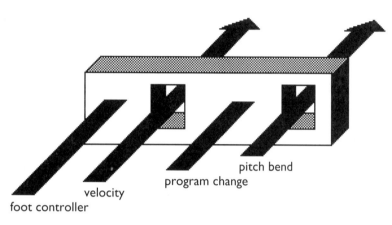

pitch bend

program change

velocity

foot controller

Fig. 2.29: A MIDI filter is used to block the transmission of specific MIDI messages.

Chapter 3

Hardware

Software can be thought of as the subjective digital chameleon that lets us stretch our imaginations by allowing a system to perform an almost infinite number of audio, graphics, and text-based tasks. But it's up to a system's hardware design to make sure that these tasks work reliably, or just plain work.

Several factors determine the types of hardware required by a random-access audio system. These factors include: the specific duty or duties that the system is to perform, the desired speed, the amount of memory and processing power needed, and the type of interface required for connecting the system to the outside audio world.

One of the advantages of most random-access audio systems is their ability to utilize existing equipment and technologies that already exist within the computer field. Therefore, hardware can often be assembled from standard off-the-shelf subsystems that go together to create a basic computer system or digital device (such as a processor, disk drive, or monitor display).

Hardware can also exist as dedicated cards or stand-alone systems that have been specially designed to allow computers to communicate with other devices, such as VTRs, MIDI instruments, and so on. Devices such as these are often used to transform a "traditional" personal computer into an integrated system for performing a wide range of creative tasks, such as MIDI, digital audio, digital graphics, etc.

This chapter will introduce you to many of these off-the-shelf hardware systems, as well as a number of dedicated interface systems that have become commonplace fixtures in music and digital audio production.

Solid-State Memory Storage

In terms of solid-state memory, an integrated circuit (or IC) is a binary logic device that incorporates a large array of electronic switches. Each of these switches can act as memory storage for retaining the series of 1's and 0's that are required for storing digital audio and related program data.

Once binary data has been stored into this memory storage, access time to any memory location is virtually instantaneous and the data can be called up at any time and in any order. Such memory can be designed to store raw digital data in either of two ways:

- As read-only memory (called ROM)
- As random-access memory (called RAM)

Read-Only Memory

Just as its name implies, read-only memory, or ROM, only allows digital data to be read from its storage memory. Data cannot be written into ROM, nor can the data be altered in any way (although it's common for user-programmable memory to be used in conjunction with ROM memory to alter the way that this data can be read). In addition, such memory storage devices do not require a power source to retain data. Thus, a ROM-based system can be turned off without fear of losing all those precious bytes.

Data is encoded into the ROM chip at a factory in one of two ways. The chip can be designed from the ground up with a specific memory pattern (as is often done with mass-produced large scale integrated circuits). Alternatively, the chip can be a limited run of special ROM chips (known as an EPROMs), which have had data "burned" into memory by the programmer.

Any type of digital data can be encoded into a ROM chip. This includes program- and function-related data (such as the data that provides the brains for your calculator, clock, blender, or latest gadget). The ROM chip can also store raw audio, graphic, or file-related information.

An excellent example of a ROM-based system for outputting factory-loaded digital audio is the drum machine shown in Fig. 3.1. This popular device uses ROMs to store and output specially recorded samples of drum sounds. The sound can be triggered either manually from the drum machine's playing pads (located on the "Beat box") or externally via MIDI. Once a trigger is activated, the digitally encoded sample data that is stored in ROM is routed to an output channel and . . . BLAM!

Random-Access Memory

Unlike its read-only counterpart, random-access memory, or RAM, allows data to be both written to, and read from, its memory store (Fig. 3.2). Thus, a user can store personal and program-related data (such as text, graphics, sound, and video) into memory and then later retrieve and/or process it to change its content.

Also, unlike read-only memory, RAM requires a power source in order to retain data. Should RAM lose power, for any reason, the stored data will be lost. There are two ways to prevent this major headache.

The first involves the use of a power backup. Certain systems (such as synthesizer patch banks and computer clock/calendars) are designed with an internal battery so that a power source is still available when the power switch is turned off. This power backup eliminates the need to reprogram basic functions every time you turn on the system.

The second way makes use of a disk-drive storage medium. This magnetic or optical medium doesn't lose its data upon powerdown and is suited for larger program-dependent files. Once the RAM data is stored on such a medium, it can be restored at any later time.

A straightforward example of an audio device that makes use of random-access memory is a sampler. With this device, you can record sounds into RAM and then edit and manipulate the sounds so that they can be output under internal or external trigger control (Fig. 3.3).

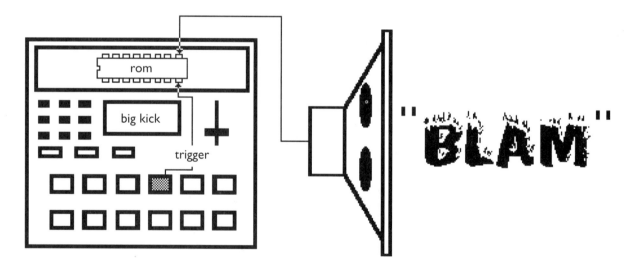

Fig. 3.1: A drum machine is most often used to trigger audio directly from read-only memory.

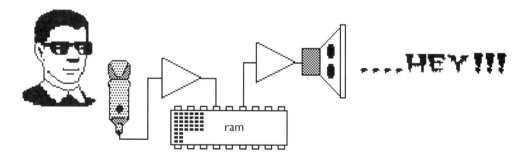

Fig. 3.2: Data can be both written to and read from random-access memory.

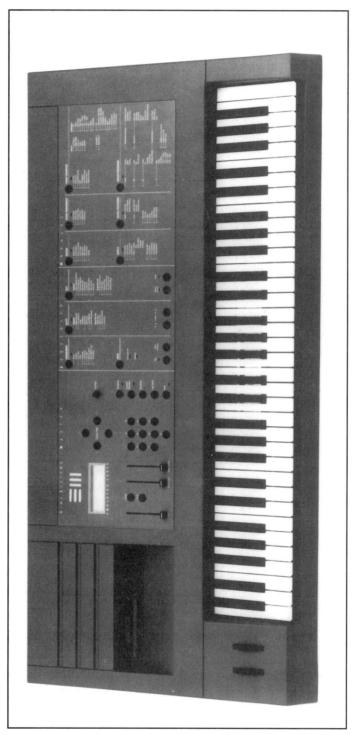

Fig. 3.3: The E III Sampling system. (Courtesy of E-mu Systems, Inc.)

Disk-Based Memory Storage

Solid-state memory (such as RAM) is needed to provide a computing system with immediate access to program and/or soundfile information. However, this medium is extremely expensive for storing large amounts of data, particularly data that isn't being used at the moment. A lower-cost medium that is more space-effective is needed for storing large amounts of on- and off-line data. Data storage on magnetic or optical disk has long been an answer to the ever-growing demand for more memory.

Disk media (particularly magnetic media) physically store data within concentric rings (known as tracks) that circle the disk surface (Fig. 3.4). Each circular track consists of data segments (known as blocks or sectors), which are often defined as being 512 bytes in size. Each block contains a unique header address that allows the computer and drive controller to link and locate data quickly and easily. Depending on the disk and drive formats, data can often be written onto both sides of the disk.

Disk drive systems (such as hard drives) capable of storing large amounts of data will often use a multiple disk surface and magnetic head pickup drive system. These disks, which are physically connected by a common rotating spindle (Fig. 3.5), map the layered disk surfaces into multilayered areas known as sectors and cylinders. A cylinder consists of tracks that share the same concentric ring location on each drive. Likewise, a sector is a vertical alignment of the same block area.

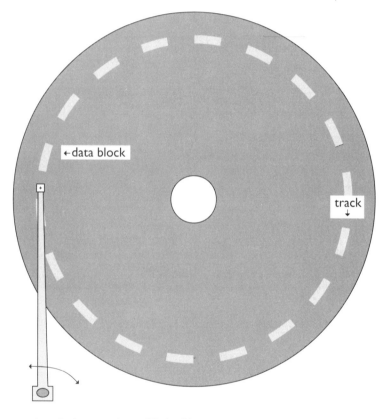

Fig. 3.4: Disk media store data in concentric tracks that are made up of blocks of data.

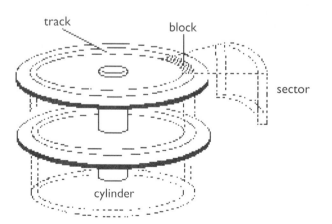

Fig. 3.5: The multiple platters in a hard drive system.

The purpose of segmenting disk surfaces into tracks, blocks, cylinders, and sectors is to provide a location map for the pickup head. The mapping system lets the pickup head quickly move to a particular location. The process is similar to the way you might use a street map to get to a particular address. By breaking the disk into the block location points, the drive's controller is able to instruct the pickup head to find a specific block of information located, for example, on the 2nd disk surface and 23rd track, within the 5th data block.

In addition to disk mapping, a cataloging system allows data to be placed into a hierarchy of directories (analogous to file drawers) and subdirectories (file folders). This system was developed as a way to organize information and help users keep track of their affairs on disk.

As you have seen, digital data exists on disk as a series of finite memory blocks, which are often 512 bytes in size. This suggests that data must be written to, and read from, disk media as a series of data bursts instead of as a continuous stream of digital information. To deal with these noncontinuous bursts, a device known as a buffer is used. A RAM buffer is probably best explained with an analogy that has long been chronicled in digital lore: the water faucet analogy.

Suppose that you have a bucket that has been partially filled by a steady drip from a leaky faucet. At the bottom of the bucket is a tap that lets you regulate its outgoing flow. If the tap is

closed, the drip will fill up the bucket. If the tap is opened, a steady stream of water will flow from the bucket, even though the dripping source isn't continuous (Fig. 3.6). In the same manner, digital data can be fed into a buffer. The buffer serves as a temporary storage medium while allowing the data to be read out as a constant stream (Fig. 3.7).

Still keeping in mind the bucket analogy, assume that the water flow scenario will continue as long as the leaky source can keep up with the outbound flow from the tap. If the source isn't equal to or greater than the tap's flow, the bucket will empty and the output tap will likewise begin to drip in a noncontinuous fashion. Conversely, if the water source is too great, the bucket will fill up, causing a new set of problems.

This analogy can be applied to a buffer's empty and full states. The buffer's noncontinuous data source represents the stream of digital blocks that are periodically routed to and from the magnetic or optical memory media.

The amount of memory capacity (measured in kilobytes, megabytes, and gigabytes) that can be stored within a disk medium is determined by the size of the medium and the physical density of the data on the disk. One kilobyte=1,024 bytes, 1 megabyte=1,024 kilobytes, and 1 gigabyte=1,024 megabytes.

Magnetic media commonly use disk platters that vary in diameter. In recent times, the 31/2-inch drive has become a popular format because of

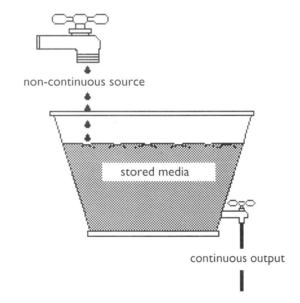

Fig. 3.6: *Example showing how a bucket can be used to buffer water.*

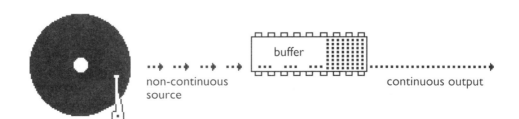

Fig. 3.7: *Example showing how a digital buffer regulates the flow of digital data from a hard disk.*

its smaller size and because of its data densities, which range from 20 megabytes (MB) to greater than 1 gigabyte (GB).

The time needed to transfer to, or access data from, a disk is known as its access time. This delay time (measured in milliseconds) is the time required for the pickup head to move from one track to another and for the correct data block to move under the head, at which time the data can be written or accessed. This rating indicates worst-case timing, which for most professional audio applications needs to be less than 24 ms.

The storage media most often used for storing digital data, and also the most cost-effective, are magnetic disks. With this media, magnetically encoded data is recorded to, and read from, one of a series of rotating disks in a way that is both straightforward and economical.

The most common forms of magnetic disk media are:

- Floppy disk
- Hard disk

Floppy Disk

The floppy disk, or diskette, is a low-density, removable magnetic medium for the recording, storage, and reproduction of digital data, including program data, text, and graphics. A floppy disk can also be used as a backup for data stored on a hard disk. If the data stored on the hard disk is lost or inadvertently destroyed, the data can be recovered from the backup diskette.

Common floppy disk formats include the IBM-style 51/2-inch disk available in 360-kilobyte and 1.2-megabyte capacities, as well as the higher-density 31/2-inch "Stiffie" disks commonly used with IBM, Macintosh, Atari, and other types of systems.

Because diskettes have limited storage capacities, only a few seconds of audio data can be placed onto a single diskette. For example, a 31/2-inch high-density IBM diskette can store 1.44 megabytes of data. However, one minute of 16-bit audio (sampled at 48 kHz) requires about 5 megabytes of storage space. This factor, along with slower access times, makes them useful only for the archival storage of short samplefiles (an application that is still widely used by sampling artists).

Hard Disk

By far the most commonly found medium for storing large amounts of data is the hard disk drive. A number of drive types and sizes are available for use as an external add-on or stand-alone system. Some of these drives can be mounted away from the computer (every little bit helps to reduce drive and fan noise) and can be easily disconnected for on-the-go users.

Current hard-drive storage capacities range from 40MB to greater than 2GB (1 gigabyte = 1024 megabytes). Although hard drives are often nonremovable by nature, they are widely known for their reliability, access speed, and cost-effectiveness.

Most hard disk designs (Fig. 3.8) are based on a series of magnetically recordable disks that are physically connected to a single spindle, which rotates at high speed. These platters are often made of a highly polished aluminum and are coated on both sides with a thin oxide recording surface.

Data is transferred to and from the surface by means of a series of read/write heads (one per disk surface). The heads are positioned close enough to the high-speed surface that they "fly" over the rotating disks on a cushion of air. The tolerance of this aerodynamic cushion must be very tight because each head has to be close enough to the disk surface to read and write data without physically touching the surface. The gap between the "flying" read/write head and the disk surface is about one-third the wavelength of green light, a figure that has been compared to a 747 aircraft flying 500 miles an hour 1/10 of an inch above the ground.

Should the head and the disk surface make contact, physical damage could be done to the written data, as well as to the disk itself. (Such a head crash isn't the end of the world, however, since the drive's controller could reformat the disk so that future data would be clear of this damaged area.)

The magnetic head assemblies are physically connected to a series of arms. The arms, in turn, are connected to a single processor-controlled actuator that positions the heads over the disk surfaces. In addition to the rotating disks, heads, and actuator assemblies, a controller is used to position the heads over the proper data area while simultaneously controlling the flow of data to and from the device.

Technically speaking, the access times of most modern, large-capacity drives have been lowered into the 24- to 9-ms range. This is often well within the minimum access time required for most professional audio applications (assuming that the CPU speed, drive controller, and disk interleave settings are fast enough for the process).

Optical Data Storage

The storage of digital data onto optical disk leads to one of the greatest success stories of recent decades: the compact disc. However, other forms of optical storage are becoming increasingly familiar to multimedia producers. These include:

- CD-ROM
- WORM (write once-read many)
- Erasable optical media

The use of an optical disk as a data storage medium is attractive because an optical disk offers greater data densities at a very cost-effective price per megabyte. (For a given area, an optical disk

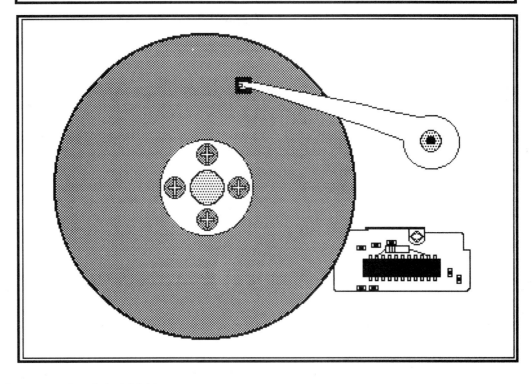

Fig. 3.8: Side and top cutaway views of a hard disk drive.

can often store more than 20 times the data that a conventional hard disk can.) An additional selling point for optical technology is its removability, meaning that when the music is over or when the dreaded "disk full" indicator appears, you need only pop in a new disk and you're back in business.

On the minus side, optical drive systems tend to have slower access times than hard disks do. This drawback is due to the physical restraints of moving an optical assembly as opposed to a much lighter, more agile magnetic head.

In the not-so-distant past, these access constraints meant that optical's only use in an audio production environment was as a read-only medium or as an archive for soundfile data. However, recent technological advances have sped up their access times to the point that optical has become a viable medium for on-line audio production.

Compact Disc

The compact disc, or CD, is a highly efficient means of storing audio data, as can be seen by its overwhelming acceptance in both the professional and consumer markets. This mass-produced read-only format allows up to 74 minutes of 16-bit stereo audio to be played. It has an overall data capacity of about 15.6 billion channel bits of information, with about 625 megabytes of this

being reserved for audio data quite a feat for a disc measuring less than 4 3/4 inches across.

The information on these silvery, polycarbonate discs is encoded within the reflective underside of the disc in the form of microscopic "pits." These pits (which are aligned in a continuous spiral from the inner to the outer edge of the disc) are impressed within the disc's plastic substrate.

This encoded surface is then coated with a thin layer of aluminum. The aluminum surface allows a low-level, infrared laser to be reflected off the disc's surface and back to a photosensitive pickup. The reflected beam takes the form of a stream of digital audio data. The data is modulated on the disc so that each pit edge represents a binary 1 and the absence of a pit edge represents a binary 0 (Fig. 3.9). When inserted into a compact disc player, this standardized information is read, demodulated, and converted back into its originally recorded form.

An additional benefit to having data recorded on CD is that the user can either play the audio data from beginning to end or make individual selections at random. Track location, numbering, and timing data are encoded into index and subcode information, which is placed within a lookup table at the beginning of each disc. Once loaded, this reference table provides the player with information regarding index start, stop, and location point markers.

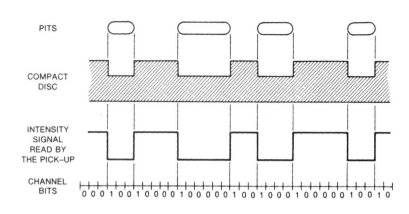

Fig. 3.9: *The transitions between a pit edge (binary 1) and the absence of a pit edge (binary 0).*

CD-ROM

CD-audio is the best-known application of compact disc technology, but it is not the only one. Since the CD is a digital storage medium, it follows that any kind of digitally related data or program material can be encoded onto such a disc. As a result, the CD-ROM (Compact Disc Read-Only Memory) format was developed to extend the digital audio CD format to the application of information storage in general.

This read-only medium is quickly gaining in popularity because it can store up to 680 megabytes of data relating to computer programs, database information, text, MIDI, graphics, and video data. According to Ken Pohlmann in his book *Principles of Digital Audio* (Sams, 1991), such a storage area is roughly equivalent to either

- 1500 half-megabyte floppy disks
- 275,000 pages of alphanumerics
- 18,000 pieces of computer graphics
- 3,600 still video pictures

In audio production, a very popular CD-ROM application is the storage of edited samplefile data for loading into a performance sampler (see Chapter 4 for more discussion of this). With the growing integration of sampling systems into computer-based applications and hardware, a number of sound effects and sample production houses have released prerecorded soundfiles on CD-ROM disc. Most commonly, these samples can be loaded into a computer soundfile editing program and then dumped to a sampler, although sampling systems now exist that allow such data to be directly loaded into sample memory.

WORM

Optical media needn't be only ROM in nature. Media that allow data to be recorded directly onto disk also exist. One form of removable optical memory, shown in Fig. 3.10, goes by the name of WORM (write once-read many). As its name implies, data can be written (recorded) to a WORM disk only once but can be accessed from disk an indefinite number of times.

This method of storage is useful for archiving data into a large information databank. For example, once a sample has been edited, it could be permanently written into a central optical WORM library for future access.

In addition to standard WORM systems, drives exist that conform to the standard compact disc format. These systems, which are commonly known as CD-WO, are quite flexible in production since they can also read data from standard CD-ROM and CD-audio discs.

Erasable Optical Disks

The last and the most recent newcomer to optical technology is the erasable optical disk. Unlike other optical media, an erasable disk can be written to, read from, erased, and rewritten an unlimited number of times. Given its high data density and ability to rewrite data to a removable disk, such a medium would certainly satisfy the mass cry for more memory.

Although erasable disk systems are useful for a number of computer applications, their use in audio production has been limited in the recent past by access times that are slower than those of most magnetic hard disks. Fortunately, this has begun to change.

The access time required for an optical pickup (or head) to finish reading data, move to a new address position, and begin reading new data has recently improved enough that this removable media is fast becoming the storage medium of choice for professional hard disk recording installations.

Three types of systems presently exist for encoding and rewriting data to optical disk:

- Magneto-optical
- Phase-change
- Dye-polymer

Magneto-Optical

Like standard magnetic recording media, the magneto-optical disk (MOD) uses the orientation of tiny magnetic particles to encode digital information. The major difference between the mag-

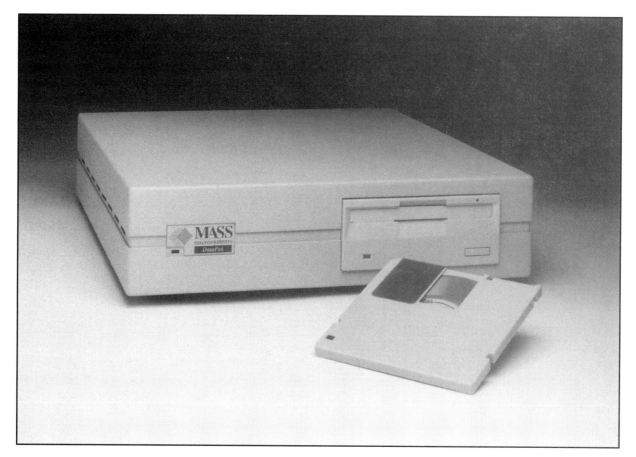

Fig. 3.10: WORM disk and drive system. (Courtesy of Mass Micro Systems.)

netic media and the magneto-optic media is that standard magnetic heads are used to orient particles at normal room temperatures, while particles in the optical media can be oriented only at extremely high temperatures.

To provide the necessary heat and particle orientation, a laser beam is focused on a small region of the medium. The laser heats the area to a temperature that will allow it to be magnetized by a magnetic field (Fig. 3.11).

To read the recorded data, a phenomenon known as the Kerr effect is applied. The Kerr effect is a rotation in the polarization plane that a light beam undergoes when it is reflected off a magnetic medium. Depending on whether the encoded magnetic field is pointed up or down, the rotation will be either clockwise or counterclockwise. The data can then be read from the disk by detecting this rotation in polarization as the polarized laser beam reflects off the medium (Fig. 3.12).

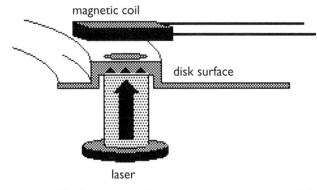

Fig. 3.11: *Digital data is written onto a magneto-optical disc by heating a small surface area to a temperature that will allow it to be magnetized by a magnetic field.*

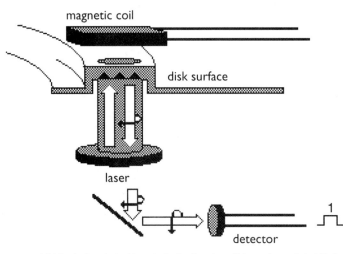

A *Light that's polarized in a clockwise direction will be read as a digital "1."*

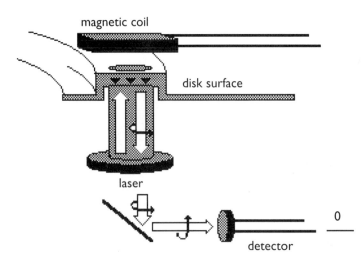

B *Light that's polarized in a counterclockwise direction will be read as a digital "0."*

Fig. 3.12: *Data can be read from a magneto-optical disc by detecting the polarized rotation of the laser light as it is reflected off the disc's magnetic surface.*

Phase-Change

A phase-change optical system uses a disk that is coated with a tellurium film, which can be altered between a crystalline (0) and a noncrystalline (1) state. This recording process is accomplished by heating the disk surface with a laser source so that the heated surface is changed into an uncrystallized (nonreflective) state, while unheated surface areas remain reflective (Fig. 3.13).

Erasure is accomplished by heating an area greater in size than the original recording surface. In so doing, the disk's surface area can be slowly heated so that the affected track will be changed back to its original reflective state.

Dye-Polymer

An opto-chemical system, known as the dye-polymer recording process, makes use of a disc that incorporates two polymer layers. Each of these layers (the expansion and retention layers, respectively) contains a dye that is sensitive to different light wavelengths in the infrared band.

To write a digital 1, for example, a laser, which is tuned to the expansion layer's wavelength, hits the surface and heats this layer, without affecting the retention layer. As a result of the tension between these two layers, the surface deforms into a "bump" that won't reflect light back to the device's laser detector and is read as a digital 1 (Fig. 3.14).

Erasure is accomplished by applying a laser to the surface at a wavelength that will affect only the retention layer. Once this layer is heated, the tension holding the bump together is reduced and the disk surface returns to its reflective 0 state.

The Central Processing Unit (CPU)

Technically speaking, the central processing unit, or CPU, is an electronic digital device that performs binary calculations for the purpose of accomplishing a specific task (or number of tasks). In short, the CPU is the brain of the computer.

A CPU can take many forms. It can exist as a single integrated circuit (IC) chip that is dedicated to a limited range of program tasks. Such microprocessors are used in controlling calculators, clocks, microwave ovens, TV sets, radios, car engines . . . the list goes on.

A CPU can also take the form of a personal computer (PC) that provides control over task-related hardware devices in an overall processing system. Bigger, more expensive systems, which handle large amounts of audio, communication, and signal processing data (such as is required in a multichannel audio environment), will often make use of a number of dedicated and separate CPUs. This arrangement allows more complex signal-processing functions to be handled, while leaving the simpler functions such as system control and screen drawing to a PC.

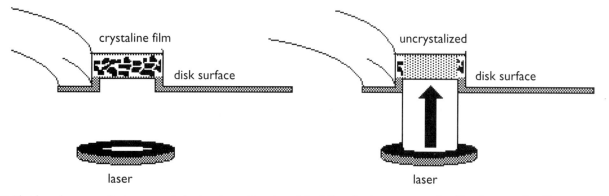

Fig. 3.13: The phase-change recording process works by changing small portions of the disk's surface between a crystalline (0) and noncrystalline (1) state.

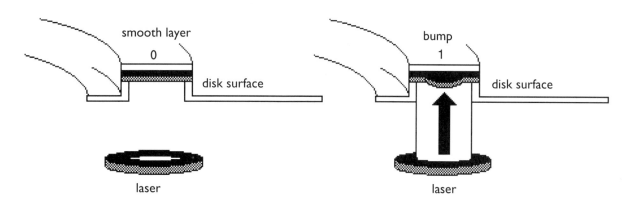

Fig. 3.14: The dye-polymer disk works by creating a tension between two surface layers in order to form either a smooth surface (0) or a bump (1).

The PC in Hard Disk Audio Production

One of the chief advantages of building a system around a personal computer is that the user/artist can customize the system to fit his or her production needs by adding software, peripheral options, and cost-effective hardware.

Probably the best options are the numerous software packages and the growing number of hardware systems that are available for the PC. These options have turned PC systems into "digital chameleons," capable of changing function to fit the necessary task at hand.

Three basic families of personal computers are commonly found at the hub of most random-access audio systems:

- Macintosh
- IBM-compatible
- Atari

Each computer family offers several computer models that bring their own distinct advantages and disadvantages to the art of personal computing.

The Mac

A personal computer system (PC) that is widely accepted by music and audio production professionals is the Macintosh family of computers from the Apple Computer Corporation (Fig. 3.15). One of the major reasons for the success of the "Mac" is its processing power and its graphical user interface located within a friendly window environment. This environment allows various application windows to be moved, expanded, tiled, and visually stacked onto the system's monitor. Users can easily interface with the system by manipulating graphic icons and using on-screen mouse commands.

An example of the Macintosh product line are the Quadra 660av and 840av personal computers. These PCs use a 68040 central processor that provides up to three hardware expansion slots for the 840av and one slot for the 660av, which allows third party hardware to be added for increased processing, graphics, video, or audio power.

Both of the av computers are shipped with full-color video capabilities and include a built-in AT&T DSP-3210 chip that supports the recording and playback of digital video and 16-bit audio.

The IBM Compatible

Because of its cost-effectiveness, acceptance, and sheer numbers within the business and production community, the IBM-compatible personal computer has become increasingly popular in both music and random-access audio applications (Fig. 3.16). In fact, there are more IBM compatibles in the marketplace (musical or otherwise) than any other type. As you might guess, a huge selection of cost-effective IBM-compatible PCs is currently available, and audio production-related hardware and software peripherals are on the rise to meet this demand.

Although there is a huge number of manufacturers and options, the one thing common to all IBM compatibles is their basic set of operating instructions. These instructions have long been standardized to work with various versions of Microsoft's disk operating system (DOS) which provides the PC with instructions for carrying out basic management and processing tasks.

IBM compatibles are usually categorized by the type of central processor that they use. For example, an XT is an older 8- or 16-bit system that often makes use of the 8088 CPU. These processors generally operate at too slow a speed to offer enhanced graphics or to permit digital audio processing. The IBM AT (which includes the 16- and 32-bit 286, 386, and 486 family of processors) offers far greater speeds and improved usage of on-board RAM memory.

These systems can run applications directly under MS-DOS or under Microsoft Windows' graphical operating system. The Windows environment has a Mac-like graphic interface that is likewise capable of switching between open programs, as well as running more than one program at a time (a feature known as multitasking).

In addition to its multitasking capabilities, the latest version of Windows (3.1 as of this writing) offers the advantage of using a system's shell known as a multimedia environment (MME or MPC). Multimedia acts as a computerized conduit for providing simultaneous control over, and interaction between, text, audio, graphics, and other on-line media. Chapter 9 has more in-depth information on multimedia.

Atari

Another computer that uses a strong graphical interface environment is the Atari ST line of personal computers. Included in this line are four models: 520 ST, 1040 ST, Mega 2, and Mega 4. All four models are compatible (and nearly identical) in design and operation. The major difference is the amount of memory that each computer is fitted with (512K, 1024K, 2048K, and 4096K, respectively). Any ST, however, can easily be upgraded to a RAM size of 4 megabytes. The Mega computing systems offer detachable keyboards, an expansion slot, and an expanded graphics processor. The 520 and 1040 don't have these features.

The ST makes use of a window-based graphical operating environment known as GEM (Graphic Environment Manager). This environment lets the user interface with programs by using drop-down menus, moving and resizable windows, icons, and desk accessories.

A cartridge port acts as an expansion slot by providing direct access to the CPU for external hardware/software processing systems, such as

Fig. 3.15: The Macintosh Quadra 840av running with OSC's Deck II 16-bit Multitrack Audio Workstation Software. (Courtesy of OSC.)

Fig. 3.16: Digidesign's Session 8 running on an IBM-compatible computer. (Courtesy of Digidesign.)

ROM-based desktop accessories, hardware RAM systems, video systems, and digital audio workstations.

The next generation in the Atari MIDI-compatible PC line is the TT, a true 32-bit processor that utilizes the speed and power of a 68030 microprocessor (running at 33 MHz). This system includes 2MB of RAM as standard (expandable to 8MB) and is compatible with Atari's entire ST product line. The TT has all of the standard Atari ports, plus 8-bit digital stereo sound, a floating point option, and six graphics modes.

Task-Specific Hardware Systems

All three of the PC systems mentioned earlier are capable of performing a wide range of basic programming tasks (such as word processing, financial and database calculations, graphics, etc.) without the need for additional hardware or processing systems. However, for certain specific tasks, more processing power is often needed. Also, hardware interfaces may be required to connect the computer to the outside world of digital peripherals.

To make this expansion process as straightforward as possible, PCs have a number of standardized slots that directly interface with a wide range of commercially available hardware cards. Once plugged in, this hardware combination makes it possible for an otherwise generic PC to perform processing or data distribution functions that are geared towards a specific task (Fig. 3.17).

These tasks are carried out within the card by translating the digital language spoken by an external device to a language that is understood by the computer's own CPU (and vice versa). Once translated, the computer can then deal with the distribution and storage of data in its usual man-

ner. Examples of the tasks that can be carried out by such hardware slot/card combinations are:

- Graphics monitor adapter
- Graphics scanning
- MIDI
- Digital audio
- Modem
- Fax
- Processing acceleration

The Audio Interface

Audio interface is a generic term for a hardware card or card/module combination that is used to integrate the personal computer with the world of digital audio. This interface design often includes analog-to-digital (A/D) converters and digital-to-analog (D/A) converters for connecting the digital world to the human world of analog.

Once in the digital domain, sophisticated processing and system-related functions are internally executed so that the system can do its intended job: namely that of recording, editing, processing, and reproducing digital audio in a straightforward manner. Some of the functions carried out by this central interface include:

- Interpreting control commands from the CPU and the user
- Displaying program and waveform data onto a monitor screen
- Routing digital audio data to and from RAM memory
- Routing samplefile data to and from various disk memory media
- Performing digital signal processing

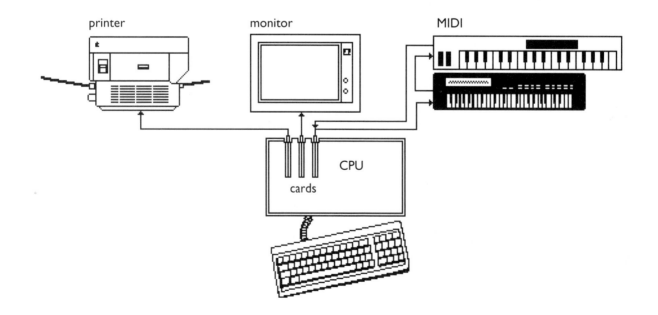

Fig. 3.17: External devices can be interfaced to a PC through hardware cards that are plugged into the computer's main processing board.

The Co-processor

Systems exist that dedicate the computer's main CPU to dealing with the task of handling digital audio and signal processing. However, the bit-stream's data density and number-crunching requirements are often too intensive for such systems to carry out anything but the most basic audio functions.

To provide for greater processing speed and advanced and/or real time DSP (digital signal processing), a device known as a co-processor is often used. Just as the name implies, a co-processor is a processor that works in conjunction with the main CPU to perform a dedicated processing task. Its main function is to take much of the processing load off of the computer's main CPU by performing specialized and mundane calculations.

For example, the process of playing back a soundfile while performing real-time digital equalization would place too great a strain on a computer's main CPU. A co-processor could be used to handle digital audio processing, and the task of routing the data from disk and to the audio interface could be left for the main CPU.

One of the most common co-processing chips used by the professional digital audio community is the Motorola DSP 56001. This 24-bit processor is capable of carrying out 20 million instructions per second (a speed usually associated with larger computing systems rather than with single-chip processors). This chip can often be found at the heart of an audio interface card, and additional 56001s can be found in systems that provide real-time multichannel signal processing.

Getting off the Bus

As you have seen, the job of the audio interface is to connect the main computer (and its associated functions) to the world of digital audio processing. Even though many systems reduce the computer's burden by using a co-processor, the computer itself is still an integral part of the file management and processing chain (Fig. 3.18A).

This is all well and good with a basic two- or four-channel hard disk system. However, the trend is to integrate personal computers into larger, more powerful multitrack systems. In such cases, the PC's main CPU can quickly sap your system's speed or, worse, you can run out of hardware slots just when you want to install that new whizbang DSP card that you've been drooling over.

To get around these potential problems, manufacturers are beginning to design modular systems whose processing functions are self-contained and don't use the PC's main processor for intensive number crunching (Fig. 3.18B). Instead, the PC is assigned the simple task of delegating control throughout the system and processing on-screen graphics. In this way, a system can easily be expanded to incorporate new hardware-based processing applications and processing speeds that are not dependent on the PC.

Systems Interface

The basic function of an audio interface is to connect analog audio and soundfile data to a computer. However, most integrated production systems require that the computer be connected to other media devices within the network. These devices require hardware interfaces such as:

- Control interface
- Digital audio
- MIDI
- Synchronization timing

Control Interface

A very important component that can't be underestimated in the day-to-day workings of audio production is that of control interface, or the way in which we as humans interface with digital devices. The methods used by different manufacturers to interface nonbinary humans to the world of digital audio (or digital anything for that matter) is a subject that could easily fill a book on its own.

The forces that drive systems design and human interface often depend on the manufacturer's subjective viewpoint of how the system should "look and feel." Market demand (how many can we sell if we make it this way versus that way?) is certainly another major factor. Additionally, the basic (or not so basic) function of the device will determine its design.

It's also interesting to note the differences in design from culture to culture. For example, American designs for hard disk recorders have chosen to follow the path of building a system around a PC and monitor screen. In the American scheme, control over on-screen waveform functions is accomplished by using a mouse or trackball (a hand-controlled device for manipulating the computer's cursor).

In contrast, certain systems have opted to design workstation systems from the ground up, using processors and controls that have been specially designed for audio applications. Instead of a standard computer monitor, such a system might show waveforms and command buttons on a touch-sensitive screen (Fig. 3.19). To execute a command using such a device, the user simply touches a "soft function key" on the screen.

In addition to standard computer controllers (such as the mouse), new task-specific controllers are appearing on the market. These controllers are a result of the increased power and integration showing up in recent PC-based audio workstations. Such workstations offer direct, hands-on control over such otherwise familiar audio functions as level mixing, transport remote controls, and waveform scrub alpha dials (Fig. 3.20).

It is important to realize that the many systems and interface types now on the market all have their own strengths and weaknesses. Since you (or

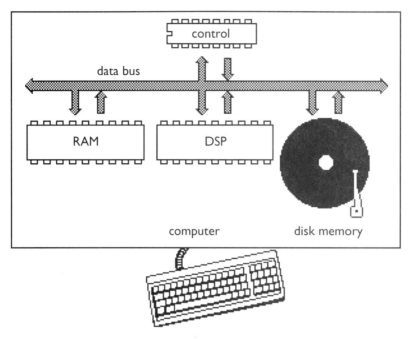

A. All disk and processing functions are carried out by the computer.

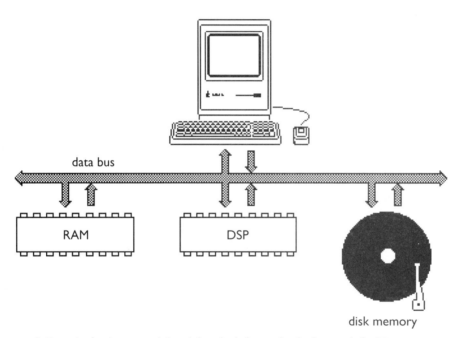

B. Processing functions are carried out independently from, and under the control of, a PC.

Fig. 3.18: Data processing methods.

those in your production facility) will be the one who will have to interact with your chosen system, take the time to find the system and design that best fit your particular application and your personal working style.

Digital Audio Interface

The digital I/O (input/output) interface is an audio communications port that allows the direct import and export of digital audio data between devices, such as digital tape recorders, digital audio workstations, and DAT and DCC machines.

In a computer-based system, a digital interface allows audio digital data to be received by the system and translated into a soundfile structure that can be understood by the audio-related

processing hardware and software. Chapter 6 has more information on these digital transfer formats.

MIDI Interface

The Musical Instrument Digital Interface, or MIDI, is a digital communications language and compatible hardware specification that enables electronic instruments, performance controllers, computers, and other devices to communicate with each other in a connected network (Fig. 3.21). MIDI translates performance or control-related actions into equivalent digital messages and then transmits these messages to other MIDI devices, where they can be used to communicate sound generation and control parameters in a performance setting.

Fig. 3.19: *The Foundation 2000 non-linear recorder - editor - mixer. (Courtesy of Fostex America.)*

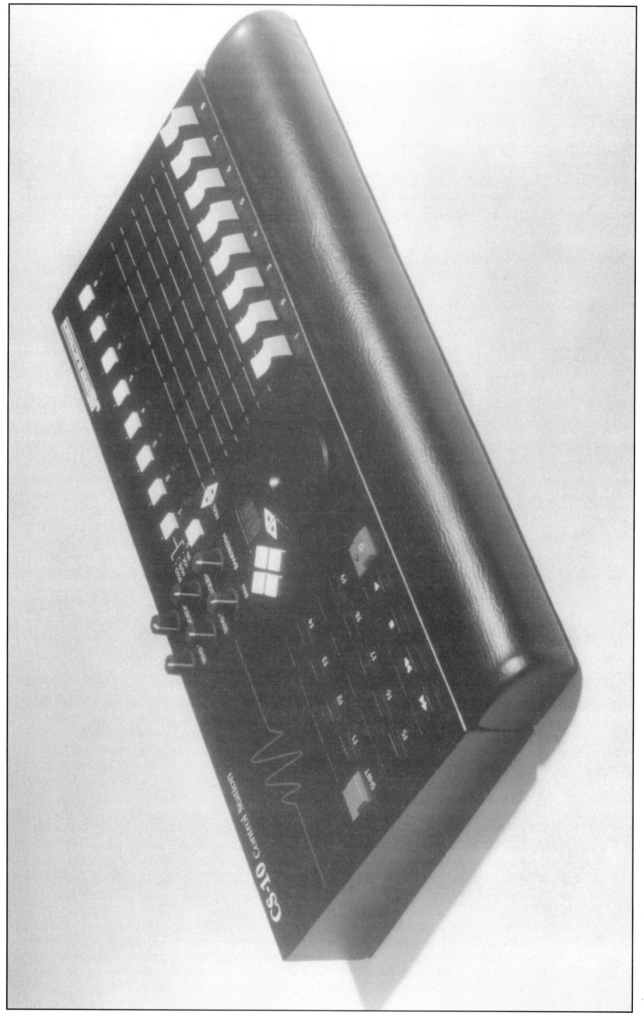

Fig. 3.20: The CS-10 Control station. (Courtesy of JLCooper Electronics.)

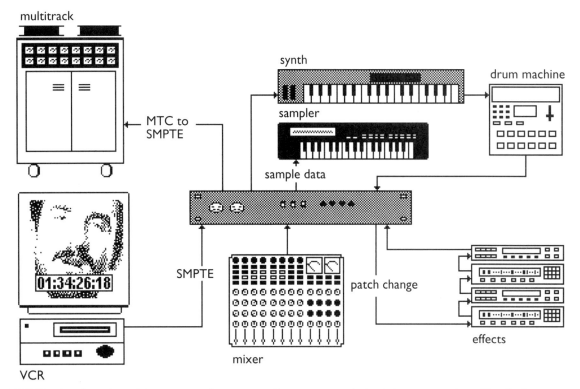

Fig. 3.21: A MIDI interface allows electronic instruments, performance controllers, computers, and other devices to communicate with each other.

Although MIDI devices and the personal computer both communicate via digital data, a hardware device known as a MIDI interface must be used in order to translate MIDI's serial message data into a structure that can be directly understood by the computer.

MIDI interfaces are available for most computer systems (Fig. 3.22). Such hardware devices are either passive or intelligent in nature. Passive systems essentially provide external MIDI ports and rely on the computer to provide the conversion. Intelligent systems incorporate sophisticated internal processors for routing MIDI data and performing mundane commands that would otherwise be left to the computer's internal processor.

Synchronization Timing

In most integrated production systems, it is very important that digital audio, MIDI, and external program material operate in a synchronous environment. Such an environment ensures that related events occur at the same time.

To provide system-wide synchronization, or "sync," various types of hardware devices are used to output and receive timing-related information. Such hardware devices are often used to provide and/or communicate accurate timing information between systems that carry analog audio, video, digital audio, and MIDI program data.

Although stand-alone "sync boxes" can be found nestled in many a MIDI and digital audio system, the more common setup is to integrate sync facilities into a modern-day intelligent MIDI interface or digital audio interface. Chapter 7 has more information on this subject and provides further discussion of sync (including SMPTE, MIDI time code, and video sync).

Power Line Conditioning

Now that you've looked at some of the hardware devices used in creating a computer-based system, you should be aware of a potential threat to this expensive and often sensitive circuitry that can lurk within the electric company's power lines. These potential problems exist in the form of power surges, "brownouts," and AC line noise.

In the day-to-day life of an electric line, power surges (also known as voltage surges or "spikes") can make their way into your computer. Such spikes can cause a system to overwork, leading to circuit damage if the surge levels are overly large.

Just as spikes can cause potential problems within a computer-based system, voltage sags, or brownouts, can also cause hardware headaches. Brownouts can cause a system (most often its power supply) to overwork and overheat, resulting in failure or damage. Localized brownouts are often caused by overloaded building circuits and by increased demand from power hogs such as refrigerators, air conditioners, or heavy industrial equipment. During hot summer months when power demands are high, utility companies are often forced to reduce voltage to customers in order to avoid total power blackouts.

Another frequent occurrence is line noise the reception of unwanted RF (radio frequency) and EMI (electromagnetic interference) through the power lines.

You can easily protect your system from these power gremlins by investing in a surge protector, uninterruptable power supply (UPS), or power conditioner (Fig. 3.23). The less-costly surge protector does exactly what it says it'll do: it

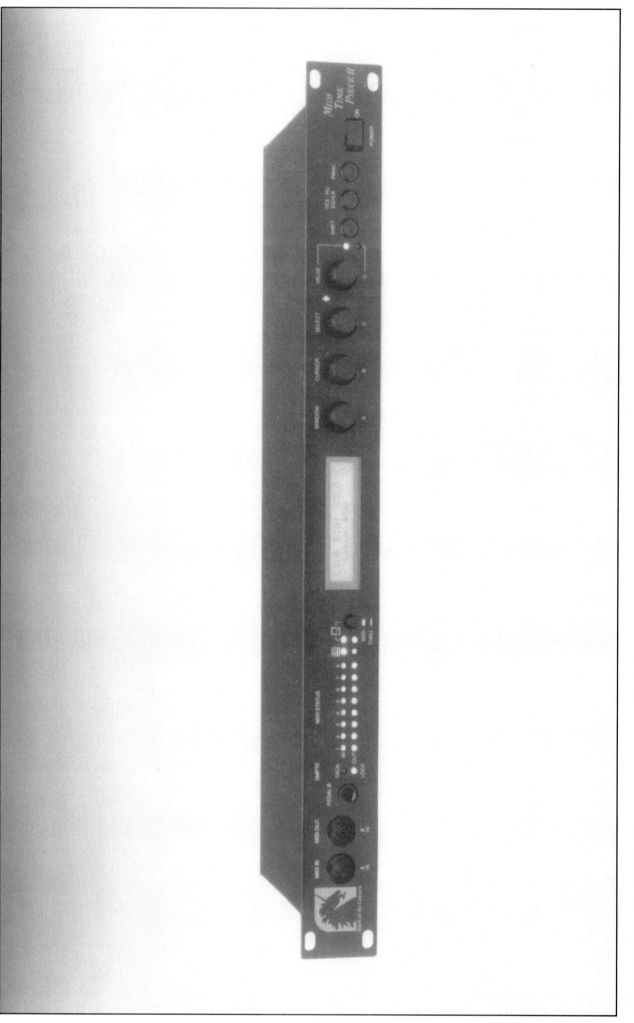

Fig. 3.22: *The MIDI Time Piece II MIDI interface/routing system. (Courtesy of Mark of the Unicorn, Inc.)*

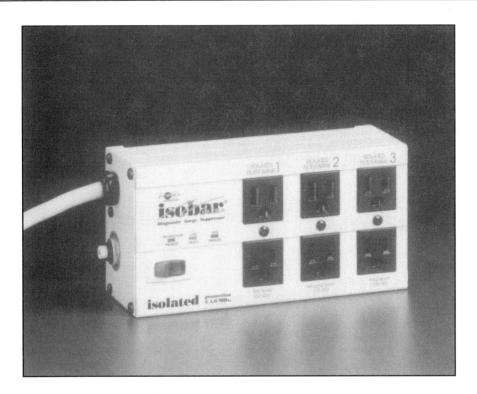

Fig. 3.23: An AC line filter and noise suppressor. (Courtesy of Tripp Lite.)

protects your power line against surges. A power conditioner is often more expensive but can guard against brownouts and can filter out AC line noise. Some power-regulating devices offer the worthwhile feature of temporary battery backup. In the event of a total power failure, this backup could give you the time needed to save your data before the system goes down.

Chapter 4
Sampling Technology and Techniques

In its most basic form, the term sampling refers to the process of encoding digital audio into RAM (and in some cases, ROM). Once data has been stored into this instant access media, it can be accessed, reproduced, and even played in a musical fashion.

Along with digital delay devices and early recording systems, sampling technology was one of the first digital applications to be used in commercial music production.

Today, this technology has grown to become an integral part of modern music production, both on stage and in the studio. It has become an invaluable tool in the placement of dialog and sound effects for film, audio-for-video, and broadcast production.

The importance of sampling technology in commercial music and sound production is due to the benefits that it brings to production:

- Repeatability
- Editability
- Instant access
- Ease of storage

This chapter looks at the sample itself and at the ways that it can be recorded, stored, edited, and played back. Then the various types of sample-based devices and musical instruments used in present-day production are discussed. The chapter concludes with a section on applied sampling techniques to help you get the best possible sample by using tried and true methods.

The Sample

In its simplest form, a sample exists as a recorded block of digital audio representing an acoustic event (such as a vocal line, sax solo, etc.) or an electro-acoustic event (such as the electronically generated sounds of a guitar or synthesizer). Such a block of sampled audio has both a finite duration and a bandwidth.

Once a sample has been digitally encoded, it can be easily stored onto disk for later recall. However, a sample's true power can be seen (or rather heard) once it has been loaded into a solid-state memory medium, such as RAM or ROM.

After a digital samplefile (such as a horn hit, James Brown scream, snare drum, etc.) is loaded into memory, the fast access speed of RAM or ROM allows all or portions of the event to be instantaneously accessed and reproduced, any number of times and at any time.

This instant access is possible because the device is capable of "mapping" the samplefile at precise sample address locations within its memory (Fig. 4.1A). By addressing a particular address location, the sampler can instantly retrieve and reproduce any part of an encoded sample.

Assuming that sufficient memory is available, it's possible to load any number of recorded samples into a system (Fig. 4.1B). These can then be accessed either one at a time or simultaneously, depending on the system's design type. The latter system type lets the sampling artist have simultaneous access to a number of musical instruments, sound effects, or any other sound combination that he or she might dream up.

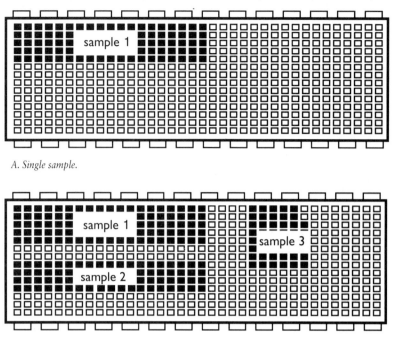

A. *Single sample.*

B. *Multiple samples.*

Fig. 4.1: *Representation of mapped sample address locations within a memory chip.*

Two types of sampling systems are available for accessing samples from random access memory:

- Monophonic
- Polyphonic

Quite simply, a monophonic sampling device is capable of reproducing only one sampled sound at a time, whereas a polyphonic device is capable of reproducing more than one sampled sound (commonly called voices) at a time. For example, a 16-voice, polyphonic system would be capable of reproducing up to 16 simultaneous sampled events (often over one or more user-selectable output channels).

A sample is accessed and reproduced through the use of an event start switch known as a trigger. A trigger can be initiated manually (by pressing a button or key, by hitting a pad, or by performing on a music keyboard), or it can be initiated automatically (as a time code or MIDI event).

Another advantage of most sampling systems is the ability to shift the pitch of a reproduced sample up or down in real time. This useful feature is most notably used when playing music on a polyphonic sampling keyboard. Quite simply, musical pitch shifting occurs by reproducing a recorded samplefile at various sample rates. Samples that are reproduced at rates higher than the originally recorded rate will play back as being higher in pitch, while lower rates will play back as lower in pitch. By dividing the number of possible sample rate shifts into ratios that match standard musical intervals, it's possible to play these samples using the keys of a standard MIDI keyboard. Likewise, a number of different samples can be triggered from the same keyboard, so that a richer orchestration or individual sounds can be easily played.

Sampling is a technological artform, and as such the "first rule" of recording applies: There are no rules, only guidelines.

That is, a sample might be created for any number of possible applications, and its recorded source can be taken from any imaginable instrument, object, or sound-producing device. It can also be of any length (depending on available memory) and can range from the transient burst of a studio snare drum to a 5-minute sample of an endangered rain forest in Central America.

A sampled sound that has been created for the specific purpose of emulating a musical instrument would most likely have been taken from a recording of the original instrument itself. Such a sampling session often involves the practice of recording various instrument sounds onto digital or possibly analog tape in a carefully controlled studio environment. In this day and age, however, an enormous range of previously recorded and edited samplefiles containing instruments, effects noises, etc., can already be found on disk, CD, and CD-ROM. Such commercially available sample libraries are the mainstay of both electronic musicians and visual post-production facilities.

Commerical sample libraries need not be the only option. The practice of creating personal sample libraries is also widely used by professional and nonprofessional artists alike. Such personal samples can be created from original acoustic or electronically generated sound sources, although it's also a common practice for samples to be "lifted" from previously recorded source material (such as records, CD, TV, videotapes, etc.).

When a recorded sound of any origin is transferred into a sampling device, the source material invariably contains extraneous sounds that exist both before and after the desired sound (Fig. 4.2). This undesired sound might include breath noises

Fig. 4.2: Example of an unedited sample.

before the desired sample, extraneous fidget sounds from an antsy musician, or unwanted wingflap sounds just after the perfect peacock screech. At this point, the sonic waste can be edited out in order to clean up or process the sound into its final form.

Sample Editing

A basic form of editing offered by any sampling system is the ability to trim the in-points and out-points of an edit. This eliminates any undesirable sounds surrounding the unedited sample. Trimming is accomplished by instructing the system's microprocessor to ignore (do not access and reproduce) all samples that exist before a user-defined in-point, and/or those following a desired out-point (Fig. 4.3).

This memory access function has the overall effect of cleaning up the sampled sound, while at the same time tightening the in-point of a recorded sample, so that the sample will immediately sound when it is triggered.

Looping

Another powerful editing technique often used in performance-based sampling systems is a process known as looping. One of the basic facts of life for a keyboard-based sampler is that it can store only a few seconds to a few minutes worth of sound. Looping, as a tool, has two important functions. It efficiently stores music data within a limited amount of memory space, and it serves to sustain notes (known as a sustain loop) that are well past the length of the original sample (thereby preventing the sound from abruptly stopping while the keys on a keyboard are being held down).

Such a loop is created by defining and then repeatedly accessing a marked segment of a recorded sample from RAM in a continuous fashion. This is done in a way that sustains the sound for as long as the note or sound is to be held (Fig. 4.4). This loop (or loops) can be created from waveform segments that are very short (consisting of a few periods), or they can be longer in length. In general, the segment to be looped will be taken from a portion of the original waveform that doesn't change over time (is cyclic in nature). Such a segment can often be found in the final sustained portion of the waveform.

When you are creating a looped splice, life can be made easier by following this simple rule: Match the waveform shape and amplitude at the beginning of the loop with the waveform shape and amplitude at its end.

By this I mean that a loop can best be created by finding a waveform segment that contains a series of repetitive waveforms. Once this area has been spotted, you can place a beginning marker at the beginning of the section to be looped and, likewise, you can place an end loop marker at the end. The next task is to match up the waveforms at the beginning and end markers so that their levels are the same (Fig. 4.5A). This avoids a signal jump or distortion at the loop joint (Fig. 4.5B).

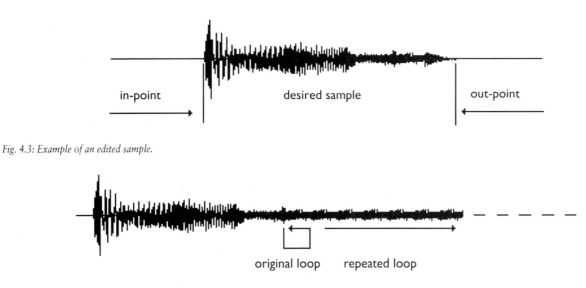

Fig. 4.3: Example of an edited sample.

Fig. 4.4: Example of a sample with a sustain loop.

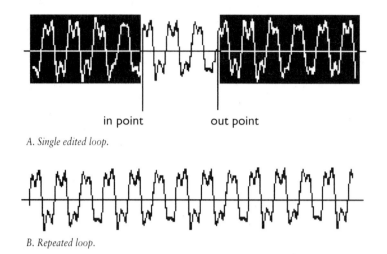

in point   out point

A. Single edited loop.

B. Repeated loop.

Fig. 4.5: A loop can be created by placing markers at the beginning and end points of a repetitive waveform.

Certain performance sampling systems (devices that allow samples to be played as music) allow more than one loop point to be programmed into a samplefile. This has the effect of making the sample less repetitive and more natural and adds to its range of expressiveness when played on a keyboard. In addition to sustain loops, a release loop (Fig. 4.6) can be programmed to decay the sound when the keyboard note is released.

The Samplefile

Once edited, a sample and its edit information can be saved and archived as a block of digital data onto a storage and/or backup medium. This stored sound data is often referred to as a samplefile.

Several industry standard and system-specific file formats make it possible for personal or commercially available samples to be easily stored, transported, and distributed. Most recently, a series of standardized samplefile formats are being supported by an increasing number of computer-based sampling hardware and software systems. This allows samplefiles to be easily distributed between production facilities and different sampling systems.

Samplefile Media Storage

A number of data recording media are currently available, with each type having its own strengths that are best suited for a particular range of applications. The following are the most commonly found media for storing and archiving digital samplefiles:

- Floppy disk
- Hard disk
- CD
- CD-ROM
- Erasable and write-once optical disks

Floppy Disk

The floppy disk is commonly used by sample artists to store samples that are of short duration. It is a popular, low-cost format, since many music-based sampling systems and PCs are equipped with a floppy disk drive.

Hard Disk

A major advantage to storing samplefiles onto hard disk is the ability to store larger samples and/or a greater number of samples onto disk. This increased capacity often means that a larger sound library can be created. The library can then be cataloged for the quick search and retrieval of files. Removable hard disk drive packs let you build and catalog sample libraries without the filespace and nonremovable drawbacks of a standard hard disk.

CD

A sizable number of CD sound effects (SFX) libraries are available on the commercial market. Instead of offering sampled sounds in a samplefile format, these libraries must often use the standard CD-audio format for storing the audio data. This allows sounds to be copied to any sampler or

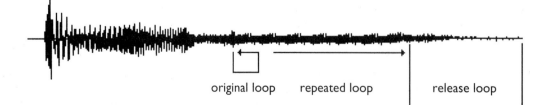

original loop   repeated loop   release loop

Fig. 4.6: Example of a looped sample with an added release loop.

audio storage medium by using a standard CD player or CD-ROM equipped to play back CD-audio.

These libraries vary greatly in size, content, and style. Collectively they constitute a large, in-depth database of mechanical, animal, and almost any other type of sampled sound that you could imagine. Instrumental sample libraries are also available on CD. These are created for the purpose of transferring various sounds, styles, and playing nuances into a keyboard-based sampler for performance purposes.

CD-ROM

Sample libraries are also available on CD-ROM. These discs are often encoded with standard or sampler-specific file formats (such as Sound Designer II, E-mu E-III, Roland S-770, and other popular formats). Because the discs are encoded with raw digital data, preprogrammed information such as edit and multiple loop points is often embedded in the data, along with sampled audio, to make the loaded sounds "performance ready."

Erasable and Write-Once Optical Disks

Erasable and write-once optical disks offer both high data storage densities and removability. In addition, they offer the ability to store (write) personal samplefiles onto optical disk.

Other Sources

Besides the sources already mentioned, a common source of samplefiles is raw audio data "lifted" from prerecorded sources (such as commercially available CDs, tapes, records, and old TV shows). Previously released samples have shown up (or have been featured) on countless modern productions. The practice of lifting sounds has actually become so widespread that royalty and copyright controversies have arisen over who owns portions of the rights to the new performances that are based (in whole or in part) on previously released samples.

This brings up the not-so-simple point that the lifting of copyright performance segments can be an act of illegal piracy. Always take care to ensure that the material is currently not under copyright, or if it is, make sure that the appropriate royalties are distributed to the rightful copyright owner. When in doubt, consult a music layer or sample clearinghouse (a service that makes noncopyright performances available to sample artists).

Finally, it bears mentioning that samplefiles in various formats and content can often be found on many larger computer bulletin board services (BBS), such as those that include a section for performing musicians. However, with the onset of desktop multimedia production and programming, the availability of low-resolution sampled sounds for consumer sound boards is increasing rapidly.

ROM-Based Samplers

One of the first sampling systems to appear on the market for music performance purposes (as well as other applications) was the ROM-based sampler. As its name implies, this device reads and outputs samplefile data from internal memory storage. Depending on its application, this type of device might directly output audio in its originally stored form. Or, in the case of music performance modules, the information might be further processed and output (by providing musical shift pitching, sample looping, modulation, and other waveform modifiers).

Early music samplers of this type were loaded with a limited variety of carefully recorded samples that represented a number of original instruments and effects. Often, these sounds were factory-encoded onto EPROMs and inserted into the device. An EPROM is an integrated memory chip that can easily be programmed to retain digital data, without the need for a constant power supply. Usually these chips could be replaced easily by the user so that additional sounds could be accessed as needed.

Today, with improved mass production and design technology, large-scale integrated circuits can be designed containing hundreds of sampled sounds and related edit information, often providing megabytes of storage memory.

The Drum Machine

The drum machine (Fig. 4.7) was one of the first applications to make use of ROM-based sample technology. This musical instrument (also loosely known as a "beat box") contains a factory-loaded ROM that is encoded with carefully recorded and edited samples of the assorted instruments making up the modern drum and percussion set. More recent drum machines offer a number of percussion styles, including examples of heavily processed rock drums, gated samples, orchestral hits, and maybe even a few James Brown screams.

In addition to the simple reproduction of percussion sounds from ROM, each sample can be individually edited. This gives control over such parameters as tuning (sample rate adjustment), level, output assignment, panning, etc.

Most drum machines can be triggered from one of two sources: from its controller pads or via MIDI. Controller pads are a set of large, rugged "buttons" that are located on the machine's top or front panel. They provide a straightforward playing surface that often includes velocity and aftertouch capabilities.

The true power of the drum machine is best realized when it is being triggered from an external MIDI source, such as a sequencer, MIDI keyboard, or external controller. Since most drum machines can both respond to and transmit MIDI messages, each sample can be programmed to a specific note message (and its associated parameters).

For example, we could set our music keyboard

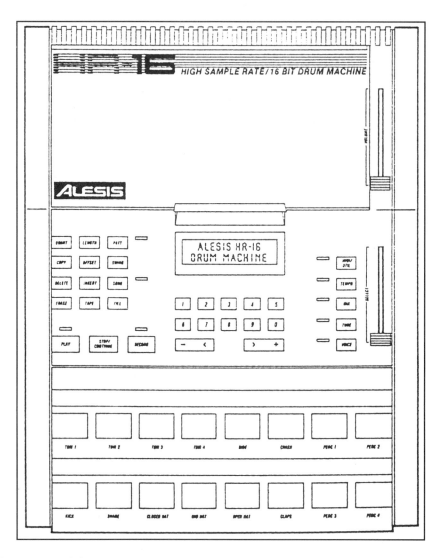

Fig. 4.7: HR-16 drum machine. (Courtesy of Alesis Corporation.)

to transmit on the same MIDI channel that the beat box is set to respond to. By pressing the lowest note on the keyboard, a series of MIDI messages are sent to the drum machine and the kick drum is heard. By pressing other keys, the entire drum set could be heard.

At this point, it is a simple matter to record all of these messages into a MIDI sequencer at once, or we could individually build up each drum in the kit into the sequenced drum pattern, one at a time. In addition to being externally controlled, the drum machine's own playing pads can be used to transmit MIDI data to a sequencer, or even as a trigger for controlling other MIDI devices.

Most drum machines have a number of audio outputs that allow individual or grouped sounds to be routed to one or more output channels. This feature makes it possible for samples to be routed to a channel on a mixer or recording console so that they can be individually processed (using equalization, reverb, etc.). It also makes possible the recording of isolated drum samples onto the separate tracks of a multitrack tape recorder.

Many drum machines also incorporate some kind of basic internal sequencer for the creation and storage of drum rhythms (known as patterns). The design and the operation of these editor/

sequencers often vary from one system to the next. However, a common way to program rhythm patterns into a drum machine's internal memory is to use step-time note entry. Step-time is a process that allows musical or rhythmic notes to be entered and edited into a pattern, one at a time (Fig. 4.8).

Often, the individual voices of a drum machine are triggered directly from standard MIDI performance sequencers. However, a number of computer-based sequencers are also available that have been especially designed so that drum patterns can be easily built up, using simple on-screen graphics. In this way, patterns can be programmed by simply clicking the mouse on a graphic grid. The grid plots individual sounds over time and then provides the means to assemble these patterns into a final arrangement.

ROM-Based Performance Samplers

Of course, performance sounds are not strictly limited to percussion sounds. Any number of instruments, percussion, or effects can be captured into a ROM. This is the case with many of the recent keyboard and rack module ROM-based performance samplers. These devices often use standard sampling technology to store hundreds of

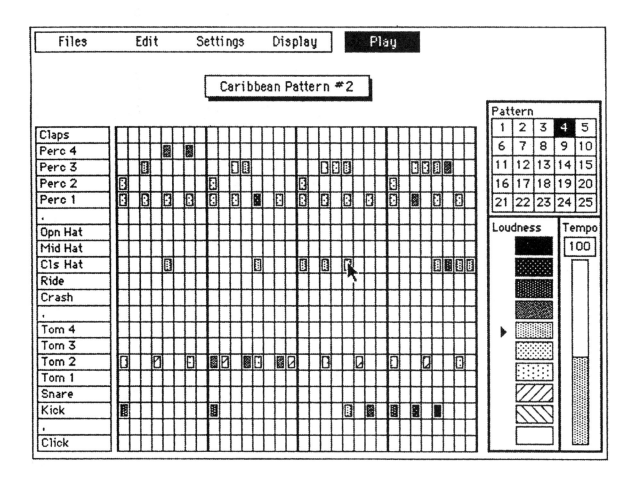

Fig. 4.8: Example of a step-time sequencing program.

edited sounds onto a large-scale ROM chip. Although the sample's loop information is factory-programmed, these devices offer extensive user-edit capabilities. For example, samples can be combined or layered to produce a richer, more complex sound texture. Sound parameters (such as frequency and amplitude modulation, envelope editing, and effects programming) are also available and can be stored into a memory bank as a patch (a user-named setup file that contains sound parameter data).

By far the most popular ROM-based systems of this type are the newer generations of digital "synthesizers" (Fig. 4.9). Although certain systems are capable of combining both synthesis and sample technology into one box, many of these keyboard and rack module devices are not really synthesizers at all. Instead of generating sounds, these devices reproduce and process an impressive number of high-quality percussion and specially designed performance samples. Since these devices are not promoted as sampling systems, the prerecorded sounds are often freed from the restriction of having to emulate an acoustic instrument. Thus, these sounds might also include sounds that range from analog and digital synth sounds to wild space-age blast effects.

Another popular system is the ROM sample module. Billed as a sample playback system rather than a synthesizer hybrid, this device is often (but not necessarily) used to emulate musical instruments from a wide range of traditional and ethnic styles. As with sample-based synthesizer systems, control parameters can be fully modified by the user and saved as patch data. These devices are generally equipped with multiple audio outputs for routing isolated or grouped voices to the individual inputs of a mixer or multitrack tape machine. As with most modern modules, each voice can be played over the entire keyboard's range in a polyphonic fashion (often reproducing up to 32 simultaneous voices).

One of the most notable of the ROM sample modules is the Proteus family of 16-bit multi-timbral digital sound modules from E-mu Systems. These 32-voice, single rack-space devices use custom VLSI (very large scale integration) technology to encode some of E-mu's most notable sounds from their E-III sound library into a 4MB ROM chip (internally expandable to 8MB via an expansion ROM kit).

The original Proteus module offers a wide range of sampled voices that include pianos, organs, strings, horns, guitars, basses, drums, latin percussion, etc. The Proteus/2 version has 8 megabytes of new 16-bit samples, which include solo violin, viola, cello, ensemble strings (both arco and pizzicato), a full range of orchestral woodwinds

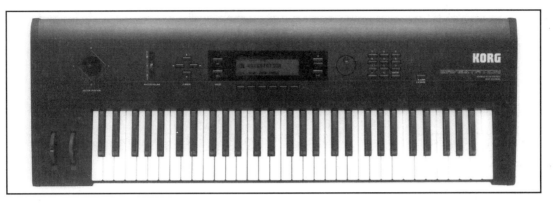

Fig. 4.9: The Korg WaveStation digital synthesizer. (Courtesy of Korg USA Inc.)

and brass, harp, celesta, timpani, tubular bells, and a wide selection of orchestral bells. The Pro-Cussion version offers a large library of sampled drum and percussion sounds in a number of instrumental, ethnic, and signal-processing styles.

RAM-Based Samplers

Unlike ROM-based samplers, RAM-based samplers make it possible for sampled audio to be both written into (recorded) and read from (reproduced) its internal solid-state memory. This means that the user can sample and edit his or her own sounds. The only limitations are those of the system itself and the amount of available memory (determining the total recording time). Once sampled and edited, the newly created sounds can be used to assemble your own personal library.

One-Shot Samplers

One-shot sampling is a loose term for a system that is capable of recording, reproducing, and editing only a single samplefile at a time from a block of RAM memory. Such a system allows a short sample to be entered into memory, where it can be triggered manually from an external trigger or time code.

RAM-based sampling capabilities such as these are often found in professional multifunction digital effects devices. These devices are able to sample monaural or stereo audio into soundblocks ranging in length from only a few seconds to a couple of minutes.

Usually some degree of editing is offered. This might include in- and out-point edit facilities for the purpose of cleaning up individual samples and facilities for a limited amount of pitch transposition.

One-shot sampling functions can be used for a number of purposes. However, they are particularly useful whenever a samplefile of limited size is repeatedly used (as might be found with a snare sound or short vocal chorus). Sample triggering can be done manually from a panel button, by MIDI note trigger, automatically through an external key feature, or by a MIDI sequence. The external key feature allows a sample to be triggered from an external sound source, such as a trigger pad or recorded audio track.

Some of the multifunction processors currently on the market have no means of storing soundfiles onto magnetic disk. This implies that a sample is lost once the system is powered off or once the device's program function is changed, thus requiring that the sampled audio be replayed back into memory. Although the sampling capabilities of these devices are limited, should you find yourself without a dedicated sampler and need to manually trigger a vocal backup line or shrill Crusty-the-Clown laugh into a mix at various points, these straightforward devices can come in quite ha-ha-ha-handy.

RAM-Based Performance Samplers

A RAM-based performance sampler is much like its one-shot sampling counterpart in that it allows the user to record, edit, and modify sampled audio from the device's internal RAM memory store. However, what sets the RAM-based performance sampler apart is the sophistication of its edit capabilities. Once digitized samples have been loaded into the system, in- and out-points and looping edit parameters can be configured, and a standard range of signal modifiers can be applied to further shape the sample into a musical sound.

One other major difference between the ROM- and RAM-based samplers is the RAM-based system's ability to import and distribute samplefile data. Commonly, both keyboard samplers and their module counterparts will sport a floppy disk drive that allows edited samples to be saved to disk and reloaded at will. This is necessary since the sample and edit data would otherwise be permanently lost should the unit be shut off.

This disk format is both cost-effective and easily transportable. The major drawback, however, is the fact that only a few seconds worth of sample data can be saved into each floppy disk.

Many high-end sampling systems include an internal, high-capacity hard disk drive. This allows a greater number of samplefiles to be stored and greatly improves the system's data access time for calling up samplefiles from disk.

Mapping Samples

Most samplers, of both the ROM and RAM variety, are polyphonic and will often have multiple audio outputs to which individual sounds that are played on a music keyboard can be routed. The control function that determines which keys on the keyboard will trigger a particular sample, and how, is known as its mapping function.

When mapping a sample over the keyboard's playing surface, it's usually a simple matter to program the range of notes that will output a particular sound. Such a mapping arrangement could be limited to a single note (which might be the case when drums or sound effects are triggered from a keyboard, as is shown in Fig. 4.10A), or it could be mapped over one or more octaves, as shown in Fig. 4.10B, so that the sample could be musically played. Each sound, in turn, could then be assigned either to the device's main stereo output pair or to any of its individual outputs.

Since the individual voices of a polyphonic device can be assigned to a range over the keyboard's playing surface, it most likely would be a simple matter for a musician to play a bass part with the left hand, piano/strings with the right, and brass hits over a single octave of the keyboard (Fig. 4.11). A multiple mapping setup such as this is often known as a split setup, or split.

In addition to key selection, it's possible to select the velocity (MIDI volume messages) settings that will trigger a sampled voice. For example, our octave of brass samples could be set up so that when the notes are softly played, muted trombones sound, but when the notes are played loudly, both trombones and trumpets sound. Alternatively, a single sound effects note could be programmed so that a "soft" velocity touch outputs the distant cry of a hawk, and a "loud" velocity touch outputs a less distant sample of a screech.

The Akai S3200 MIDI stereo digital sampler is a popular example of a performance sampling system. This rack-mounted device (Fig. 4.12)

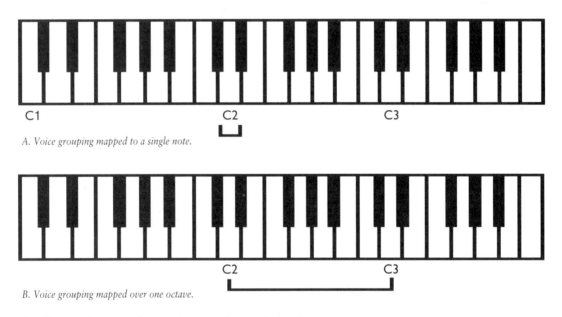

C1   C2   C3

A. Voice grouping mapped to a single note.

C2   C3

B. Voice grouping mapped over one octave.

Fig. 4.10: Examples of how sample voices can be mapped onto a performance keyboard.

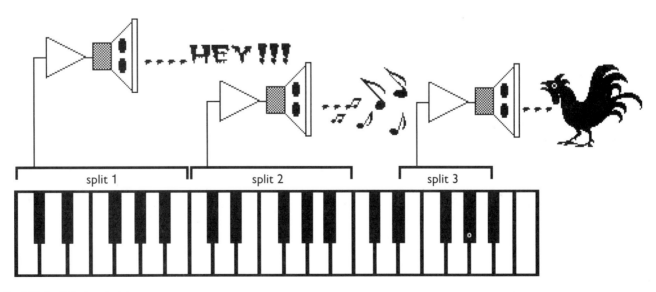

split 1   split 2   split 3

Fig. 4.11: A split keyboard setup.

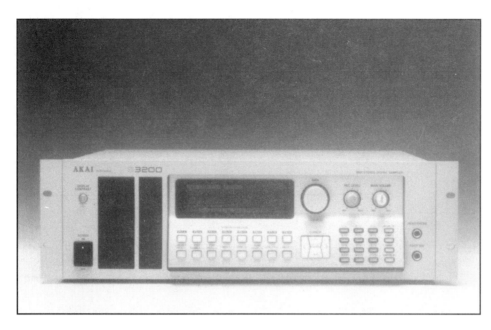

Fig. 4.12: The Akai S3200 MIDI *stereo digital sampler. (Courtesy of Akai Professional/Digital.)*

offers 16-bit, 32-voice polyphonic playback, with each voice being assignable either to a stereo output mix or to any of its 8 individual outputs. A few of the S3200's features include a standard memory of 8 Mb (expandable to 32 Mb), SMPTE reader/generator, SCSI interface, digital I/O and direct to disc recording (to a 105 Mb internal hard disk or optional 3.5" removable magneto-optical drive).

Computer-Based Performance Samplers

Since the latter half of the 1980s, powerful performance sampling systems have been especially designed to be incorporated into computer-based production systems. Systems such as New England Digital's Synclavier are examples of how sample and mapping capabilities can be used to create highly expressive sonic textures.

With the advent of the 1990s, however, sampling systems that can be incorporated directly into the personal computer have begun to appear on the market. These lower-cost systems provide the power and setup programmability that come with their ability to communicate directly in real time with other computer programs (such as a MIDI sequencer, hard disk recorder, sample editor, etc.).

An example of this type of system is Digidesign's SampleCell II 16-bit stereo sample playback card for the Macintosh or IBM-Windows family of computers (Fig. 4.13). These RAM-based card inserts directly into an open slot on the computer, which makes it possible for up to 32 simultaneous, CD- quality voices (at a 44.1-kHz sample rate) to be polyphonically routed to any of the card's eight polyphonic audio outputs. In addition, up to 32MB of on-board memory can be installed by the user with standard off-the-shelf Macintosh SIMM kits.

SampleCell II's system edit program includes a range of tools that take advantage of the computer's point-and-click graphic environment to load sampled sounds and to edit their performance setup, as well as to save or recall a particular setup under a given filename. The program's mixer-like interface (Fig. 4.14) provides on-screen control over each sampled sound (or group of samples), through the use of level, panning, balance, output assign, and a range of MIDI mapping tools (such as key range/velocity assignments and envelope contours).

The sample map window allows keygroup and velocity assignments settings to be visually controlled from an intuitive graphics screen. To change a note or velocity range assignment, you simply use the mouse to select the vertical or horizontal assignment "bar" that you wish to change and move the bar to a new position. A matrix modulation window provides control over MIDI modulation, envelope design, as well as controller source and destination assignment.

SampleCell II is capable of reading any Sound Designer II 44.1-kHz soundfile, and thus can access user-sampled files from any number of compatible sources. This package comes shipped with Sound Designer editing and Sound Designer II SC sample editing software and two factory-encoded CD-ROMs that incudes hundreds of acoustic and electronic soundfiles that are edited and ready for loading into the system. In addition to this, over 25 third-party CD-ROMs are commercially available for this card.

Distributing Sampled Audio

Because sampling systems are often part of a larger integrated MIDI and digital audio production system, samplefile data must often be communicated between devices or programs within a connected network. In order for most samplers

Fig. 4.13: *SampleCell 16-bit stereo NuBus sample playback card for the Macintosh. (Courtesy of Digidesign, Inc.)*

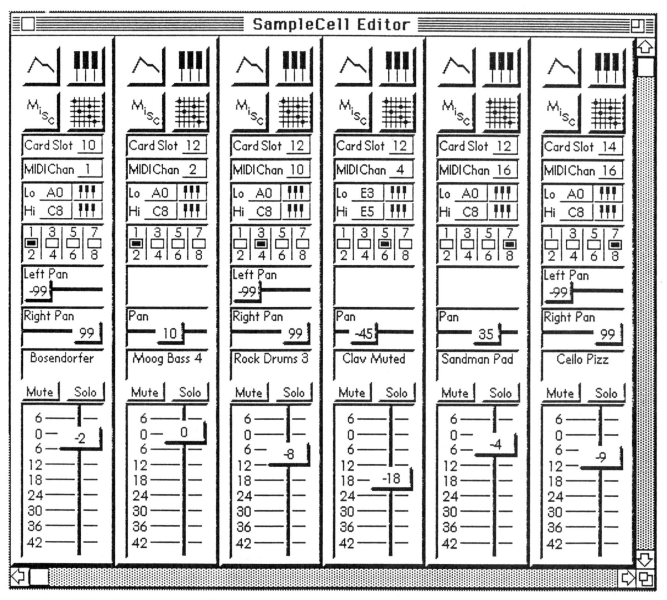

Fig. 4.14: SampleCell II's editor screen. (Courtesy of Digidesign.)

and related software management programs to communicate systemwide, standards have been adopted for importing and exporting samplefile data. These include:

- The MIDI SDS (sample dump standard)
- The SCSI (small computer systems interface)
- The SMDI (SCSI musical data interface)

MIDI **Sample Dump Standard**

The sample dump standard (SDS) has been adopted as a protocol for transmitting sampled digital audio and sustain loop information from one sampling device to another. This handshake protocol is transmitted as a series of MIDI system exclusive (Sys-Ex) messages for successful data transfer between sampling hardware.

Although most samplers share common characteristics, many sampling devices can recognize only device-specific Sys-Ex messages. Should this likely event occur when transmitting samplefile data from one sampler to another (such as those sam-

plers made by different manufacturers or even those having different model numbers), a computer-based system (such as a sample editor or digital audio workstation) would be required to make the necessary Sys-Ex code translations.

One of the greatest drawbacks of SDS is its speed. The data transfer can be a rather slow process, since it conforms to the MIDI standard of transmitting serial data at a rate of 31.25 kbaud.

SCSI

More recently, computer-based digital audio systems and sampling devices have been able to transmit and receive sampled audio via SCSI (small computer systems interface). SCSI is a bidirectional parallel communications protocol that is commonly used by personal computer systems to exchange digital data between devices at high speeds.

When used in digital audio applications, it provides a direct data link for transferring sound-files at a rate of 500,000 bits/second (nearly 17 times the speed of MIDI) or higher. Such an interface can provide a fast and straightforward means for transferring audio, program, and setup data between devices and for transferring archived samplefile data from sources such as CD-ROM or hard disk.

SMDI

As already mentioned, a number of sample editing programs use SCSI to transmit and receive soundfile information between samplers and the computer systems. Unfortunately, special drivers (special communications subprograms) must be used for each specific sampler, and SCSI cannot be directly used to dump data between samplers.

This, however, seems to be changing with the implementation of SMDI (an acronym for SCSI musical data interface). SMDI was developed by Matt Issaacson for Peavey Electronics as a non-device specific format for transferring digitally sampled audio between SCSI-equipped samplers and computers at speeds that can range up to 300 times faster than MIDI's transmission rate of 31.25 Kbytes per second. This means that all you'd need to transfer digital audio directly from one supporting sampler to any other device is to connect the SMDI ports (via a standard SCSI cable). It's just that simple.

Although SMDI is loosely based upon MIDI SDS, it has more advantages over its slower cousin than just speed. For example, it can distribute stereo or multichannel samplefiles, isn't limited to files that are less than two megawords in length and can transmit associated file info (such as filename, pitch values and sample number range). Sound patch and device-specific setup parameters can also be transmitted and received over SMDI lines through the use of standard System Exclusive (Sys-Ex) messages.

SMDI is not, however, designed to replace MIDI. Although MIDI isn't the fastest at shuffling samples around, it is still the best way for communicating real-time performance and control data. Therefore, SMDI should simply be thought of as a fast side-chain for distributing samples and Sys-Ex data.

In the applied real world, SMDI could let you save all your samples to disk (possibly within a single database) and then quickly distribute these sounds to any supporting sampler. Sample editors wouldn't really require that your computer have an internal DSP sound card because edited samples could be quickly shuffled to and from your sampler for auditioning. Inexpensive sample players could have easy access to tons of samples, and sample dumps from a central library could be managed much more easily during a live performance.

Sample Editing Software

To take full advantage of the process of transmitting digital audio within an electronic music system, sample editing software has been developed for most popular personal computer systems (Fig. 4.15).

Such program-related hardware systems are capable of performing a variety of important sample-related tasks:

- Loading samplefiles into a computer. This allows them to be stored onto a central hard disk, arranged into a library, and transmitted to any sample-based device within the system (even to samplers having different sample rates and bit resolutions).

- Samplefile editing. Standard cut and paste edit tools are provided, in addition to multiple segment looping.

- DSP: Samplefiles can be digitally altered or mixed with other samplefiles (using such tools as gain changing, mixing, equalization, inversion, reversal, muting, fading, cross-fading, and time compression).

An example of a sample waveform editor for the Macintosh computer and a range of supported samplers is Alchemy from Passport Designs. Alchemy is a 16-bit stereo sample editing program (Fig. 4.16) that allows samples to be imported into the computer via SCSI, the MIDI sample dump format, the Sound Designer II format, and the

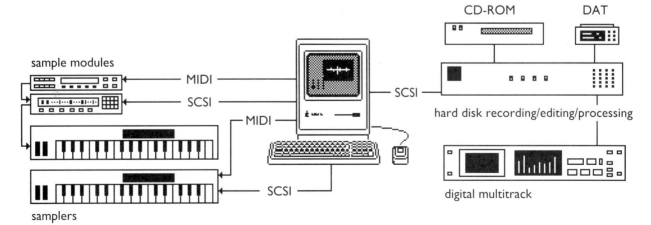

Fig. 4.15: Example of a sample editor network diagram.

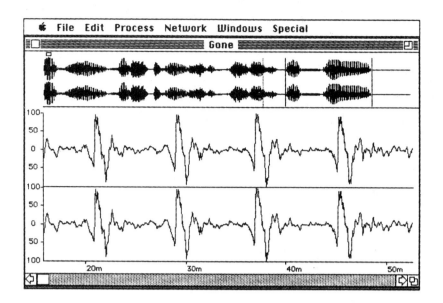

Fig. 4.16: Alchemy main visual editing software screen. (Courtesy of Passport Designs.)

Apple SND resource file format (for integration with Hypercard, Videoworks, Mac Recorder and others).

Once sample data is loaded into the software, Alchemy functions as a 16-bit sample editor, processor, and network support to most industry standard samplers. It can also be used to create new waveforms from original existing samples. Alchemy also acts as a universal sample translator, allowing samplefiles to be transferred between samplers or to be distributed systemwide from a centralized sample library. Other similar programs are available for the Mac, PC, Atari, and Amiga.

Synthesis and Sample Resynthesis

In addition to computer-based sample edit and signal-processing functions, software packages exist that can perform synthesis (designing synthesized samples from scratch) or resynthesis (import-ing a sample and resynthesizing the existing sample so as to alter its sound and shape according to program parameters). Once done, these programs use various samplefile and sample dump formats to export the new samplefiles to hard disk or external sampling devices.

Digidesign's Turbosynth (Fig. 4.17) is one such modular synthesis and sample resynthesis program. It combines the elements of digital synthesis, sampling, and signal processing in order to create new sounds from an existing sample through the use of a Macintosh computer and sampling system.

Modular synthesis works by combining various modules into a sound patch to generate or modify a sound. Turbosynth's modules include oscillators to generate basic waveforms, filters to modify the harmonic content of the oscillator's signal, and amplifiers to vary the volume of the sound. In addition to these traditional analog-style modules, Turbosynth includes several digital processing modules, not existing in analog modular synths,

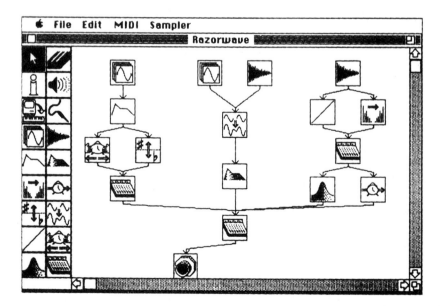

Fig. 4.17: Turbosynth modular synthesis and sample processing program. (Courtesy of Digidesign.)

that allow the production of a wider range of sounds. Once created, a sound patch can be saved to disk in a Sound Designer or Sound Designer II format or transferred to a number of currently available samplers.

Sampling Techniques

Like any art form, the process of sampling sound follows the "first rule" of recording. Remember? There are no rules, only guidelines.

An important part of what is generally called the "art of sampling" is choosing the best way to capture the sampled sound source and then applying it appropriately to the music, video, film, or computer program.

Although a lower sampling rate will directly increase the audio storage capacity of diskette or hard disk, it's important that a high enough sample rate be selected to reproduce the signal's entire bandwidth. For example, should you choose to sample a small brass bell at a rate of 22 kHz, you would find that the playback was dull and lifeless. This is because a Nyquist cutoff frequency for a 22-kHz sample rate requires that frequencies above 10 kHz be filtered out.

By raising the sample rate to the 44.1-kHz and above range, the bell's full spectrum would be heard during playback. On the other hand, if the sampling system were capable of multiple record/reproduce sample rates, and memory space were a consideration, it might be worth the slight loss in the extreme high overtones to sample a limited bandwidth signal (such as a deep kick drum) at a lower rate.

Avoiding the Dreaded "Clipped" Signal

One of the "kinder and gentler" attributes of analog audio gear is its relative tolerance to overload or clipping distortion. Many engineers and musicians feel that adding a moderate amount of analog distortion adds "feel" and "guts" to a sound. On the other hand, a clipped digital signal is one of the harshest sounds that you could imagine. In fact, upon reaching its maximum levels, the digital circuit will quickly begin to add large amounts of rather ugly third-harmonic distortion. To avoid this, it is a good idea to keep average and peak signals at levels that are at least 3 to 6 dB below the clipping point.

Sampling a Direct Signal Source

When recording a sample, remember that the signal to be recorded should be kept as clean and free of audible noise as possible. When recording an electronic instrument, you can ensure a clean, quality signal by recording a sample direct from one of its audio output jacks. From a signal standpoint, sampling electronic sources is a piece of cake. All that's required of devices such as guitars, synths, and electronic keyboards is that you find a clean signal source and a high output level (well

below the threshold of distortion) and simply plug it into your sampler.

Miking Tips

When miking a sound source, you must take great care. In fact, you need to take as much, or more, care when miking a sampled sound than you would if you were miking for a live studio session. This is mostly because a favorite sound might end up being used repeatedly within a song or production. That killer snare sound may show up more than a hundred times during a song. If noises such as a rattle or background noise are noticeable upon first hearing the sample, the noises could drive you nuts after the hundredth snare shot.

In miking an acoustic source, the following simple guideline can help you get the best results. I call it the "good rule."

Good Source + Good Acoustic Placement + Good Mike = Good Sound

A good source refers to the quality of both the performer and the acoustic sound source. Before diving in, ask yourself such questions as: Will the player bring life into this sample or recording? Is the instrument right for the part?

A close-miked sound is generally considered proper placement when recording a sample. This guideline has been adopted because close miking will often reduce the pickup of unwanted room ambience and other extraneous sounds. Remember to take your time when close-miking an instrument, since the sound's character is generally dependent upon placement.

One of the best ways to be assured of attaining a quality sample is by using a good mike. You might find that adding at least one high-quality condenser or electret-condenser microphone to your tool chest will be invaluable in helping you add life and a full-range punch to many acoustic sounds. Beyond this hint, use the best possible pickup that fits the application at hand. If you're unfamiliar with microphones, consider purchasing a good book that explains the various mike types and placement techniques, or simply experiment on your own.

Sampling from Tape

Some sounds just can't or won't wait around for the "right" sampling conditions. For example, one of my favorite sounds in nature is created by the emu, a large ostrich-like Australian bird that sounds sort of like the percussive sound of a 5-foot tall Coke bottle . . . truly amazing. However, these animals aren't known for their patience. So what's the option record it.

When recording a sound to tape, take the same precautions that you would during a live sample. If you are making an analog recording, the recorder should be of the highest quality and should be aligned for optimum results. To get the most out of your recorder, use a quality low-noise, high-output tape and record the signal at the highest possible levels while avoiding distortion.

A better method for capturing live samples is to record the signals digitally. Digital recording media, such as digital audio tape (DAT), greatly reduce noise and sideband distortion found in analog machines. There are a number of portable DAT machines that can be battery operated, allowing field recordings of your favorite sounds to be brought back into the studio and sampled to your heart's content.

To Process or Not to Process

After you've attained the best possible direct or miked signal, try to keep the signal as clean as possible throughout the rest of the signal chain. This can be done by reducing or eliminating any nonessential devices between the sound source and the sampler that might add small but measurable amounts of noise and distortion to the signal. Serious technocrats will often bypass the input strips of a recording console or mixer, preferring simply to use a high-quality, discrete microphone preamp when sampling a live signal.

At times, however, outboard effects and processing equipment can be of benefit to the sampling artist. For example, should corrective equalization be necessary, you should equalize (EQ) the signal before it is sampled. This saves you from having to EQ it every time that it's used.

When sources containing a large percentage of high-level transients (such as a cymbal or car crash) are sampled, a compressor or limiter might be placed into the audio chain. These devices are sometimes necessary to keep transient or high-level signals below the sampler's clipping level while maintaining an optimum signal-to-noise ratio.

Give careful thought to mixing effects, such as reverb, delay, and echo with the signal to be sampled. An old recording adage says that "You can add effects to a recorded track, but you can't take them away." This also holds true with the sampling process. The resulting processed signal could be very complex and could end up being very difficult to edit or loop.

On a Final Note

As you're probably aware, a large number of prerecorded sample and sound effects libraries are commercially available on disk, CD, and CD-ROM. These can get you started in the biz of sampling. However, the foundation of the music and recording industry is rooted in individuality and creativity. Time permitting, the art of making, resynthesizing, and/or mixing your own original sounds (including augmenting store-bought samples) can add to your personal sonic palette and can be a rewarding tool for breathing your own style into a production.

Chapter 5

Hard Disk Recording and Editing Systems

In my view, one of the most powerful aspects of random-access audio production is the ability to record a soundfile onto hard or optical disk. Of course, recording data to disk is only part of the story; the real fun and flexibility lie in the ability to edit, process, and reproduce these soundfiles.

This chapter examines the process of recording digital audio to hard disk and discusses the various "tools" that are available in the form of digital signal processing and editing techniques. This bag of tricks allows you to access, alter, resynthesize, and rearrange recorded sounds in ways that have been difficult or even impossible to achieve using traditional analog technology.

In addition, the chapter takes a closer look at practical tips for saving and keeping the valuable data that has been recorded onto disk. It discusses several types of hard disk recording systems that are currently available.

Hard Disk Recording

The term hard disk recording refers to the recording of a soundfile onto a permanent, high-density, fast-access, and random-access recording medium. "Hard disk" refers to the fact that most early systems, and even current ones, use a hard disk drive as the primary storage medium. Given the increased access times of most high-density optical drives, it's fairly safe to say that the term "hard disk recording" will stay in our language as a matter of habit rather than as a reference to the media type.

A hard-disk recording system furthers the basic concepts of sampling technology by allowing the recording, manipulation, and access of digitized audio directly to and from a high-capacity digital storage drive. These systems differ from a sampler in that the digital audio isn't stored directly into RAM. Instead, it is recorded directly to disk in the form of a continuous stream of audio data that can vary in length from a fraction of a second to well over an hour. As far as recording time goes,

this means that a monaural, two-channel or multichannel system is limited only by the amount of memory available on the storage medium itself.

Although hard disk systems don't have the instantaneous access speeds of a sampler, the time taken to access and output is impressive (typically less than 25 thousandths of a second), and even this time lag can be eliminated by the proper use of short-term memory buffers. This means that once the data has been recorded onto disk, any portion of the sound-file can be accessed at any time and in any order. To drive this concept home, take a look at XYZ Records' recent hit single "I'll Move Anywhere for You," which began to hit the charts last week. This chart buster made the company so happy that it asked the group to make a remix version for release later next month.

After listening carefully to the song, the group knew that they could use their producer's hard disk recorder to copy the hit to disk (along with a few remix cuts from the original master) and make it into a hot, new mix. For spice, the producer suggested that the main verses be repeated and extended and that the solo and chorus lines be altered to create a new extended version for the dance market. By using a hard disk recorder, the producer was able to move these segments around in any order with a minimum of time and money which made everyone very happy.

Hard Disk Editing

In addition to its advantage in recording larger soundfiles, another important advantage of hard disk recording is its ability to offer extensive editing features. What would otherwise represent minutes or even hours of cutting, copying, and reassembling snippets of analog tape can be performed much more quickly in the digital domain. Also, if you don't like the results, these changes can often be easily undone or redone until the edit is right. Try doing this in just a few minutes or seconds with analog tape.

75

Non-destructive Editing

In straightforward terms, non-destructive editing means the ability of a random access system to edit a recorded soundfile without in any way affecting the audio data that was originally recorded onto the disk. With non-destructive editing, defined portions of the original soundfile can be accessed, processed, and reproduced in any order (and any number of times). Thus, a revised, edited production version can be created by accessing portions of the soundfile without affecting its original integrity in any way.

This form of editing points out how disk-based reproduction doesn't always access and reproduce data as a continuous stream of audio. Instead, it randomly accesses defined regions and reproduces them in any desired order. As an example, suppose that you were given the task of cutting the "my dear" out of Rhett Butler's famous line from Gone with the Wind, "Frankly, my dear, I don't give a damn." If you were using the linear medium of analog tape, you could do this only by physically cutting out the words "my dear" and splicing the remaining tape pieces back together (Fig. 5.1A).

By recording the same line onto hard disk, you can make this edit in several ways. The simplest way is to define the segment that you want to delete and then cut it from the on-screen graphic display (Fig. 5.1B). When played back, the segment will be reproduced up to the cut point and will bypass the data that was cut, immediately skipping to the segment following the cut. It's important to note that, although the cut segment was ignored during playback, it remained unaltered and intact on the hard disk (on some systems though, the cut segment would be erased). To recall the soundfile in its original form, you may be able to select the Undo command (which returns the cut segment to the active file for playback), or you can simply reload the original soundfile into the system.

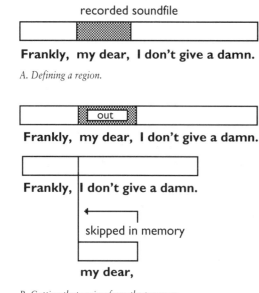

recorded soundfile

Frankly, my dear, I don't give a damn.

A. Defining a region.

out

Frankly, my dear, I don't give a damn.

Frankly, I don't give a damn.

skipped in memory

my dear,

B. Cutting that region from the program.

Fig. 5.1: A random access exercise.

Another way to edit this soundfile into its new form would be to define the segments to be reproduced and then instruct the system to output them in a desired order. For example, in Fig. 5.2, you could define the phrase "Frankly, my dear, I don't give a damn" into three segments. Then by instructing the system to reproduce these segments in various orders, you could create an entirely new sentence structure.

segment 1 segment 2 segment 3

Frankly, my dear, I don't give a damn.

A. Segment defined into three segments.

segment 2 segment 1 segment 3

my dear, Frankly, I don't give a damn.

B. One possible edited combination.

segment 3   segment 2 segment 1

I don't give a damn. my dear, Frankly,

C. An alternative combination using all three segments.

Fig. 5.2: A recorded soundfile can be edited by defining various segments, which can be reproduced in any edited order.

Destructive Editing

Destructive editing occurs whenever original soundfile data is altered and overwritten. It is the process of permanently rearranging or changing actual sample values on disk to alter the way that a soundfile will output.

This editing form is often used in soundfile management and archival, allowing soundfiles that have been edited into a final form to be saved to disk (or other data medium) as a single soundfile. This edit style is also used for preparing short soundfiles so that they can be easily transmitted to a sampler's ROM memory.

Basic Editing Tools

Both RAM and disk-based memory include options for performing a number of editing functions. Since data is stored as a series of numbers, it's a simple matter to perform basic editing functions in a standard computer "cut and paste" fashion. This section details many of the basic editing functions that can be found in most modern toolboxes.

Terminology

When compared with analog technology, hard disk recording is new to music production and other communications media. Its newness has an unexpected drawback when you study the disk-based systems currently on the market: a lack of standardized terms to describe basic functions from one company to the next. Although this situation is improving, in an effort to sound "new and different," one company might use a certain name for a common program function, while another might use an entirely different "term du jour" for the same or similar program function. For example, the portion of a soundfile that has been highlighted (selected) for further processing might be called a "region," "segment," "snippet," or other term. For the immediate future, your choice of terminology will depend on your familiarity with a particular manufacturer.

In writing this chapter, one of the hardest choices that I had to make was whether to choose the adopted terminology of certain leading companies or whether to use general terms. In trying to remain true to my strong feelings about the need for standardized terminology, I decided to use terms that are familiar to most system users.

Keep in mind that certain terms and functions in this chapter may be referred to by several different names. This is unavoidable until standardization of at least the most basic terms happens. If you are in doubt about the meaning of a term in relationship to your system, consult your owner's manual for a listing of terms used by your system.

Defining a Region

A defined segment of audio that exists within a soundfile is known as a selected region (Fig. 5.3). A region is commonly displayed on a computer monitor or LCD display as a highlighted area (containing user-defined in- and-out edit points). Once defined, a selected edit or DSP function will be performed only on the range that is highlighted.

For example, once a region has been defined, it can be cut from the waveform display, reversed, changed in level, etc. In any of these cases, only the waveform data within the selected region will be affected.

Markers

A marker (Fig. 5.4) is an identification flag that can be placed anywhere in a soundfile. Depending on the system, a flag can be displayed in a number of ways. However, it is often represented as a simple graphic identifier that can also have a number, letter, or short text note assigned to it.

Most systems make provisions for moving the playbar or actively selected region so that they jump to a desired marker point. In this way, you can easily mark the beginning and end points of an important segment, move to another place in the soundfile, and then jump back to the previous marker location at will.

Auditioning a Soundfile

An on-screen waveform display is a powerful tool for graphically locating in-and-out edit points or loud transients. However, the need to hear the sound is equally, if not more, important.

The number of options for playing back parts of a soundfile will vary from system to system, but a few basic playback options are almost always available. These include:

- Play Soundfile. This audition function is used to play the soundfile from its beginning or from the current cursor bar position. In the latter case, you need only scroll the soundfile to the desired waveform position and press play.

- Play Region. Once a region has been defined, this simple function can be used to hear only the selected range.

- Scrubbing. The scrubbing function (Fig. 5.5) is an important audition tool that is used for a wide range of applications (such as defining segments or placing markers in a soundfile). Quite simply, scrubbing is a tool that lets you move the playbar over a soundfile in either direction and at any speed while simultaneously listening to the sampled audio that is at the current cursor position. In other words, you can directly audition any point in a soundfile by placing the bar cursor at a desired location and moving it. This is most often used during slow-speed searching of a soundfile.

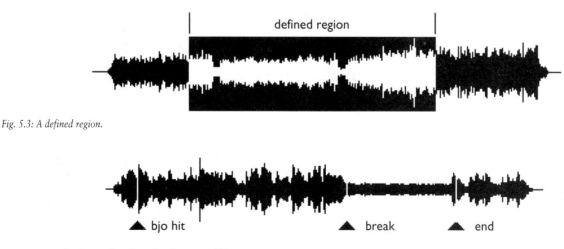

defined region

Fig. 5.3: A defined region.

▲ bjo hit   ▲ break   ▲ end

Fig. 5.4: Example of a set of markers placed in a soundfile.

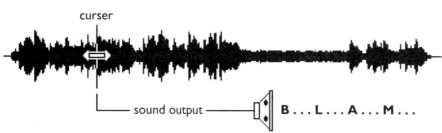

Fig. 5.5: Example of a system in scrub mode.

On most systems, the cursor's speed and direction can be controlled by moving a mouse or trackball in either the right (forward scrub) or left (backward scrub) direction.

Other systems might use a computer's keyboard arrow keys, continuous alpha dial, or light pen/pad combination to move the scrub cursor.

Scrubbing is often used to audibly locate the in- or out-point of a region. As an example of how you might put this to use, suppose that you need to locate an eight-measure segment that falls near the middle of a song. Then you want to copy it and repeat it at the end of the song while the song is being slowly faded out. Here is a possible scenario of how you might accomplish this:

1. Move the cursor bar to a position that is in the general area near the segment.
2. Select the scrub mode and "scrub" over the area until you find the exact beginning point.
3. Define this point as the beginning of the region range and continue to scrub (or return to play mode) until the general ending point has been found and defined.
4. Copy the region and paste it at an appropriate point near the song's end, allowing enough time for a slow fadeout.

There are two scrub modes commonly used for reproducing a waveform:

- Jog
- Shuttle

In the jog mode (Fig. 5.6), only those samples that are at the current cursor bar position will be reproduced. By moving the cursor bar over the soundfile (over a range of speeds and in either direction), you can play back the scrubbed samples in direct relation to the cursor's movement. This method is good for pinpointing precise events in a soundfile.

In the shuttle mode (Fig. 5.7), the software program will sense the initial direction and speed of the cursor and will then begin to reproduce the scrubbed audio at a speed and direction that is analogous to the initial cursor movement. For example, if you grab a mouse and move the scrub cursor slowly to the right, the system will compute the cursor's speed and direction and will begin to slowly scrub the waveform from its initial cursor position, even though the mouse is no longer being moved. You can change the scrub cursor's speed and direction again by moving the mouse at a different speed or in another direction.

Cut and Paste Commands

Once a region has been defined, probably the most basic editing tools that you can use are those belonging to the cut and paste family. These commands are the same basic applications that can be found in almost any window-based program.

Once a region has been selected, the Cut command (Fig. 5.8) will delete the selected region from its current position and will then place a copy of it in the computer's clipboard memory. The Clipboard is a block of memory that actively resides in

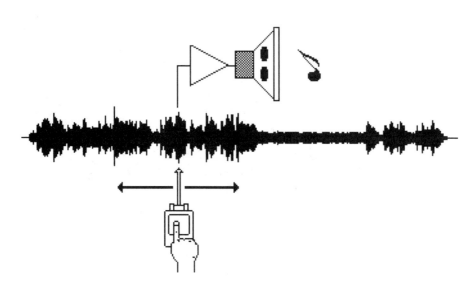

Fig. 5.6: In the jog mode, only those samples at the play cursor position will be heard.

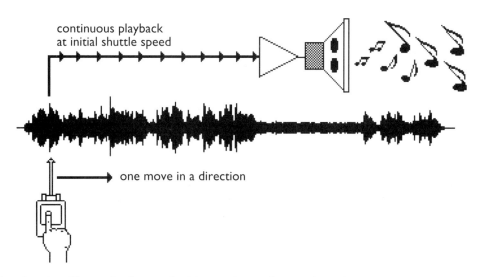

continuous playback
at initial shuttle speed

one move in a direction

Fig. 5.7: In the shuttle mode, audio will be reproduced at a speed and direction that is analogous to the initial cursor movement.

region to be cut

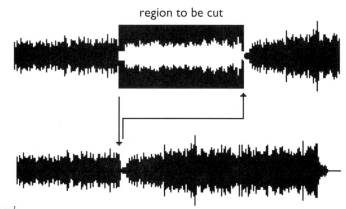

Fig. 5.8: An example of the Cut command.

the background and is set aside for temporarily storing text, graphics, video, or audio data. On some computer systems, the Clipboard may be referred to by another name.

The Copy command (Fig. 5.9) places a copy of the selected region into the computer's Clipboard. However, the region will not be deleted from its current position.

The Paste command (Fig. 5.10) copies the waveform data from the Clipboard memory and inserts it back into the active sound-file at a point beginning immediately after the cursor bar.

Depending on a system's available options, the Paste command can be used to copy waveform data into a soundfile in one of two possible ways:

• Shuffle

• Replace

Selecting the shuffle command causes any audio that originally followed the cursor bar (prior to pasting new data into the soundfile) to be moved to a point immediately following the newly inserted segment (Fig. 5.11).

The Replace command (Fig. 5.12) causes the contents of the Clipboard to be placed into the soundfile directly over the audio that immediately followed the cursor bar. The overwritten audio will, of course, last only for the duration of the pasted segment.

region to be copied

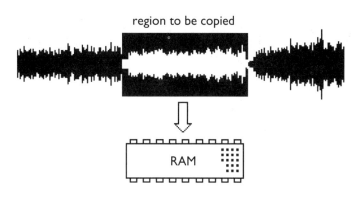

RAM

Fig. 5.9: An example of the Copy command.

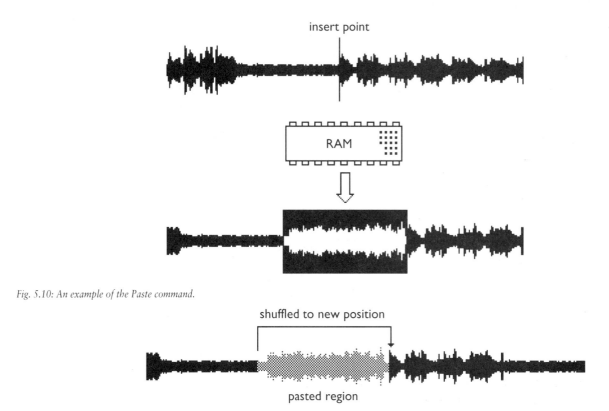

Fig. 5.10: An example of the Paste command.

Fig. 5.11: The audio following the pasted insert will be shuffled to a point directly following the insert.

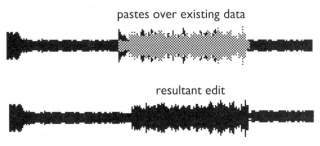

Fig. 5.12: An example of the Replace command.

DSP Editing Functions

In addition to the basic editing tools offered by almost every hard disk recorder, some systems also offer digital signal processing (DSP) functions. DSP alters digital sample values by performing extensive mathematical calculations on them. This process changes their numeric value in such a way that an effect is created or a particular function is performed. This section briefly introduces many of these processing tasks. For more information on DSP, refer to Chapter 8.

Crossfade

Crossfade (or X-fade) can be used to smooth the transition between two joined regions at a digital splice, or edit point. Quite often, when two dissimilar waveforms are joined at a digital edit, the instantaneous break in continuity will be audible.

This "bump" in the sound can often be digitally smoothed over by overlapping the regions by a defined length of time (often stated in milliseconds) and then fading out the first segment while fading in the second (Fig. 5.13). The effect is to average the two signals over the length of the crossfade and mask the offending edit point, so that it is much less noticeable to the ear.

A second use of crossfades involves longer durations lasting from a fraction of a second to several seconds. Such a long fade might be used, for example, to create a transition between two songs in the production of a final edited master. Using a computer-based system to carry out this function makes the crossfade extremely smooth and, since the original data isn't altered by the fade, changes can easily be undone and reexecuted.

In addition to control over the length of a crossfade (time), a number of systems allow for user-control of the slope of a fade curve. This is done by controlling the various shapes and durations of the in and out curves. Many hard disk systems offer a choice of basic in and out curve types (linear or logarithmic). However, a growing number of systems also offer parametric control over these curves, which allows the user to design crossfade types to fit the program's needs, as shown in Fig. 5.14. For example, you may want to join two songs together so that the outgoing song will not fade out until the very end, while the incoming song will begin to slowly fade in at a point 5 seconds before the preceding song ends.

Note that a crossfade is a tool that is available to the user but it need not always be used. In certain cases, a butt splice (the joining of two regions without a crossfade) can be very effective and even preferable when joining similar sounds, particularly those that are random in nature. As with all audio production, your ears are often the best judge.

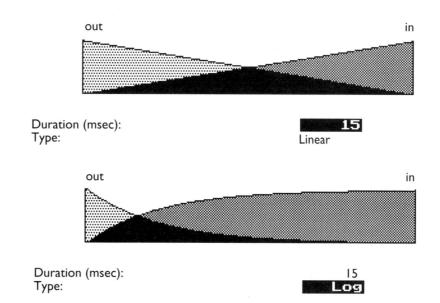

Duration (msec): 15
Type: Linear

Duration (msec): 15
Type: Log

Fig. 5.13: Examples of a linear and logarithmic crossfade curve.

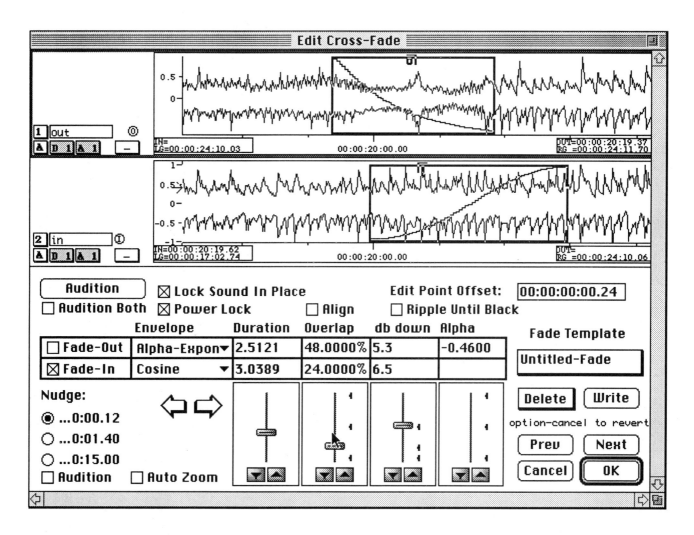

Fig. 5.14: Example of a parametric fade and crossfade screen. (Courtesy of Sonic Solutions, Inc.)

Real-Time and Disk-Based Crossfades

A crossfade is by nature a DSP function. In effect, the two waveform areas to be crossfaded are digitally merged over its duration according to a set of parameters. This is done in such a way that the outgoing segment is reduced in level over time, while the incoming segment is increased.

These mix calculations must be performed in RAM memory and will often take up their fair share of processing power and time.

Some systems make use of number-crunching co-processors that are fast enough to perform these and other calculations in real time. That is, these calculations are performed in RAM at the same time that the soundfile is being played.

Many systems, however, perform crossfades that are not done in real time. The co-processor will dedicate itself solely to the task of calculating the crossfade. Once done, a file containing the newly calculated samples is written to disk. Upon playback, the system will seamlessly play back the soundfiles up to the crossfade point, then will access and reproduce the written crossfade file, and finally will begin accessing the second soundfile at the precise time following its fade-in point.

Calculating crossfades in real time has the advantages of saving disk space and calculation time. However, calculating crossfades in non-real time is a cost-effective approach that sacrifices very little in lost time on most modern processing systems.

Fading

The fading-in or fading-out of a soundfile region is a DSP function that is very similar to the crossfade. During a fade, the calculated sample amplitudes are either proportionately reduced or increased in level, according to a defined curve ramp. For example, when performing a fade (Fig. 5.15), the signal will usually begin at a level that is 100% of its current value and will reduce over the defined time to 0 percent (full attenuation).

Like crossfades, fades in certain systems can be accomplished by using parametric control over in and out amplitude values, as well as over the selection or drawn shape of the curve. In a similar fashion and depending on the system, a fade can be either written to disk in non-real time or calculated directly in RAM in (real time).

Gain Change

Often, a system will allow the sample amplitude in a soundfile or region to be proportionately changed (either up or down) to a new value in order to affect overall gain of the signal (Fig. 5.16). As with the DSP functions mentioned earlier, these amplitude changes can be calculated in non-real time and written to disk as a separately tagged file, or they can be calculated in real time.

Normalization

Whenever digital audio is sampled at levels that are below its maximum gain value, the resolution of the recording (at the bit level) may be below the full 16-bit or greater capabilities of a digital audio system. For example, a 16-bit sample that has been recorded at very low levels may be encoded with an effective resolution of 8- or less bits (as these bits represent the number of steps at these low

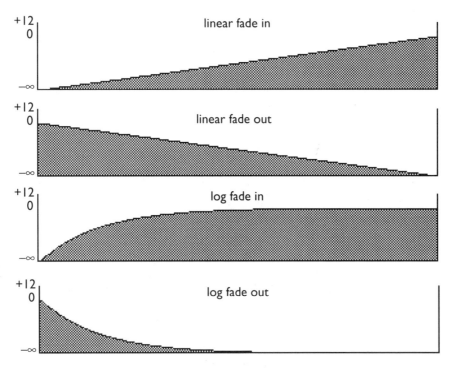

Fig. 5.15: Examples of various fade curves.

Fig. 5.16: Example of a segment that has been increased in gain by 6 dB.

level values). Turning the recording up will not only increase the system's internal noise, it will also reveal a grainy or possibly distorted signal that's inherent to 8-bit recordings.

In order to improve the soundfile's resolution, a feature known as normalization can be used to digitally boost the gain of the recorded sample to a level that will make use of the full range of available bits. This is done by calculating an increase in gain that would be required to boost the highest peak signal to the system's maximum bit level and then proportionately changing the soundfile's gain by this value.

Obviously, the best solution in this situation would be to re-sample the original source at a higher level, however, if the low level soundfile is all you have to work with the normalization function wont reduce the perceived noise level, but it will eliminate or reduce side effects due to quantization error.

Advanced DSP Functions

In addition to offering basic DSP calculations that relate to the amplitude characteristics of a soundfile or region, high-end systems commonly offer advanced signal-processing calculations.

Added DSP power and programming can provide extensive control over such functions as equalization, dynamic range, effects processing, and time/pitch ratios.

Equalization

A number of computer-based systems are capable of performing digital equalization (EQ), either on an entire soundfile or on a defined segment within a soundfile (Fig. 5.17). Depending on the system, this useful function can be performed in real time or in non-real time.

The advantages of digital EQ over its analog counterpart are many. Digital EQ allows sounds to be processed without the added noise and ringing distortion sometimes associated with analog EQ circuitry. In addition, it allows a greater degree of control over frequency, band width, and level. Since calculations and control over EQ parameters are performed entirely in the digital domain, complex EQ "patches" can be easily saved to disk or attached to a file. This makes it possible for these settings to be saved for recall at a later date.

Dynamic Range Change

Using another popular DSP function, you can change the dynamic range, or amplitude content, of a signal. This allows for real-time or non real-

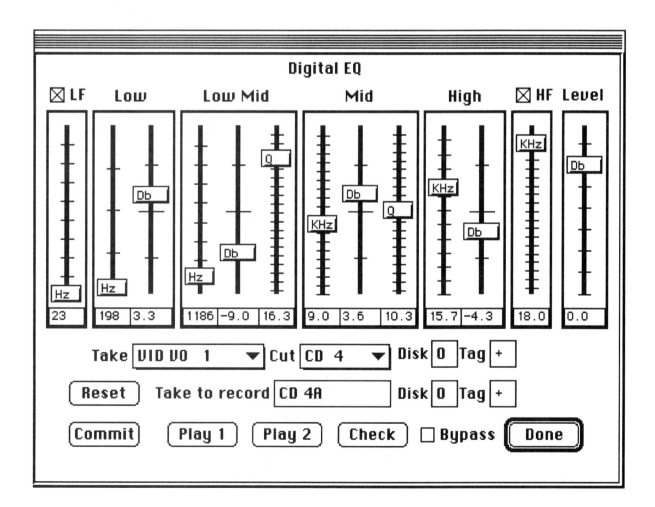

Fig. 5.17: The DD-QMac equalization screen for the Akai DD1000 Magneto Optical Disk Editor. (Courtesy of Akai Professional/Digital.)

time control over the gain structure of a recorded soundfile or region, without the need for external analog processing equipment. These dynamic range options include:

- Compression. This reduces gain above a definable threshold according to a variable input versus output level ratio.

- Limiting. The amplitude of a signal is limited so that it can't increase in level above a user-defined threshold. The resulting signal level will be limited to this maximum level even though the original samples might be greater.

- Expansion. This occurs when the soundfile's amplitude is either increased in level when it's above a defined threshold or conversely lowered in level below the threshold. The effect is to increase a signal's overall dynamic range.

Pitch Change

Pitch change is a DSP function that allows a soundfile or region's relative pitch to be shifted upward or downward, without affecting its relative time or length. These changes are often measured as a plus or minus percentage value of the original pitch or as a relative musical pitch interval.

It should be noted that changing the pitch of a digital signal is effective only within a limited shift range (typically only a few semitones up or down), since shifts beyond this range can introduce distortion side effects. How much distortion is added can vary from one system to another and often depends on the complexity of the waveform being processed. For example, a less-complex voice or solo flute track can often be shifted over a wider range, without getting into distortion troubles, than a complex rock music passage can.

Time Change

The advanced DSP function of time change is related to pitch change, although its task is that of changing the duration of a samplefile or region without changing its relative pitch.

Time-change functions are tools used by those in video post-production, film, and broadcasting to allow changes to be made in the overall length of a soundfile or region while maintaining the original program's pitch. For example, such a function could be used to lengthen a 26-second radio spot so that it would fit into a 30-second time slot without affecting the program's natural pitch.

On-Screen Soundfile Editing

In the past, the only tools for locating, editing, and manipulating sound were your ears. When you performed an edit, the in- and out-points were located manually by "rocking" the reels of an analog tape machine. This process allowed the audio signal to be heard while the magnetic tape moved over the playback heads.

Once you found an edit point, you marked it with a grease pencil and then cut the tape using an edit block. After you found the second edit point, you could physically cut out the section or splice it onto a new reel. You could then splice together the tape and audition the resulting edit points.

Although this process is still standard procedure for many communications industries and is still a handy skill to have, it is no longer the only production option. As computer-based editing systems have moved onto the scene, an entirely new dimension to the editing process has been added. You now have the ability to visually display and manipulate audio waveforms by using a computer monitor screen.

In general, sound waveforms are displayed on-screen in one of two basic ways:

- As a symmetrical amplitude display
- As a nonsymmetrical peak amplitude display

The symmetrical amplitude display (Fig. 5.18A) graphically shows signal amplitude as a series of vertical bars that are drawn so as to symmetrically stem out (in both a positive and negative direction) from a central zero-level reference line.

A peak amplitude display (Fig. 5.18B) shows amplitude as a series of vertical bars that rise in a positive direction from its zero reference line.

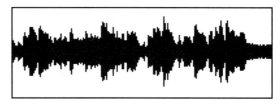

A. Symmetrical.

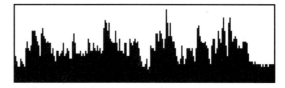

B. Peak amplitude.

Fig. 5.18: Waveform amplitude displays.

It should be pointed out that these display techniques are used roughly to represent a soundfile's audio level over time. When a portion of a soundfile is "zoomed" into an area that's small enough to show individual sample values, both display types will generally show the signal's true waveform shape instead of a representative amplitude graph (Fig. 5.19).

This ability to graphically manipulate a soundfile almost invariably speeds up the editing and processing of audio data, since the identification of individual soundfile events is usually made easier.

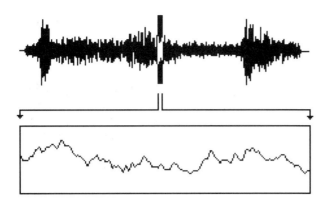

Fig. 5.19: *Example of a zoom function.*

When you are using an on-screen display, it's generally a quick matter to visually identify and access an audio event. For example, a quiet passage is often immediately visible as having little or no amplitude; a loud, transient event will, likewise, be easily identifiable (Fig. 5.20). Once you're use to it, this correlation between sight and sound will speed the process of locating, marking, and listening to particular events.

As already mentioned, waveform editing can ease the process of locating a particular point in a soundfile. Its other strongpoint is the ability to identify and define a marked region. For example, during the process of defining a region, the selected waveform area is commonly identified by being reverse-highlighted (Fig. 5.21). Once the in- and out-boundaries of a region have been defined, any number of editing or processing functions can be performed on it. Additionally, a number of systems allow these regions to be named and to graphically retain the edit boundaries for easy search and access at a later time.

Although most systems display waveform data in much the same manner, the way that this data is organized and manipulated into a final, edited product can differ from system to system. Currently, there are four basic graphic ways to edit raw soundfile data into a final, edited form:

- Graphic editing
- Playlist editing
- Disk-based mix editing
- Object-oriented editing

Graphic Editing

One of the most common forms of on-screen editing is graphic editing. It is used to display and manipulate waveform data (Fig. 5.22). Graphic editing is basically WYSIWG in nature (what you see is what you get), since it graphically displays soundfile data as a continuous waveform data stream that flows from left to right (from the beginning to the end of the soundfile).

When the soundfile is longer than what the screen can show at one time, only a portion of the soundfile will be shown. The screen can be scrolled forward or backward to see the off-screen data. Generally, instead of smoothly scrolling the off-screen data into view, most systems will refresh, or redraw, the screen to show the entire updated waveform page.

With this edit style, the cutting, copying, or reversing, of a region would at all times be visually reflected directly on the screen. However, keep in mind that on most systems the original hard disk soundfile data will remain intact. In other words, the moving of a defined region to another area in an edited production will not alter the original soundfile data, but will mean only that this region will be accessed in an order that is different from the way that it was originally recorded.

Playlist Editing

Playlist editing is another popular way to organize unedited soundfile data into its final, edited form or to trigger defined regions from an external time-related source (such as time code). A playlist (Fig. 5.23) is a listing of named regions that can be reproduced in either a sequential fashion (with one region immediately following

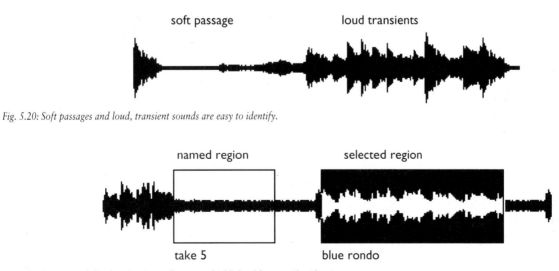

Fig. 5.20: *Soft passages and loud, transient sounds are easy to identify.*

Fig. 5.21: *An active, defined region is usually reverse-highlighted for easy identification.*

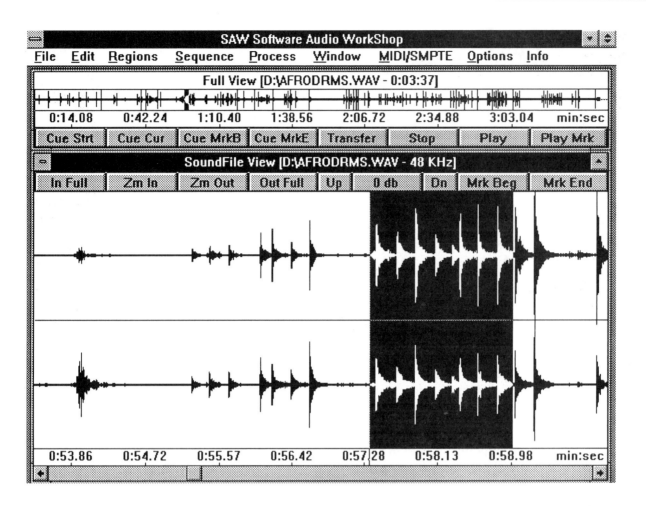

Fig. 5.22: Example of a screen in the graphic edit mode. (Courtesy of Innovative Quality Software.)

the other) or at a particular event time (that is triggered from a time-coded event source).

Once a soundfile region has been defined and given a name, that name will thereafter appear in a source list. By choosing any number of defined regions from this available source list and placing them in an edited playlist, you can play them back in any order. Since this edit style is non-destructive and accesses only parts of a soundfile recording, you can select a region any number of times and place it into the playlist in any order.

As an example of sequential playlist editing, have some fun with the following example. Assume that you have a DAT master of "Do Da House," a house dance piece that's sure to be a hit on both sides of the ocean. The producer has just handed you a few solo lead-vocal samples, and your job is to create an intro to the extended play version. Upon playing the tape, you hear, "Let's do it, let's do da house!"

You transfer the tape to hard disk as a stereo soundfile and name it "Da House Intro." Now, you define a few regions. With your mouse, you mark the beginning of the file and scrub through "Let's do it." You mark this point as the end of the region and define it. Now you mark and define a few other regions, such as the L in "Let's" and the phrase "do it." After you've auditioned the regions, a playlist is created that instructs the system to access portions of the hard disk as

defined by the regions. From this list, these sound-bites might play as: Let's . . . L-L-L-Let's do it, do it, do it, . . . Let's do da house!

Since the edits are non-destructive, the soundfile and playlist perform two entirely different functions. The source list refers to defined regions of digital audio data that are recorded on hard disk, while the playlist (that is stored along with the soundfile data) contains only parameters that tell the system how these regions are to be accessed and reproduced. The audio data is actually not duplicated; rather, it is accessed according to the playlist's set of instructions. Since it's possible to access and play back these regions in any imaginable combination, numerous playlist edit versions can be created from a single soundfile source. Because the soundfile is not changed only the way that the soundfile data is accessed changes you can create as many playlists as you want while taking up almost no additional memory.

An example of playlist editing that is externally triggered from time code might occur in the production of a made-for-TV movie or music video. Here, you might place the raw soundfile data onto disk, define the appropriate regions, and then place them into a playlist so that they could each be triggered to time code. This feature means that any number of soundfile regions can be synchronized to film, video, or other time-related sources.

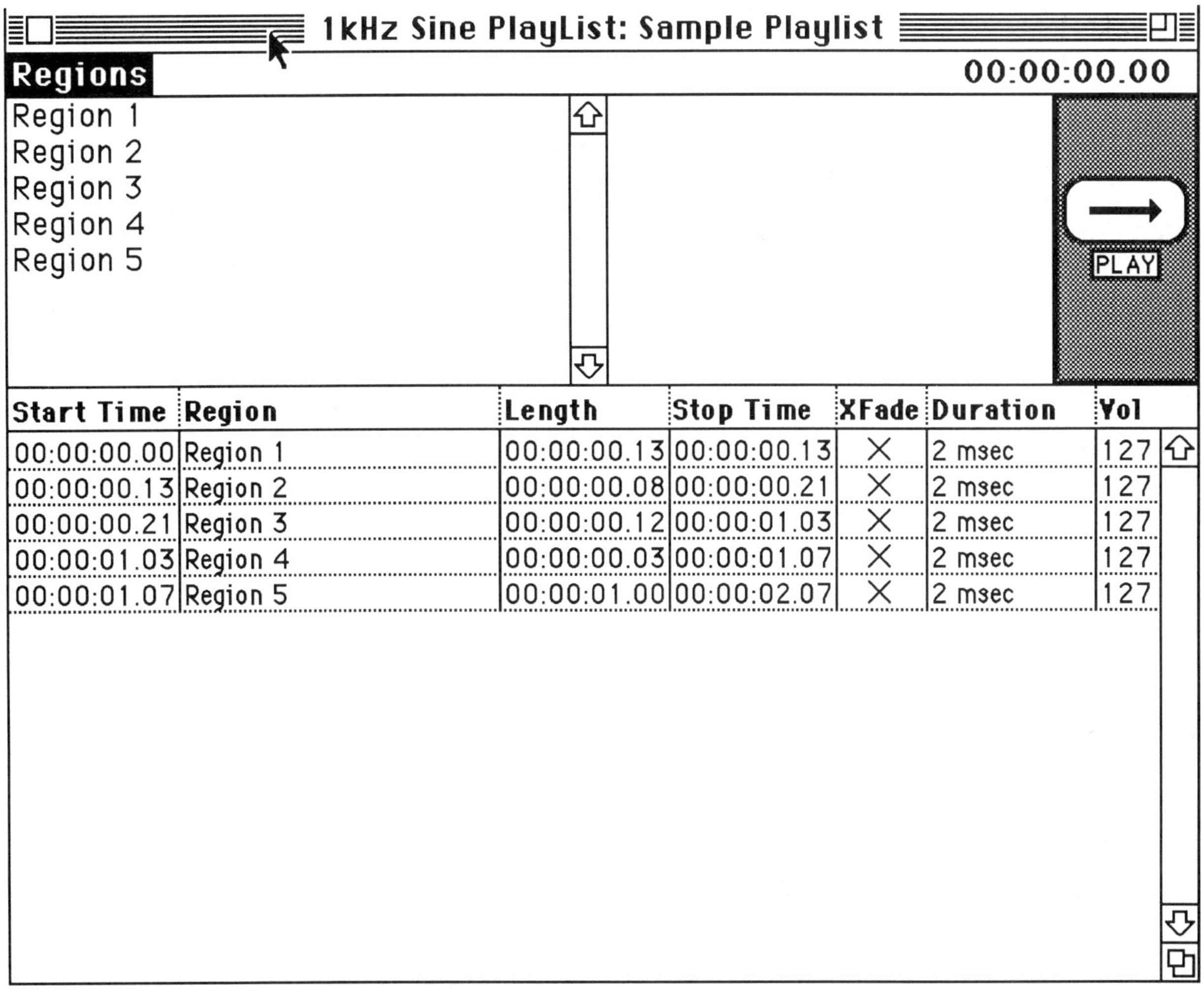

Fig. 5.23: Example of a playlist. (Courtesy of Digidesign, Inc.)

But let's get back to your latest project. Since the producer knows that this dance tune will be a hit, it's music video time! The video has already been shot to the soundtrack. However, the director has created a new video intro that begins with a panorama of New York City shot from a helicopter. The camera scene slowly tightens into Times Square at 3:45 a.m. Then, POW!, a full face shot of the lead singer singing "Let's do da house!" And it's into the standard dance mix.

In order to recreate the intro, you have set up a VCR (providing a picture, time code, and a window dub that shows burned-in time code numbers) and a hard disk recorder. Once you've loaded the hard disk recorder with the rough vocal edit cuts, you create a new playlist to match the picture. Once the videotape is rolling, you see that the aerial shot ends and that the vocalist's line begins at exactly 15 seconds. This calls for a slight remake of the playlist, requiring that you define and name a few more regions. Now you create a new playlist that will trigger regions at a predetermined time code address.

After a few minutes work, you have a playlist that looks like this:

01:00:05:27	"Let's do it"
01:00:07:08	"Let's do it"
01:00:09:15	"d"
01:00:09:26	"d"
01:00:09:31	"d"
01:00:11:15	"do it"
01:00:15:00	"Let's do da house!" (dance mix version)

After auditioning the sound to video, the producer loves it, and you're ready to lay down the sound to a synchronous soundtrack or back to the videotape's audio tracks . . . it's all in a day's work.

In addition to the two editing options mentioned, almost every playlist system will include information boxes that detail the event start, stop, and duration times. Another common feature allows crossfades to be entered between the listed regions. The times and types of crossfade (linear, log, etc.) can be easily changed in order to smooth any noticeable breaks or bumps that might occur during a transition from one region to the next.

Disk-Based Mix Editing

Disk-based mix editing is an editing method used by only a few random access systems. This rather inventive edit style is capable of bringing many of the advantages of multichannel operation into a two-channel editing system.

The disk-based editor (sometimes known as a layer editor) is similar to a playlist editor in that it depends on defined and named regions for its operation. However, instead of displaying these regions as a vertical events list, the named regions are represented as a series of horizontal bars that are stacked on top of each other in a vertical array (Fig. 5.24).

Although these defined regions are separated vertically, it is their horizontal placement in this stack that determines when the regions will be played. Thus, a series of bars that sequentially follow each other in the stack would effectively play back as though they were in a standard playlist.

The advantages begin to be evident when you realize that each of these bars can be horizontally "slipped" in time, thus changing their starting times. Should one or more bars overlap in the vertical stack, only the sample values that exist within the overlapped regions will be digitally mixed together and stored to disk as a separate "mix file." When such an overlapped area is reached, the system will begin to access and output the newly mixed sum of the involved sample values in a butt edit style. Once the end of the overlapped file is reached, the system will again return to accessing the original or next region's soundfile data.

This method of mixing together only overlapped regions is both time- and memory-efficient, since only the data contained in overlapped files needs to be processed and written to disk. The main drawback is that these mix files are usually written in non-real time, and this processing time can last anywhere from a few seconds to a short coffee break.

If the previously mixed data or any other edited portion is moved so that it overlaps with another region(s), a new summation mix file will be created, written to disk, and output upon playback.

Object-Oriented Editing

One of the most recent systems for editing soundfiles is known as object-oriented editing (Fig. 5.25). This on-screen style relies on the definition and naming of a region, which will thereafter exist as a graphically defined block or "object." The selection of such an object can be made simply by clicking the cursor anywhere within its defined boundaries. Once selected, any number of editing and processing functions can be carried out upon this highlighted region.

Such a point and click method adds new dimensions to the editing process, since editing can be extremely interactive and intuitive in its graphic nature. For example, should you wish to move an object from one point in a project to another, you need only select the desired object, cut it from its current position, and paste it in at the new position.

The moving of an object within an edited file can take either of two possible forms. The first method, known as shuffling, allows an object (or selected range of objects) to be inserted into an edited file by simply placing the cursor between two existing objects and selecting the paste command. The new object will then be inserted directly between the two objects in a butt splice fashion. If needed, a crossfade can be performed at either boundary to smooth the transition.

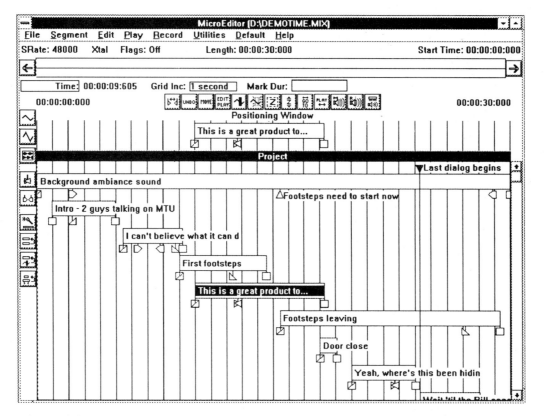

Fig. 5.24: Example of a disk-based mix editing screen. (Courtesy of Micro Technology Unlimited.)

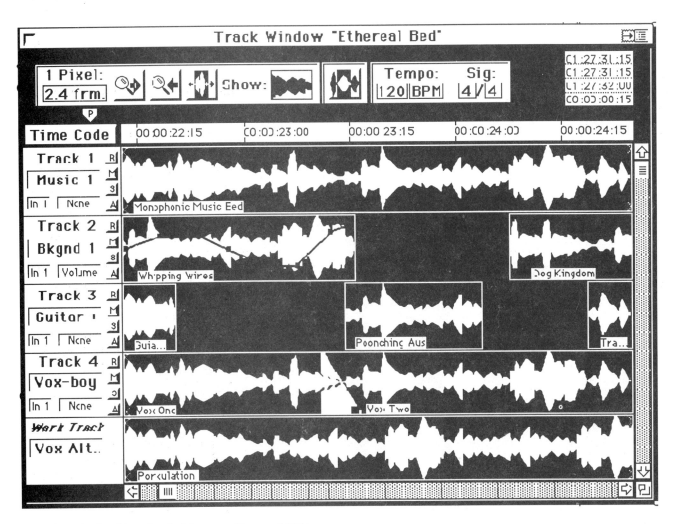

Fig. 5.25: Example of an object-oriented editing screen. (Courtesy of OSC.)

The second method, known as slipping, allows one or more selected objects to be moved in time, without changing the relative start time of any other edited object. In other words, a selected object can be slipped, while unselected objects remain in place. This editing system can affect a file in ways that differ from all other edit styles.

For example, suppose that you define an object from within a continuous music segment, and you slip its boundaries backward in time (toward the beginning of the song) by 1 second. Since the other boundaries have not moved, the result is an existing gap of silence that follows the moved object and lasts 1 second.

Conversely, if you slip the object forward in time by a second (towards the song's end), the object's trailing edge overlaps and hides a second's worth of the trailing soundfile data, while a gap of a second exists before the slipped object.

Note that the audio data hidden or layered behind other data is not lost, only hidden from view. It can again become active after an object covering the data has moved to another position. Alternatively, layers can be selectively switched to the foreground or background on certain systems, allowing the user to select between alternate takes.

Although slipped audio may have limited applications in two- channel production (where gaps and overlaps could cause problems), it can be of tremendous value in a multichannel environment. For example, time slipping is useful when you need to fix timing problems in music, film, and audio-for-video applications, since particular start times can be altered to match a particular event's timing.

On a final note, certain object-oriented systems have the ability to attach real-time DSP attributes to each object. For example, a system might allow an object to be given a number of equalization attributes, which are not stored in the soundfile itself but are processed in real time as the object is played. Should this object be copied or moved within the production, these EQ attributes can be attached to, and would follow, the object to its new or alternate position.

Practical Soundfile Fundamentals

As you know, a soundfile is raw, digitally encoded data that is stored onto a memory medium. The process of storing, manipulating, and retrieving this data is certainly not a failproof procedure. Murphy's law usually prevails, and @#%& happens. The practical fundamentals discussed next can keep your valuable data intact and may indeed save your day.

Housecleaning Tips

Recall from Chapter 3 that disk-based memory media store blocks of data onto a rotating medium by using a systematic arrangement of tracks, cylinders, sectors, and blocks. Like many logically oriented systems, a computer and its associated program will always work best when this data is accessible in a straightforward fashion.

Initially, when data is stored onto a disk, it is encoded as a contiguous file (Fig. 5.26). That is, blocks of data are laid down to disk one after the other, in a way that allows for the easiest disk access. The process is very straightforward. However, as other programs are added to the disk, or as files are updated, the number of available sectors that do not already have valuable data written on them decreases. This computerized fact of life makes it necessary for the disk controller to write data to disk in a noncontiguous fashion.

Essentially, the blocks of data are spread over the multiplatter surfaces, while the computer tries very hard to write data anywhere it can. Data will thus be written to, and read from, a fragmented disk (one containing fragmented data) in a non-contiguous form. Such disk fragmentation often leads to reductions in access time or, in rare instances, program crashes as a result of over-working the hard disk's controller.

One of the first rules for reducing fragmentation (and avoiding disaster) when writing digital audio soundfiles to disk is to keep audio soundfiles separate from all program-related files. The mixture of these data types would, almost certainly, result in excessive fragmentation of sound file data.

To separate the two types, store your program data on one disk and dedicate another, larger disk to audio. Should a system be limited to a single drive, you can usually partition the drive into two logical drives. In this case, a user-defined number of cylinders can be assigned to be one drive, while the remainder are assigned to another logical drive. For example, a 360Mb drive might have 60Mb assigned to store program data and the remaining 300Mb assigned for storing soundfile data.

Whenever soundfile data is continually written onto a disk that already contains various audio files, it's often a good idea to periodically use a disk optimizer. These programs are capable of

reading fragmented data off a disk and rewriting it back to the disk as contiguous data, leaving lots of fresh, open space for your new, favorite files.

Saving the Day! Data Backup

I'd like to stress a very simple but important guideline that applies to hard disk recording or to any type of computer-based audio production:

ALWAYS SAVE YOUR WORK AND MAKE A BACKUP WHENEVER POSSIBLE!

Remember that random access audio is not exempt from one of the greatest laws of all Murphy's law. By far, one of the best ways to guard against a potential disaster or major headache is to save and back up your work.

When working for long periods of time, human nature often steps in and we sometimes do the perfectly natural thing: we screw up. Let's say it's 3 a.m. and you've been working on a series of song edits for over four hours. In your bleary bliss, you take the last, carefully defined region and accidentally invoke the Replace function, thereby losing several beats of carefully edited music. When you use the Undo command to get the data back, Mr. Murphy steps in and the computer locks up . . . ARRG! You've probably lost several hours of editing time.

Yes folks, things like this do happen. However, in your short term sorrow, you remember to save a copy of the editlist, just minutes before the major mishap. Since the editlist contains all of your precious edit information, you need only reload the list, redefine the last region, and call it a night. The day's been saved, because you saved the data.

Like saving datafiles, making backups of both program and soundfile data can be a life preserver in the sea of mishaps. The backing up of soundfile data to a removable storage media can serve either of two purposes: a safety backup of an original or edited soundfile, or an archive for important data.

Backup Media

The process of backing up a soundfile can take on a number of forms. The obvious questions to be asked here are: What type of data is to be backed up and what are the best media for the job?

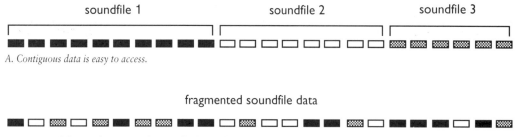

soundfile 1   soundfile 2   soundfile 3

A. Contiguous data is easy to access.

fragmented soundfile data

B. Fragmented data is often scattered across the disk surface.

Fig. 5.26: Organization of data blocks on a hard disk.

Often a soundfile will contain two distinct types of data: raw digital audio and edit information (such as region definition and playlist data). Should you need an audio-only backup or archival copy of the final edited soundfile, the best choice might be to copy the soundfile to a digital audio media (such as DAT or recordable CD). However, if both soundfile and edit data need to be backed up, a computer-based media must be used.

Computer soundfile data can be backed up in a number of ways. These include all forms of removable media (both write-once and recordable). Backing up soundfile data to traditional media (such as the floppy diskette) can be a pain, since many diskettes would be required to save files of even modest size. For such high-density applications, the use of some form of a streaming tape or optical backup media may be the best choice.

A streaming tape device is a drive mechanism that is used to transfer computer data onto a high-density digital cassette media. Systems like these can back up large amounts of data ranging into the 8GB (gigabyte) range.

Although certain systems use data cassettes that have been designed for this particular purpose, many popular systems incorporate readily available tape formats, including off-the-shelf 8mm video cassette and DAT tape formats.

Magnetic media are commonly used for backups, but optical formats are gaining acceptance in this area. This is true for both WORM and recordable disk drive systems. In fact, a fast-access erasable drive has the distinct advantage of being able to use the same drive as a working production drive and as an archival disk for saving data.

Having said that soundfile and file data must be written to a computer-based media, I'd like to point out one popular exception to this process. That is the backing up of both soundfile data and edit information to a standard DAT machine.

One example of this backup process is Digidesign's DATa, which uses the DAT medium and digital audio interface to encode playlist edit information (in a modulated form) at the header of the soundfile. This header is immediately followed by its associated raw soundfile data. Upon reloading the playlist and soundfile, DATa will reconstruct the playlist and mix so that the audio can be

reproduced in edited form, or easily changed into a new form without having to redefine each region.

Background Backup and Restoration of Soundfile Data

A common method for communicating data between high-density drives and computer systems is the SCSI transmission protocol. SCSI is capable of data communications at transfer rates of up to 15Mb per minute. Although this is fairly fast, the process of backing up to a media source or loading soundfile data from a media source can still take time, as shown in the following equation:

$$\textit{Megabytes/Minute x Soundfile Length} \div \textit{Transfer Rate = Transfer Time}$$

For example, 10.7Mb (at 44.1) x 30 (min) ÷ 15 (Mb/min) = 21.4 minutes.

With the advent of the newer, faster co-processors, multitasking (the ability to perform more than one functional task at a time) is now practical. Soundfiles can be uploaded to, or downloaded from, a disk drive in the background (Fig. 5.27) while the currently opened project is active.

This means, for example, that your next project can be loading into the system while you are still editing a current project. When you're ready for your next project, simply call it up from the newly loaded disk and dive in.

Soundfile Formats

Most file formats are system-specific and must be transferred from one device to another. However, a few systems have been widely accepted and can be written and read by a number of sample and hard disk recording systems. The following sections describe some popularly known formats.

SND Resource

The Apple Corporation has adopted the SND Resource, an 8-bit applications format, for the playback of short soundfiles by the computer's internal speaker (such as the alert sound) and for use with certain applications, such as HyperCard.

load-in new data   current project   download finished project to DAT

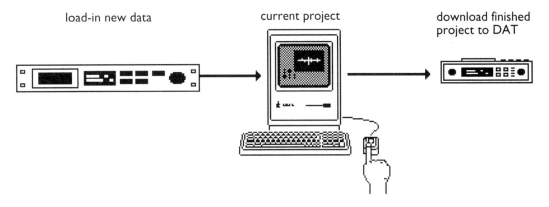

Fig. 5.27: Some multitasking systems can upload or download data while simultaneously working on a current project.

Audio IFF

The Audio Interchange File Format (Audio IFF) is another standard that's been chosen for the Macintosh computer. It allows the storage of both monaural and stereo sampled sounds at a variety of sample rates and bit widths. Each sample point is processed as a linear, two's-complement value (a straightforward system for storing positive and negative sample values), with a maximum bit width of 32. Sound data can also be looped in this format, allowing a portion of the sound to be repeated in either a forward loop or a forward/backward direction.

Wave

The Wave (.Wav) file format is a straightforward PCM encoding method that has been chosen for use with the multimedia extensions in Microsoft Windows (version 3.1 or later). It is used to encode digital audio in either 8- or 16-bit widths at such sample rates as 11.025 kHz, 22.050 kHz, and 44.1 kHz.

This standard is supported by all Windows-based multimedia hardware cards and is commonly used in audio production as it relates to CD-ROM and CD-I (Compact Disc-Interactive) games and educational software. Currently, Wave does not support the creation of loops within its file structure.

Sound Designer

Sound Designer and Sound Designer II are two commonly encountered 16-bit linear samplefile formats developed by Digidesign, Inc. Sound Designer is an earlier monaural version that is capable of encoding only two sample loops (sustain and release).

The newer, more commonly encountered Sound Designer II is a stereo samplefile and soundfile (hard disk recording) format that can be used over a wide range of sample rates and can encode up to eight loops within a single file.

The Two-Channel Hard Disk Recorder

Although many two-channel hard disk systems have been upgraded to handle four discrete channels, there are still systems on the market whose primary job is to record, process, and edit two-channel stereo soundfiles. Although these systems can certainly be synched to a MIDI sequencer to provide a pair of tapeless acoustic channels, they often manipulate and process data into a final edited form. This edited form can then be used for further production (as would happen if you were to edit several incomplete takes of a guitar solo into a final version for dumping back to tracks on a multitrack tape), or the edited results might be the finished master.

One example of a two-channel system is the CardD+ system from Digital Audio Labs. The CardD+ is an affordable 16-bit stereo hard disk recording and editing system that has been designed for IBM-compatible computers. More specifically, the hardware and software requirements call for an AT-compatible 386, or 486 computer. The system itself is made up of three separate components:

- The CardD+ interface
- The I/O CardD
- The EdDitor

The CardD+ is an AT-style interface card that fits into any available 16-bit computer hardware slot. Its single purpose is to transfer digital audio to and from the computer's hard disk at sample rates of 32 kHz, 44.1 kHz, and 48 kHz. Access to analog I/Os is provided by four RCA jacks that have been mounted directly onto the card's edge plate.

The I/O CardD interface has been designed to work with the CardD to add digital inputs and outputs to the system that conform to the consumer S/PDIF format. This optional board fits into a nearby slot and communicates digital audio to and from the CardD by way of a flat ribbon cable.

The EdDitor is exactly that, an editing program for recording, editing, and displaying waveform data. This program allows original soundfile data to be non-destructively edited into final edited form. It works by displaying stereo waveform data onto two windows: the lower Read-Only window (containing soundfile source data) and an upper Modified window (that contains the final edited program).

All of its basic functions can be easily accessed by either keyboard or mouse, providing command functions pertaining to help, soundfile playback, screen scrolling, region definition, and copying, as well as the ever-useful Undo command. Traditional pull-down menus offer access to additional system commands that relate to file, edit, mix, DSP, display, and setup functions.

The MicroSound digital audio recording and editing system from Micro Technology Unlimited has been designed to work on an IBM-compatible under Windows and can be shipped as a complete turnkey system or can be installed into an existing PC that fits all of the necessary system requirements.

The MicroSound turnkey system includes a:

- rack mount 486/66DX2 PC with 4 Mb RAM, VESA local bus and SCSI interface, 14" color monitor, mouse and keyboard

- 2.01 Gb SCSI-2 hard drive

- MicroSound AT-DSP56 system board

- 2U rack mount I/O module providing two channels balanced +4 analog in/out, S/PDIF and AES/EBU

- MicroSync board for chase-lock sysnc to SMPTE and video black burst

- MIDI Interface

- MicroEditor software and additional applications software

Micro Technology's MicroEditor software for Windows offers a series of pull-down menus and command icons for performing three of the system's basic functions: recording a soundfile, creating a segment, and creating a mix file.

The Record screen can be accessed from the **program's main window** (Fig. 5.28). It includes separate record and play sections (with associated on-screen VU metering) that can be automatically triggered via SMPTE time, MTC (MIDI time code), or MIDI channel/notes when using an optional SMPTE/MIDI card.

Segments can be created by using the program's graphics and audition functions (including a Scrub command that lets you listen to any part of a soundfile at standard, 1/2, 1/4, 1/8, or 1/16 playspeed). Once you've created the segments, they can be assembled into a final mix through the use of a **Mix screen** (Fig 5.29). The Mix screen provides a graphic interface for viewing, placing, and controlling segments in a disk-based mix environment and then for saving the edited results as a separate mix file.

The Multichannel Hard Disk Recorder

The multichannel hard disk-based system operates in much the same fashion as its two-channel counterpart, with the exception that soundfiles or defined regions can be placed in any number of on-screen tracks and assigned to various isolated output channels. This capability is often very useful in audio and audio-for-video post-production, since the defined regions can be individually edited and/or slipped in time, and the individual outputs often give the user a greater degree of mixing and signal-processing control.

Although certain hard disk recorders provide an equal number of input and output channels, many systems offer only two inputs. This design economy takes into account the fact that most productions will be assembled onto the disk from a single stereo or mono sound source. Once on disk, these soundfiles can be edited and assigned to the various channel outputs for final mixing.

Track vs. Channel

When referring to multichannel random-access systems, many people are confused by the concepts of tracks and channels. This confusion can be cleared up by comparing a multichannel random access system with its analog counterpart.

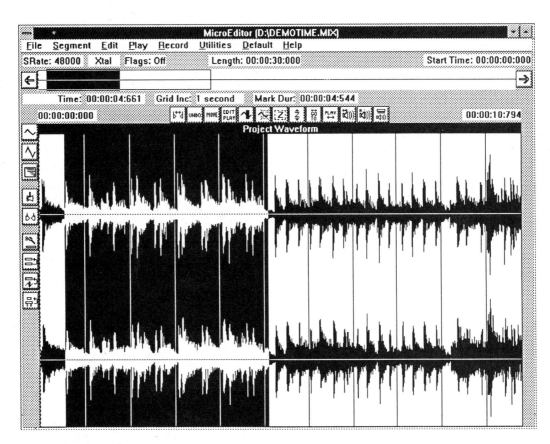

Fig 5.28: An example of MicroEditor's main screen. (Courtesy of Micro Technology Unlimited.)

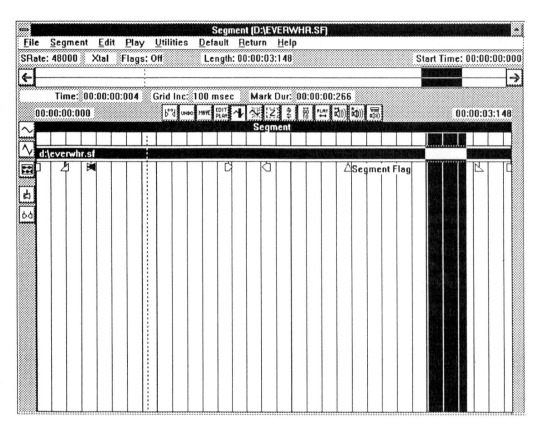

Fig 5.29: The Mix screen and Position Window. (Courtesy of Micro Technology Unlimited.)

In analog technology, the concept of the track is relatively simple and straightforward. Analog multitrack recorders use stationary heads to record and play back a longitudinal band of magnetically encoded information. Once recorded, the magnetic information is physically tied to the medium itself and can't be moved to another track or slipped in time without being re-recorded.

On the other hand, computer-based audio data is not physically tied to an output track or to a particular point in time. However, it can be assigned to a particular output destination or event time, but this could easily be changed or the same data could be output any number of times and to different output channels. Thus, the concept of the channel refers to an assigned output destination. A multichannel design might be capable of outputting 8, 16, 24, or more channels at a time.

The Virtual Track

Although multichannel systems are able to route digital audio to a number of individual outputs, it's also possible for a number of isolated sound "tracks" to be assigned to a single output. Such a series of isolated soundfile events are assigned to what has come to be known as the **virtual track** (Fig 5.30).

Unlike a sound that's recorded upon a single, dedicated tape track, any number of virtual tracks can be assigned to a single output or pair of outputs. In effect, virtual tracks allow you to place soundfiles into isolated tracks, where they can be easily processed without effecting other soundfiles that might be assigned to the same output channel.

In the recent past, only one track could be actively outputting data to a single channel at one time without physically being mixed together into a combined datafile. However, with increased processing speeds and faster-disk access times, it has become increasingly common for simultaneous soundfiles to be mixed together and delivered to a single output channel in real-time, without the need for writing data to disk.

Obviously, all of this means that a four- or eight-channel hard disk system might let you open up a much greater number of tracks. However, it's also important to note that this combined use of use of virtual tracks with real-time soundfile mixing has given birth to two-channel hard disk recorders that are capable of handling up to eight discrete soundfiles. This ability to mix soundfiles in real-time to the system's stereo output pair has given way to a number of cost-effective and yet powerful hard disk recording systems.

The Digital Audio Workstation

Since the late 1980s, the term digital audio workstation (DAW) has become familiar to many in the audio and computer industries. This term loosely refers to a hard-disk based system that incorporates basic editing tools with standard (and possibly advanced) DSP functions. Although a DAW can perform a broad range of audio-related tricks by itself, one of the main characteristics of a computer-based workstation is its ability to integrate with other devices that relate to audio, video, and music production, creating a single multifunctional environment

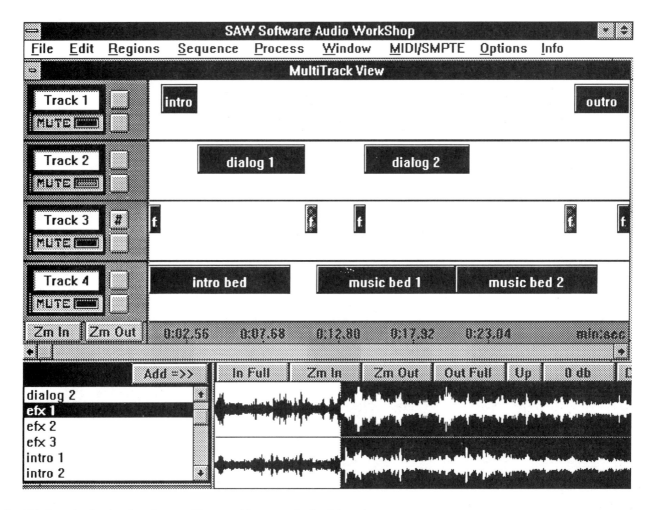

Fig 5.30: Example of a virtual track screen. (Courtesy of Innovative Quality Software.)

A digital audio workstation provides control and communication over various internal/external hardware and software systems. This frees you for the tasks of MIDI sequencing, sample/playlist editing, sampling, hard disk recording, digital signal processing, synthesis and resynthesis, and music printing all within a single production environment.

Over the many years of music production history, we've become used to the idea that certain devices were meant to perform a single task; that is, a recorder records and plays back, a compressor compresses, and a mixer mixes. Recall from Chapter 1 that a digital production system can be likened to a chameleon in that it can change functions to meet your current needs. In situations where it can't quite match the "color" of the moment, it should be able to communicate with other digital hardware/software systems to get the job done. In effect, a digital audio workstation is not so much a device but rather a systems concept that is designed to perform a number of audio production tasks, with ease and speed.

Integration

A major goal for a workstation is to provide complete control over signal recording, editing, processing and routing functions, and other tasks associated with production. Although this control usually stems from a central computer, links to other media devices (like MIDI keyboards and modules, samplers, analog recorders, and VCRs) are common extensions of the control space.

Communication

A workstation environment should easily communicate with other integrated digital hardware and software systems, as well as allow data transfer between them. In fact, one of its chief roles is that of digital traffic director.

It can communicate system-wide with other external devices through the distribution of such digital data as AES/EBU, S/P-DIF, SCSI, or MIDI sample dump standards, or through such timing and synchronization signals as SMPTE time code and MTC. For example, a powerful music system could be designed by integrating a digital audio workstation and powerful MIDI sequencing software together into a single computer package. Such an integrated system could be used to trigger a bank of electronic musical instruments, transmit setup messages to an array of effects devices for total effects automation during a mix, and output soundfiles at specific time code locations.

Expandability

The task of adding related hardware or software to such a production facility is often made easier by the addition's ability to communicate with other hardware and software. Again, the ideal workstation should be able to integrate production-related devices with little difficulty. To take a few examples, newly released programs can be added to bring your system up to date, a CD-ROM can be added to breathe new life into your sampling system, or a DAT or recordable CD system can be added with only a few minor fusses. Ideally, with the assurance of compatibility and expandability, you should merely have to tap the new device into the system and begin work. Of course, I said "ideally."

User Friendly

Perhaps the most important element of a digital audio workstation is its central analog interface we, the users. The central operating program should forego any attempt at speaking "computer-ese" and instead should be highly intuitive ("Wow, this makes sense!") and interactive ("Are you sure that you want to delete last night's session?").

Speed and Flexibility

The qualities of speed and flexibility are probably the greatest selling point of a digital audio workstation. Once you've gained some familiarity with an integrated system, any production task (such as simple editing) can usually be tackled in far less time than with similar analog equipment. With such system integration often comes production flexibility, which can result in more creative freedom. In certain cases, DSP effects (like time compression and expansion) that would have been impossible using analog technology have become commonplace in the processing bag of tricks.

The Multichannel Digital Audio Workstation

The multichannel digital audio workstation works in much the same way as does its two-channel cousin, with the exception that it is capable of outputting soundfiles to a number of isolated channel outputs. Such workstations are known for their flexibility and cost-effective speed, and have become increasingly familiar to those in professional music and audio-for-video production facilities.

The Sonic System

An example of such a workstation is the Sonic System from Sonic Solutions (Fig. 5.31). This integrated audio system is shipped as a complete hardware package consisting of a Macintosh computer, an internal hard disk for program storage, an extended keyboard, a hi-res mono-chrome monitor, a video card, and a signal-processing card. Also included is a large capacity SCSI hard drive that stores the audio data.

The signal-processing card (which incorporates four Motorola 56001 processors) plugs directly into one of the Macintosh's available NuBus slots. However, in order to improve processing and disk scheduling, a proprietary internal Sonic Operating System was developed to offer additional processing features. Among these is the ability to process most digital audio and DSP functions on-the-fly in real time.

This card is capable of simultaneously handling up to four independent channels (or two stereo pairs) of digital I/O in AES/EBU format at sample

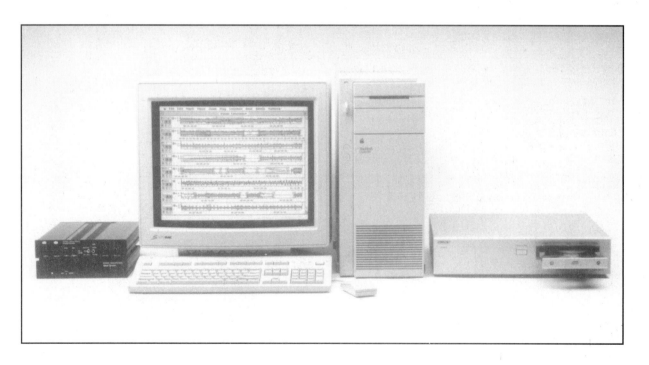

Fig. 5.31: The Sonic System. (Courtesy of Sonic Solutions.)

rates of up to 60 kHz (with most programs operating at 44.1 kHz or 48 kHz). Each card incorporates an SCSI port that is capable of handling up to four external hard disks. Because of the system's unique operating structure and speed, it is capable of simultaneously uploading or downloading a soundfile in the background while editing or processing an active soundfile in the foreground. Four RS-422 serial ports are also included to permit software control over external digital tape transports during the edit and upload/download process.

Sonic Solutions offers a number of "audio desktop" programs that are tailored to perform a particular task. Some of the most popular task-specific programs are:

- CD Premastering Desktop
- Sample Rate Conversion Desktop
- PQ Code Editing Desktop
- Sound for Picture Desktop
- No-Noise Desktop

CD Premastering Desktop

The CD Premastering Desktop applications program is designed to give the user the benefits of both digital signal processing and random access editing. The user can thus fully prepare a project for direct mastering to CD. This task is primarily accomplished from three screens: the Edit screen, the Mixing screen, and the Crossfade screen.

The Edit screen allows multiple samplefiles to be visually displayed on the screen at any point in time. Up to four channels at a time can be directly assigned to the digital I/O ports.

The Mixing screen facilitates the mixing of up to four discrete soundfiles into a final stereo soundfile (or to an output bus) by emulating an on-screen digital 4 x 2 mixer. This section includes control over EQ and dynamics and also offers real-time moving faders.

The Crossfade screen allows a wide range of user-defined crossfades to be performed within or between soundfiles. It has the expected range of linear and log crossfades and also lets users draw their own parametric crossfade curves.

Sample Rate Conversion Desktop

The Sample Rate Conversion Desktop program is a straightforward program for converting sample rates from 48 kHz to 44.1 kHz, and other rates.

PQ Code Editing Desktop

The PQ Code Editing Desktop program can be used to prepare finalized program soundfile for transfer into a completed CD premaster. It does this by generating all the necessary PQ subcodes and/or CD setup log sheets in a variety of mastering formats.

Sound for Picture Desktop

The Sound for Picture Desktop software allows the Sonic System to be fully synchronized to an external video source (via a serial controller) for audio-for-video post-production. It's also capable of generating background and dialog loops, and includes time compression/expansion processing functions.

No-Noise Desktop

The No-Noise Desktop program is a single-ended noise removal system that is commonly used to restore and clean up problematic programs from the 78 rpm record and early analog eras so that they can be remastered to compact disc. The system can be regarded as an intelligent multiband expander. In this case, however, "multi" means that the audio spectrum is divided into more than 2,000 frequency bands and requires more than 53 million computations to process just 1 second of sound.

Pro Tools

Another popular system is Pro Tools from Digidesign, Inc. (Fig. 5.32). It combines multitrack digital audio recording and editing, digital signal processing, MIDI sequencing, and automated digital mixing into a single Macintosh-based workstation.

Pro Tools offers up to sixteen independent digital audio channels in upgradable four-channel increments. In addition, it has been designed from the ground up to fully incorporate MIDI sequencing and edit capabilities, which can be synchronized to existing digital audio tracks.

The format of the Pro Tools digital soundfile is Digidesign's own Sound Designer II (SDII) mono and stereo digital audio soundfile format (at sample rates of 44.1 kHz and 48 kHz). This, of course, makes it compatible with Sound Tools (both I and II), SampleCell, Deck, and other Digidesign digital audio products. Sound Designer audio files are also supported for use by a number of products from third-party developers (such as Opcode's Studio Vision, Mark of the Unicorn's Digital Performer, and Steinberg's Cubase for the Mac).

The Pro Tools system consists of two hardware components, an Audio Card and an Audio Interface, as well as two software applications, Pro-DECK and ProEDIT.

The Audio Card is a high-speed, four-channel processor card that has been designed to occupy a single Macintosh NuBus computer slot. When operating with only one Audio Card, Pro Tools can be configured as a four-channel system (with the ability to handle up to 64 digital audio or MIDI virtual tracks. However, with the addition of a system accelerator card the system can be expanded to handle up to sixteen channels (in four-channel increments).

This optional accelerator card is used to speed up the overall system and to avoid data bottle-

Fig 5.32: Pro Tools multichannel digital audio workstation. (Courtesy of Digidesign.)

necks by providing a direct path from the audio cards to the hard disk drives (thus bypassing the Macintosh's internal processors).

The Audio Interface is rack-mountable, external I/O analog and digital interface. The front panel includes a power switch, an array of front panel indicators (showing sync, sample rate, and digital status information), and recessed multiturn level controls. I/O ports include four electronically balanced XLR analog inputs and outputs along with two digital I/O parts (AES/EBU and S/PDIF), MIDI I/O, and various other computer periphery connections.

ProDECK, a software application, includes a number of integrated software windows that are used for recording both multitrack digital audio and MIDI information. It features a main transport window that, in addition to standard transport functions, offers full punch-in/out, loop, vari-pitch, and a programmable autolocation keypad. A rather comprehensive real-time digital "mixer" has also been designed into the system. This allows any number of internal digital audio sources (such as output channels, internal effects returns, etc.) to be assigned to an input module. Each channel strip offers provisions for channel fader, metering, solo/mute, panning, record status indicator, and two independent effects sends.

The mixer's two auxiliary sends give a rather interesting design twist. When performing a real-time mix to any or all of the four (or more) channel outputs, it's a simple matter to route the two independent sends through either of the system's AES/EBU or S/PDIF digital ports.

ProDECK also has an internal signal-processing section that allows two real-time DSP functions to be assigned to any one of the mixer's input modules. In addition, the automation control window can be used to automate both the digital mixer and the DSP functions. This can be carried out by capturing static setting "snapshots" of all Pro-DECK level and control settings. Dynamic automation can also be used to automate moving control settings in real time. Both snapshot and dynamic automation information may be performed within a mix.

The system has a comprehensive MIDI sequencer that allows for the recording and playback of MIDI data in a standard multitrack linear fashion. Individual MIDI tracks can also be easily punched in or out or looped by the user.

The system's ProEDIT software provides a comprehensive approach to non-destructive graphic editing of both audio and MIDI information. Upon booting up the program window, ProEDIT will list a number of icons at the top of the screen. These provide tools for viewing, auditioning, scrubbing, and defining regions.

Plug-In Modules for hard disk recorders

In recent years, the process of routing digital audio through a computer has become increasingly standardized. For example, soundfile protocols for the Mac (AIFF & SD II) and Windows (WAV) can be processed by an intermediate software program and then routed to it's output destination. As the soundfiles and signal routing have become less and less software specific, it is possible for the software that is handling the soundfile data to be designed to perform a specific task. This form of software has generally come to be known as a "plug-in" module.

Recently a number of these modules has come onto the market for use with Digidesign's Sound Designer II soundfile formats and hardware for the Mac. The following is a brief description of a few of these products that exist as of this writing.

- UltraMaximizer - The UltraMaximizer from Waves Ltd. (Fig. 5.33) has created a plug-in dynamics tool that can perform transparent peak limiting, advanced soundfile dithering and noise shaping, as well as advanced normalizing features (for maximizing the gain and bit resolution of a file).

- DINR - The Digidesign Intelligent Noise Reduction system (DINR) is a signal-processing plug-in module that allows you to remove hum, tape hiss and other extraneous noises from your recordings (Fig. 5.34). Hiss and other broadband noises are eliminated by analyzing the audio in question (a brief, isolated noise passage is ideal but not necessary) to create a "sonic model". Using this model, it can then intelligently subtract the noise from the digital soundfile. Once the sound is analyzed, UltraMaximixer can be applied to the soundfile in real-time during playback (where it can be saved to DAT or another recording source or the file can be processed in non-real time and then saved directly to disk.

- MDT (Multiband Dynamics Tool) - The Multiband Dynamics Tool from Jupiter Systems is another plug-in for the Mac that lets you see and shape up to 30 thresholds and 5 UltraMaximixer controlled spectral bands to perform such processing functions as compression, expansion, tube emulation, gating, de-essing and vocal processing.

- Hyperprism - Hyperprism from Arboretum Systems (Fig. 5.35) is a signal processing plug-in that allows for on-screen control over time compression & expansion, equalization, delays, chorus, frequency shifting and 16 other functions. Control over these functions can be assigned to a mouse or MIDI controller and varied in real-time by moving the Ultra-Maximixer over the screen. The drawn figure (which results in a custom processed signal) can then be saved for late replay at the appropriate time.

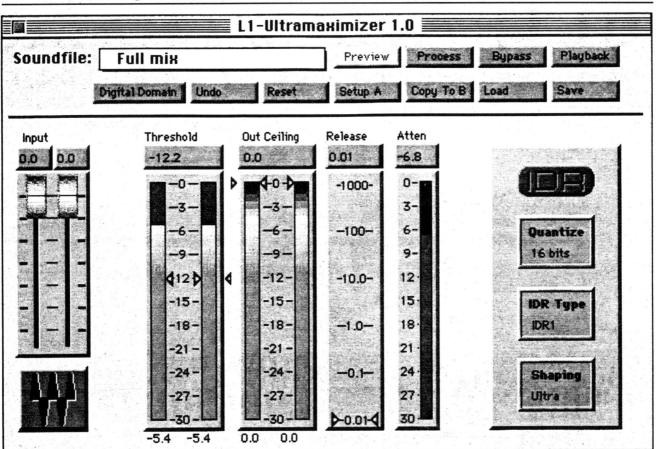

Fig. 5.33: The UltraMaximixer dynamics plug-in application. (Courtesy of Waves Ltd.)

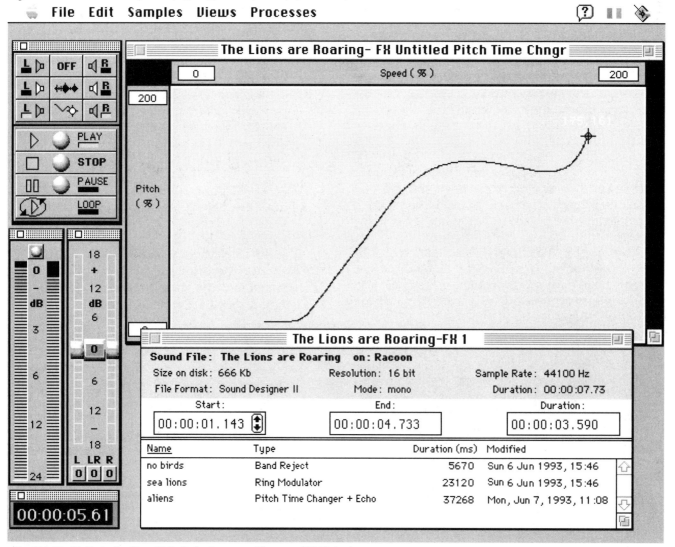

Fig. 5.34: The Digidesign Intelligent Noise Reduction system. (Courtesy of Digidesign.)

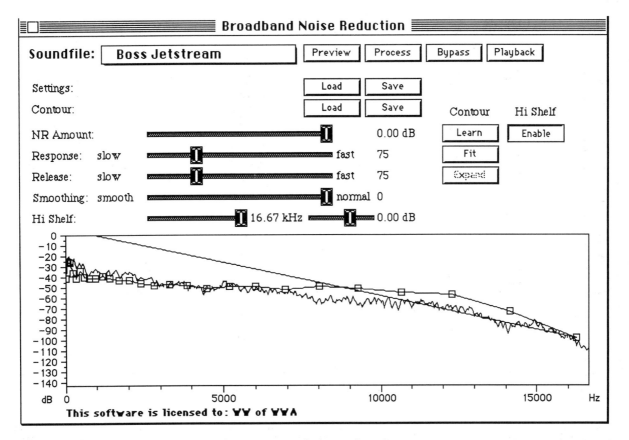

Fig. 5.35: Hyperprism plug-in signal processing application. (Courtesy of Arboretum Systems)

Chapter 6
Digital Audio Transmission

In the 1990s, it has become increasingly common for audio to be distributed between connected devices in the digital domain, without ever seeing the light of analog. With digital audio transmission, information can be distributed between devices in its originally encoded numeric form. Thus, it is possible to make an exact clone of the originally recorded program material.

This chapter discusses some often-overlooked technical aspects of transmitting audio in the digital domain. It also takes a close look at the various professional and consumer formats currently in use. In the course of doing so, it investigates the Serial Copy Management System, or SCMS, which is widely used today to prevent consumers from digitally copying program material at the 44.1-kHz sampling rate.

The Perfect Digital Clone

The concept of the "perfect digital clone" has been the subject of articles and debates. I tend to agree with Dr. Toby Mountain, owner of Northeastern Digital Recording, who made copies of a prepared digital master and then compared the numbers of a short segment between a multi-generation digital clone and the released CD. In studying the two, he could find no numeric differences, and he concluded that "the numbers simply don't lie."

In my personal experience, digital copying results in an exact clone of the original provided that certain guidelines are followed to ensure that the digital signal's integrity is kept intact. If not, it is possible that a signal's noise figure could be slightly degraded, that audible annoying clicks or tics might be introduced, or, at the extreme, that the signal could be beyond all hope (a condition that would result in a muted output signal).

Signal Characteristics

Besides keeping in mind that digital audio is relayed from one device to another by the transmission of numeric values, you should also keep in mind that the bandwidth of digital audio works in the megahertz range. This basic fact of digital life means that these signals have more characteristics in common with video than with their analog counterpart. As such, a quick-fix solution to, say, a wiring problem might not cause problems in the relatively forgiving world of analog but could severely degrade the signal when used between digital devices.

A major example of this fact are the variations in impedance values (internal resistance) that might be encountered between the output, cable wiring, and input ports of two or more digital audio devices. When copying analog audio, which is the lowest end of the frequency spectrum, minor impedance mismatches will generally not have a devastating effect on the quality of a program. However, way up in the megahertz range of digital signals, such mismatches could seriously deform the digital waveform.

Fortunately, impedance is usually not a problem when connecting one digital device to another, since digital transmission standards have set down precise input/output impedance load ratings. On the other hand, the splitting of a digital signal from a source to two devices by using a "Y-cord" is a major no-no because impedance and digital reflections at such high frequencies would invariably present problems.

One simple way to solve this problem is to daisy-chain a number of digital audio devices together (Fig. 6.1). This solution works fine if only a few devices are chained together. However, if a number of devices are connected in this manner, problems relating to time-base errors (known as jitter) could arise.

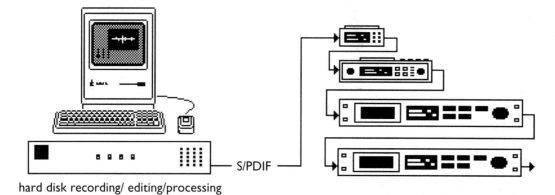

Fig. 6.1: Distribution of digital audio in a serial daisy-chain fashion.

Such problems might be avoided by using a device that is capable of distributing digital audio data (Fig. 6.2). In this way, data can be routed to individual destinations, without having to be daisy-chained through devices that might introduce relatively small amounts of time-base error.

What Is Jitter?

Jitter is a widely misunderstood digital phenomenon. It is perhaps best explained by Bob Katz of Digital Domain (NYC), who tackled the subject in his article "An Introduction to Jitter." The following is an excerpt:

Jitter is time-base error. It is caused by varying time delays in the circuit paths from component to component in the signal path. The two most common causes of jitter are poorly designed phase-locked loops (PLLs) and waveform distortion due to mismatched impedances and/or reflections in the signal path.

The top waveform in Fig. 6.3 represents a theoretically perfect digital source. Its value is 101010, occurring at equal slices of time, represented by the equal-spaced dashed vertical lines. When the first waveform passes through long cables of incorrect impedance, or when a source impedance is incorrectly matched at the load, the square wave becomes rounded and fast rise times become slow. Also reflections in the cable can cause misinterpretation of the actual zero crossing point of the waveform.

The second waveform in Fig. 6.3 shows some of the ways in which the first might change. Depending on the severity of the mismatch, you might see a triangle wave, a square wave with ringing, or simply rounded edges. Note that the new transitions (measured at the zero line) in the second waveform occur at unequal slices of time. Even so, the numeric interpretation of the second waveform is still 101010! There would have to be very severe waveform distortion for the value of the new

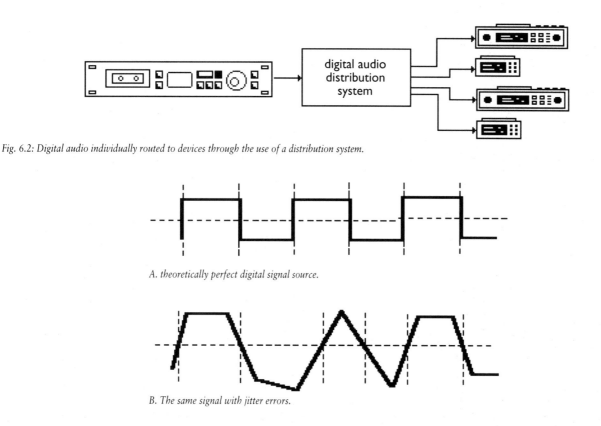

Fig. 6.2: Digital audio individually routed to devices through the use of a distribution system.

A. theoretically perfect digital signal source.

B. The same signal with jitter errors.

Fig. 6.3: Example of time-base errors.

waveform to be misinterpreted, which usually shows up as audible clicks or tics in the sound. If you hear tics, then you really have something to worry about.

If the numeric value of the waveform is unchanged, why should we be concerned? Let's rephrase the question: "When (not why) should we become concerned?" The answer is "hardly ever." The only effect of time-base distortion is in the listening; it has no effect on the dubbing of the tapes or any digital-to-digital transfer (as long as the jitter is low enough to permit the data to be read).

A typical D to A converter derives its system clock (the clock that controls the sample and hold circuit) from the incoming digital signal. If that clock is not stable, then the conversion from digital to analog will not occur at the correct moments in time. The audible effect of this jitter is a possible loss of low-level resolution caused by added noise, spurious (phantom) tones, or distortion added to the signal.

A properly dithered 16-bit recording can have over 120 dB of dynamic range; jitter can deteriorate that range to 100 dB or less, depending on the severity of the jitter. We have performed listening experiments on purist, audiophile-quality musical source material recorded with a 20-bit accurate A/D converter (dithered to 16 bits within the A/D).

The sonic results of passing this signal through processors that truncate the signal at -110, -105, or -96 dB are:

- Increased "grain" in the image
- Instruments losing their sharp edge and focus
- Apparent loss of level, causing the listener to want to turn up the monitor level (even though high-level signals are reproduced at unity gain)

Contrary to intuition, these effects are audible without having to turn up the listening volume beyond normal! Nevertheless, the effects are subtle, require the highest-grade audiophile musical material to be audible at all (as well as high resolution D to A converters), and some engineers [might] not deem the effects to be audible with most music recorded today. Jitter in the signal path can produce a subtle loss of resolution similar to the above.

Since writing the above article Mr. Katz has done additional research on jitter and wants you to be on the lookout for some surprising developments on the subject in the near future.

Digital Audio Formats

The need to understand the inner workings of digital audio transmission differs from one individual to the next, depending on the application being considered. For example, suppose you want to make a simple copy from one digital consumer recorder to another. Basically, you need only connect the digital out-port to the digital in-port, and you're in business.

However, more complicated systems may use different formats (and in certain cases a system may not even strictly adhere to an established format). This could lead to possible complications that require a degree of understanding. Even in the first example, where only two recorders were involved, it's entirely possible that even with the digital in- and out-ports of each recorder using the same format, you might still be prevented from making a digital copy. At that point, you're confronted with the question of "Why?"

The four digital-audio transmission formats discussed here are the ones most likely to be encountered in the everyday world of digital audio production:

- SDIF-2
- AES/EBU
- S/PDIF
- MADI

SDIF-2

The SDIF-2 (Sony Digital Interface Format) was adopted for the purpose of transmitting serial digital data between certain digital audio systems that were sold by Sony in the mid to late 1980s. A number of these systems are still in wide use (such as Sony's PCM-1610 and the PCM-1630 CD mastering and archive processors).

SDIF-2's interface connections are made by using three 75-ohm BNC-type connectors (Fig. 6.4). Two of these connectors are used to handle right and left audio data, while the third communicates word clock (a square wave signal whose sample rate transitions are used to synchronize the digital timing between a source and the copy deck). Although any sampling rate can be used, this format is primarily intended for use with rates of 44.056 kHz, 44.1 kHz, and 48 kHz.

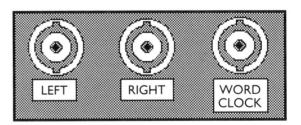

Fig. 6.4: BNC-type connectors are used in making SDIF-2's interface connections.

Digitally speaking, SDIF-2's word structure is made up of 32 bits, with the first 20 bits being reserved for audio (whenever 16-bit audio is used, the last 4 digits are automatically set to zero). The remaining 12 bits are reserved for unassigned data, preemphasis, copy-prohibit, and various sync identifiers.

AES/EBU

The AES/EBU digital audio transmission format has been adopted by the Audio Engineering Society and the European Broadcast Union for use in professional applications. It is used to convey two-channel or monaural audio and related data over a shielded, twisted pair of wires in a balanced (nonpolarized) configuration (Fig. 6.5).

Connections are made using three-pin, balanced XLR connectors, with pin 1 being connected to signal ground (shield) and pins 2 and 3 carrying signal data. Typical data waveform amplitudes range from between 3 to 10 volts peak-to-peak with a nominal impedance of 110 ohms.

These cable/connection characteristics have been defined so that readily available, standard two-conductor microphone cable could be used in the field. Cable lengths of up to 328 feet (100 meters) can be used, although greater distances can be achieved with the help of special line signal processing.

The AES/EBU format operates by transmitting channel data and information as blocks of 192 bits, which are organized into twenty-four 8-bit words. Within the confines of these data blocks, two subframes are transmitted during each sample period. The subframes are made up of both audio and non-audio channel information that is serially transmitted in an A-B-A-B . . . fashion. When two channels of digital audio are being transmitted, subframe A represents left channel data and subframe B represents right channel data. When audio is transmitted in monaural, only subframe A is used to convey channel information.

Each subframe is 32 bits wide and includes encoded data relating to sync, audio data, and various other bits associated with error, channel, and user-related data (Fig. 6.6).

Up to 24 bits can be stored within the audio data area (with the least significant bit being transmitted first). However, in most applications, only 20 or 16 bits are used, with the first 4 or 8 bits being set to "o" or reserved for other sample-related applications.

Digital data is transmitted as a self-clocking bi-phase code (Fig. 6.7). In this way, wire polarity can be ignored and a device that is receiving digital data can derive its clock timing directly from the digital source.

From a purely practical standpoint, the AES/EBU interface format isn't capable of transmitting the SCMS copy-prohibit status bits (as described in the next section) because these bits are reserved for other flag applications. Nevertheless, a major disadvantage to this professional interface is that digital copies between recorders will not receive subcode data.

For example, a digital DAT or DCC copy that is made via AES/EBU will not retain the valuable

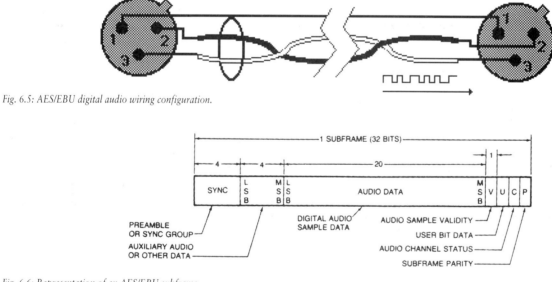

Fig. 6.5: AES/EBU digital audio wiring configuration.

Fig. 6.6: Representation of an AES/EBU subframe.

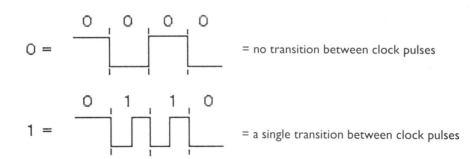

0 = = no transition between clock pulses

1 = = a single transition between clock pulses

Fig. 6.7: AES/EBU digital data is transmitted as a self-clocking bi-phase code

index markings that have been encoded onto the original tape. This is because the AES/EBU format was created before index markers were implemented into professional and consumer digital audio recorders.

S/PDIF (IEC-958)

The S/PDIF (Sony/Philips Digital Interface) has been adopted for the purpose of transmitting digital audio data between consumer devices and is remarkably similar in data structure to its professional counterpart.

S/PDIF digital parts don't use balanced XLR connectors but instead employ unbalanced phono (RCA) cables with a nominal peak-to-peak voltage of 0.5V at 75 ohms. Although most off-the-shelf phono cables will work, low-impedance video-grade cables are often recommended.

In addition to using standard phono-type connections, it has become common for standard optical links to be used for digitally connecting one consumer device with another. In such circumstances, S/PDIF is usually the spoken transmission language. More information on optical transmission can be found later in this chapter.

This format also relays channel data and channel information as a block of 192 bits. However, they are organized into groupings of twelve 16-bit words. The first two bytes in the chain indicate channel status, with byte 0 being used to detail the signal's general status and byte 1 being used to convey data relating to the source device's category type and generation status.

Alternatively, the category code for a DAT machine will tell the system to respond to setup information (such as sample rate, copy code, etc.). It will also reserve a portion of the unused 24-bit audio data for relaying data that pertains to track indexing. In this way, index information (start ID and program numbers) can be copied from the source tape onto the digital copy.

In certain cases, it's possible to make digital copies from an AES/EBU source to a device that has only an S/PDIF interface (and vice versa). This is possible, using certain machines, because the bitstream voltage level threshold is often designed to be tolerant of higher or lower signal levels, thus allowing the transfer to take place.

This conversion is often accomplished by making a simple cable (or set of cables) that modifies the AES/EBU's three-pin XLR balanced connector. This allows it to be wired to an unbalanced S/PDIF phono (RCA) connector (Fig. 6.8).

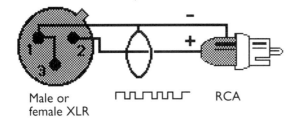

Male or female XLR   RCA

Fig. 6.8: Adapter cable for converting between AES/EBU and S/PDIF interface formats.

SCMS

Copy-inhibit codes have been a source of much confusion for both consumers and professionals alike. This is due, in part, to the lack of standardization that has arisen from record companies' fears that their products would be cloned like bunnies. The lack of standardization was also due to manufacturers who feared extensive legal battles with these record companies and their political lobbies. However, in the 1990s, a consensus regarding copy inhibitors is finally beginning. The following is a brief history, which will lead up to present day events.

Initially, the medium of digital audio tape (DAT) was intended to provide consumers with a means for making high-quality digital recordings for their own personal use. As of this writing, it is the current standard for mastering and archiving professional two-channel productions.

However, early in its development, the DAT medium was seen as a threat by certain record companies. These companies thought that such a high-quality medium would open the doors even wider for CD and tape piracy. As a result, the RIAA (Record Industry Association of America) and the former CBS Technology Center set out to create a "copy inhibitor."

The first of these developments was a copy guard notch that actually filtered out a narrow band of audio. Once this band was electronically detected as missing from the audio spectrum, a copying device would inhibit the record process. Following the defeat of this ill-fated, reactionary process (and the cause of many red-hot debates), a copy-inhibit scheme was created that resided within the structure of the digital bitstream itself. This widely adopted copy-inhibit process has come to be known as the Serial Copy Management System, or SCMS.

SCMS (pronounced "Scums") is designed to control digital-to-digital copying of audio material at a sample rate of 44.1 kHz via the consumer S/PDIF (IEC-958) interface. It does not prohibit analog copying, nor does it apply to digital copies made using the AES/EBU digital interface port or to program material that is sampled at rates other than 44.1 kHz (that is, 32 kHz and 48 kHz).

The SCMS protocol is currently being implemented in the digital interface of such professional and consumer recording devices as DAT machines, Digital Compact Cassette (DCC), and certain hard disk recording systems (many of which are capable of placing a copy-prohibit flag into a soundfile's bitstream).

Although these codes could apply to any popular sample rate, they have been adopted to relate only to the consumer rate of 44.1 kHz in order to deter consumer copying of prerecorded CD, DAT, DCC, and other such material.

Technically, the SCMS copy protection flags, which are encoded within byte 0 (bits 6 and 7) of S/PDIF's bitstream subcode area, can have only one of three possible states:

- Status 00 unlimited copying and subsequent dubbing

- Status 10 no more digital copies allowed

- Status 11 a first-generation copy can be made of the product, but the copy cannot be copied

As an example, a program encoded with a status code of 00 can be digitally copied any number of times. However, suppose that you just released a product on Digital Compact Cassette that has been encoded with a status 11 flag (Fig. 6.9). After shopping at the local record store, Joe Consumer just paid into your account by buying the tape, and he decides that he wants to make a DCC copy for his car player. No problem.

However, upon making a first-generation dub, the recorder that is doing the copying detects the 11 code and automatically changes it to a status 10. Now, six months later, Joe's best pal hears the tape and loves it. So Joe offers to make a copy for his pal from the car tape. As you might guess, the third-generation dub deck reads the status 10 code and says, "Do not pass GO and do not collect $200." Of course at that time, Joe might bypass the digital copy circuitry by getting cords and making an analog copy anyway.

These copy protection codes are to be applied when preparing the final production master (before going to CD, etc.), and their use (at the time of this writing) is entirely at the discretion of the artist, producer, and/or record company. Once encoded, SCMS can't be altered by the consumer, although considerable professional gear and audio-related software are being developed that can easily alter digital bitstream states.

A SCMS Caveat (Let the SCMS Beware)

From the preceding discussion, you might think that SCMS was a simple, straightforward matter. Well, this would be true if companies would stick to the strict definition and implementation of this standard. Unfortunately they don't a fact of life that sometimes makes SCMS a four letter word to consumers and professionals alike.

At present, here are some of the copy-inhibit incongruities introduced by SCMS:

- When a digital copy is being made of a program that was originally recorded by using a recorder's analog inputs, the status flag will be set to 11 (one more copy allowed). This setting is unfortunate because it prohibits the digital copying of legitimate original material. Should this situation occur, your choices are: (1)copy the material using the professional AES/EBU interface, (2)make the dub using the machine's analog ports, or (3)if available, strip the copy code by using a digital audio format converter (see the last section in this chapter).

- Upon recognizing a CD category code (10000000), an SCMS-equipped DAT will automatically set the copy-prohibit status to 10 (no further copies allowed).

- Copies from an unknown digital source (having a general category code of 00000000) will automatically set the copy-prohibit status to 11 (one more copy allowed). In essence, the recorder that is doing the copying doesn't know if the source is copyrighted or not and therefore takes a (so-called) safe middle-ground stance.

MADI Multichannel Transmission Standard

With the increased use of multichannel digital devices in the audio and audio-for-visual media, it is easy to see the need for a straightforward multichannel digital interface standard. Recognizing this need, Mitsubishi, Neve, Solid State Logic, and Sony met in August of 1987 to propose such a standard. Known as MADI (Multichannel Audio Digital Interface), this specification defines a method of simple, point-to-point connection between two digital multichannel devices such as a console and tape recorder (Fig. 6.10).

The MADI format provides up to 56 channels of linearly encoded digital audio, whose interface connection is made via a 75-ohm, video-grade coaxial cable at distances of less than 164 feet (50 meters). Its data structure is compatible with that of the AES/EBU twin-channel format since the data, status, user, and parity bit structure are preserved.

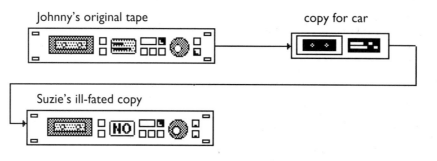

Fig. 6.9: Tapes that are encoded with a SCMS status code of 11 can't be digitally copied.

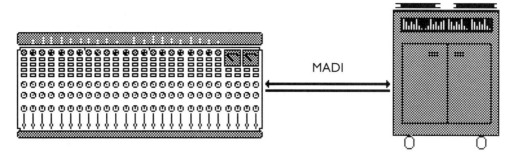

Fig. 6.10: The MADI specification defines a method of simple point-to-point connection between two digital multichannel devices.

Because MADI is a serial interface format, its channels are transmitted sequentially starting with channel 0 and ending with channel 55. It has a data transmission rate of 100 megabits/second, which results in an overall bandwidth that is capable of accommodating numerous sync codes and transmissions at variable sample rate speeds. These rate adjustments allow for the pitch of any channel to be adjusted up or down by 12.5 percent at the basic sample rates of 32 kHz to 48 kHz.

MADI is defined as having a maximum of 56 channels, and any number of channels can be active at any one time. This means that a single MADI link can be established with equipment that supports 56 or fewer channels of audio data.

Fiber Optic Transmission

In addition to transmitting digital audio through impedance-matched cables, transmitting digital audio through fiber optical links is becoming increasingly common. The use of optical links between equipment is a functional, cost-effective option wherever wide bandwidths are required (as is often the case with multiplexed digital audio or video transmissions). Currently, rates of up to 100 megabits/second can be found in digital audio and communications systems, with higher rates being possible for special applications.

As an example of the capabilities of optical links, data rates such as those just mentioned are easily capable of communicating tens of thousands of simultaneous phone conversations over a single hair-thin cable. In such a mass communications link, backup redundancy is often an important consideration. For example, in early 1992, a large portion of downtown Manhattan lost phone communications for almost two days when a nonredundant optical cable was accidentally cut. This simple occurrence resulted in a computer breakdown at a major New York airport that caused airline delays across the country.

Despite such a mishap, data transmission using fiber optic technology is superior to standard wired systems in almost every respect. Its advantages include:

• The ability to transmit information at high data rates over long distances, with very little signal loss when compared to wire

• Complete immunity to ground loops, crosstalk between channels, and electromagnetic interference (such as AC power lines and lighting grids)

• Its small size and light weight when compared with an equivalent wire layout

• Ruggedness

Within conventional wiring, data is carried by the flow of electrons through a metal conductor. Fiber optics, on the other hand, operates by propagating photons (light particles) through a thin, optically clear cable that can be made from either highly purified glass or plastic. All systems using this technology include three basic components (Fig. 6.11):

• An optical source that is used to convert electrical signals into analogous light impulses

• A fiber optic cable that serves to convey the light

• An optical receiver that is reciprocally used to convert the light impulses back into analogous electrical signals for further processing

Depending on its application, the optical source can be either an LED (light emitting diode), a laser diode, or other laser source. LEDs are used where a slower speed, limited bandwidth transmission rate will suffice. A laser is usually the optical source in faster, high-bandwidth systems. Receiv-

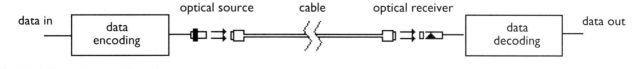

Fig. 6.11: A fiber-optic transmission path.

ers are generally constructed using light-responsive photodiodes to begin the process of converting the optical signal back into electrical impulses.

The fiber optic cable consists of a solid tube of plastic or glass (known as the core) surrounded by a highly reflective covering (known as its cladding). It is the function of the cladding to reflect stray light emissions back into the core, thereby sending as much light as possible onto its receiving destination (Fig. 6.12).

Unlike standard wire connections which can often hang by a thread and still work, optical connections can be unforgiving at weak connection points. A poor coupling between the cable and the optical transmitter/receiver could easily result in a lost or inefficient data transfer. For this reason, precision optical couplers have been designed to ensure that the surfaces of the optical couplings are properly lined up and that they are both smooth and touching.

Format Conversion and Utility Tools

In connection with the various format types and special status options that can either help or hinder the distribution of digital audio, a number of digital audio format converters are being marketed. These converters indicate and/or alter the format or status bits within a digital bitstream, and basically can be thought of as Swiss army knives that are often helpful in dealing with the dilemmas of modern day digital audio production.

One such format conversion utility tool is the FCN-1 from Digital Domain (Fig. 6.13). Its dual purpose is to act as a central distribution system for connecting together digital audio devices and for providing control over the digital bitstream's formats and status bits.

In its standard version, two separate digital audio sources can be connected to the FCN-1 by using either its balanced XLR connector (which is labelled "110W") or its phono (RCA) jack (labeled "75W"). Either input can be selected by sliding the input switch towards the appropriate connector.

On the output side, the FCN-1 can simultaneously feed up to four separate digital loads (three 75W and one 110W). This is useful for music and dubbing facilities, since it avoids the

daisy chaining of digital signals from one device to another. All inputs and outputs on the FCN-1 are transformer-isolated (including the 75W RCA jacks), thus avoiding potential ground loops and impedance mismatches that might otherwise occur.

A main feature of this device is an eight-position output format DIP switch, which is used to alter the incoming digital audio code (both pro and consumer). This switch provides direct control over important bit flags within the digital bitstream and gives the user direct control over format settings:

- PRO/CON allows the user to switch output formats between AES/EBU and S/PDIF, regardless of which format type is at its input.

- SAMPLE FREQ alters the sample frequency at which the receiving device(s) will record (32 kHz, 44.1 kHz, and 48 kHz).

- CATEGORY alters the "L bit" or generation bit, which tells the receiving device what type of device the source is (DAT, CD, PCM, etc.). When transmitting in S/PDIF, the category code will affect copy-prohibit status and the transmission of start, skip index IDs (such as the index IDs that are recorded onto DAT tape).

- COPY alters the copyright status bit, allowing the user to either assert or disable the SCMS (Serial Copy Management System) flags in the S/PDIF bitstream.

- EMPHASIS controls the presence or absence of digital pre- emphasis (a form of digital noise reduction that is no longer in common use).

In addition to the input/output ports and the format DIP switch, the FCN-1 includes four lights that are used to show the status of the incoming digital bitstream and power:

- ERROR is on if there's no signal at the selected digital input or if there is a string of bad data with a duration of more than a second. When the ERROR indicator is on, the box will automatically mute the outgoing digital signal.

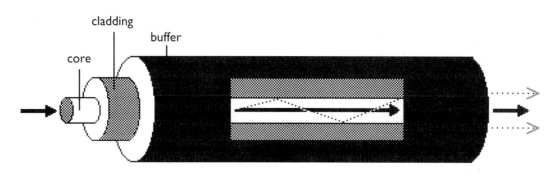

Fig. 6.12: Detail and cutaway views of a fiber optic cable.

Fig. 6.13: The FCN-1 digital format converter. (Courtesy of Digital Domain.

- indicates the presence of a copy-prohibit flag (channel status bit C2), relevant only to consumer digital sources. This flag was used before SCMS was widely adopted. If the C2 bit is a 0, the will light up, meaning that the source may be subject to SCMS restrictions.

- EMPH indicates the presence of digital preemphasis.

- POWR indicates that an AC or DC (of either polarity) power source of between 9 and 18 volts is connected.

Other options include polarity (analog phase) inversion for either or both channels, a digital "over" indicator, L/R channel reversal capabilities, standard optical (Toslink) input and output ports, as well as provisions for word clock.

In addition to its toolbox control over bitstream data, the multiple I/O structure of the FCN-1 means that it could also be used as a control center from which various dubbing and routing combinations can be made without repatching.

Another such format converter is Roland's SRC-2 Dual Sample Rate Converter (Fig. 6.14). This rack-mountable device not only convert between digital audio formats, it can also mix two digital sources (at any sample rate and in different formats) to a single destination and format.

The SCR-2 is capable of converting AES/EBU, S/PDIF and optical digital audio signals at rates of 32 kHz, 44.056 kHz, 44.1 kHz, 47,952 kHz, 48 kHz and 48,048 kHz with up to full 24-bit word accuracy (20-bit audio sampled word and 4-bit audio auxiliary). Full signal level and channel status indicators are supplied on the front panel, as are input/output gain and controls for switching between the various input and output digital audio formats. Signal lock to a multitude of sync signals (including the various video frame rates and external sync) are also provided.

Local Area Networks

Within larger audio production and post-production facilities (where a number of digital audio workstations and hard disk recorders might live under one roof) it might prove to be cost- and system-effective for all of these devices to be connected to a central data storage and distribution point. Such a system for sharing data is known as a local area network or LAN, for short (Fig. 6.15).

Basically, a LAN works by providing a high-speed digital connection between operating stations and a central memory storage device or terminal. Although Lans exist that are capable of providing real-time data transfer to a number of stations, it is equally as likely that a LAN's transmission rate might provide access to a file, which can then be copied to an individual station for local access and processing.

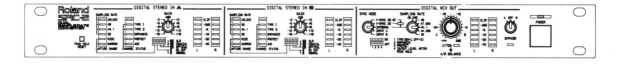

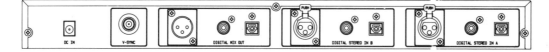

Fig. 6.14: The Roland SCR-2 Dual Sample Rate Converter. (Courtesy of Roland Corporation US.)

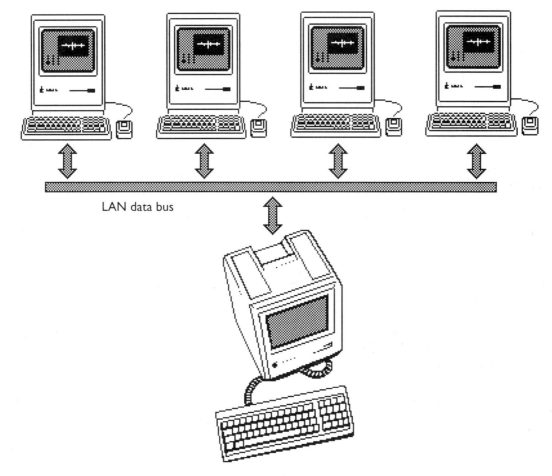

LAN data bus

Fig. 6.15: Example of a local area network that is capable of sharing audio and other types of data within a connected system.

Chapter 7
Synchronization

Synchronization (often abbreviated as sync) is the occurrence of two or more events at precisely the same point in time. When talking of audio and/or video program material, synchronization is used to ensure that an event (such as a video segment showing a door slam) will have a direct time relationship with one or more other devices in a connected system (such as the simultaneous triggering of an effect from a hard disk recorder, sampler, or recorded effect on tape . . . SLAM!).

This chapter explains the basic concepts of synchronization beginning with SMPTE time code, the time-based language used worldwide in production and broadcast media. It discusses the various time-code encoding methods, including MIDI time code, and looks at digital audio synchronization.

Analog vs Digital Synchronization

Analog audio or video sync is achieved by ensuring that the transport speeds of all the involved tape machines are locked in a precise time relationship with one another (Fig. 7.1). Without a system for keeping the relative speeds constant between two or more machines, synchronization would soon be lost as a result of tape slippage and minute differences in tape speed.

In an analog synchronization system, a change in speed in the designated control transport (known as the master) will be marked by a proportional change in each of the machines that are following the master (known as slaves).

Digital audio systems, on the other hand, deal with synchronization in an entirely different

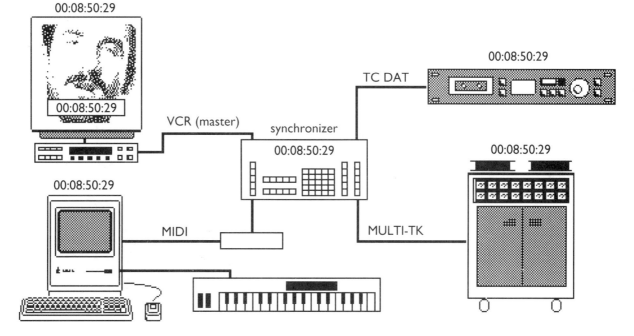

Fig. 7.1: Sync is achieved when the transport speeds of all the tape machines are locked in a precise time relationship with one another.

manner. As an example, neither samplers nor disk-based recorders have a mechanical transport per se to contribute variations in speed (such as wow and flutter). Instead, their record and playback speeds are regulated through the use of a stable crystal oscillator time-base circuit.

Although digital audio is far more stable than its analog counterpart, even these accurate timing sources are not identical from system to system, and can vary with age and temperature. This means that two digital transports that have been started at the exact same time may drift out of sync over time.

One method used by digital systems for achieving synchronous lock is to vary the system's playback sample rate (and thus its speed and pitch ratio) in order to precisely match the relative playback speed of the master transport. Another straightforward method that is commonly used when short audio passages are involved is to trigger a sample, region, or soundfile at a specified event time.

In the future, synchronization between devices will become more and more digital in nature. Right now, though, maintaining synchronization between analog and digital devices is still necessary. As a result, modern music and audio production have produced some rather ingenious systems for maintaining synchronization and for locating audio and/or video events in a multi-transport system. It's the goal of this chapter to introduce the most commonly used methods in maintaining synchronous lock between professional analog audio/video, MIDI, and digital audio devices.

SMPTE Time Code

To understand the basic concepts of synchronization, you need to first understand a time-based language that is used in virtually all production and broadcast media worldwide: SMPTE time code. (SMPTE stands for Society of Motion Picture and Television Engineers. 1) This time code is used to directly synchronize such media as analog audio, video, and often film. Its role in synchronizing digital audio, analog and digital tape machines, and triggered digital audio differs slightly from system to system and will be fully discussed later in this section.

Time code is used to mark and identify exact locations on an analog magnetic tape by encoding digital address points directly onto the media itself.

Each identifying address specifies a location along the length of the tape that cannot slip and that always retains its original time-stamped identity. These individual address locations are called frames (a term taken from film production). The frames allow the continual monitoring of tape position to an accuracy of approximately 1/30 of a second.

Basically, this system operates by tagging each audio or video frame with a unique identifying number, known as a time code address. This eight-digit address is displayed in the form

00:00:00:00

Each pair of digits represents, successively, hours:minutes:seconds:frames (Fig. 7.2).

The recorded time-code address is used to locate a position on analog magnetic tape in a way that is similar to the way a postal carrier uses a house address to deliver mail to a particular location. For example, suppose that a postal carrier has a letter for Reggie at 351 Old Reliable Lane. The postal carrier knows precisely where to deliver the letter because each house on the street has an assigned address number (Fig. 7.3A).

Likewise, a time code address can be used to locate a specific location on a magnetic tape because only one address number can (or should) exist on a reel at a time. For example, suppose that you'd like to lay down the sound of a screeching cat onto a 10-minute, time-encoded multitrack tape at an address of 00:08:50:29 (Fig. 7.3B).

By monitoring the address code (in a fast shuttle mode), you can easily locate the position that corresponds to this tape address and then lay down the sound effect.

Time Code Word

The total amount of information that is encoded into each audio or video frame makes up a time code word. Each word is divided into 80 equal segments or bits, which are numbered consecutively from 0 to 79. One word occupies an entire audio or video frame, so that for every frame there is a single, corresponding time code address. Address information is contained in the digital word as a series of bits. The bits are electronically generated as fluctuations, or shifts, in the voltage level of the time code's data signal.

This method of encoding serial information onto analog audio or video media is known as

| 00:08:50:29 |
| hours | minutes | seconds | frames |

Fig. 7.2: Example of a SMPTE time-code address readout.

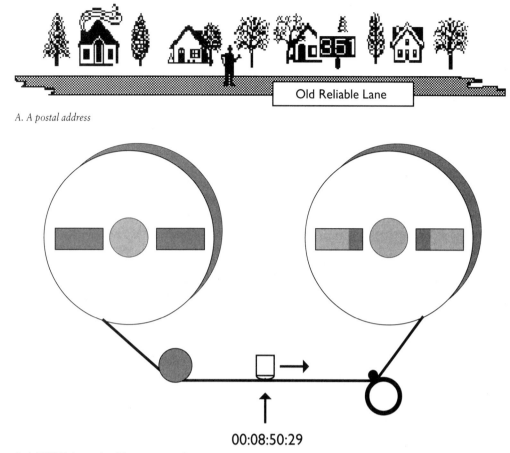

A. A postal address

00:08:50:29

B. A SMPTE time-code address on magnetic tape.

Fig. 7.3: Relative address locations.

biphase modulation (Fig. 7.4). When the recorded biphase signal shifts either up or down at the extreme edges of a clock period, the pulse is coded as a binary 0. A binary 1 is coded for a bit whose signal pulse shifts halfway through a clock period. A positive feature of this encoding method is that detection relies on shifts within the pulse and not on the pulse's polarity. This means that time code can be read in either the forward or the reverse direction and at fast or slow shuttle speeds.

The 80-bit time code word (Fig. 7.5) is further subdivided into groups of 4 bits. Each group represents a specific coded piece of information. Within each 4-bit segment is the encoded representation of a decimal number, ranging from 0 to 9, which is written in binary coded decimal (BCD) notation. When a time code reader detects the pattern of ones and zeros within a 4-bit group, it interprets the information as a single decimal number. Eight of these 4-bit groupings combine to constitute an address in hours, minutes, seconds, and frames.

The 26 digital bits that make up the time code address are joined by another 32 bits called user

bits. This additional set of encoded information, which is also represented in the form of an 8-digit number, has been set aside for time code users to enter personal ID information. The SMPTE standards committee has placed no restrictions on the use of this personal "slate code," which can contain such information as date of shooting, take ID, reel number, etc.

Another form of information that is encoded in the time code word is sync data. The sync data is found in the final 16 bits of a time code word and is used to define the end of each frame. Because time code can be read in either direction, sync data is also used to tell the controlling device in which direction the tape or device is moving.

Time-Code Frame Standards

In productions using time code, it is important that the readout display be directly related to the actual elapsed program time, particularly when dealing with the exacting time requirements of broadcasting. A black-and-white (monochrome) video signal operates at a frame rate of exactly 30

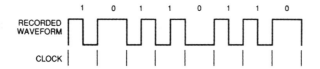

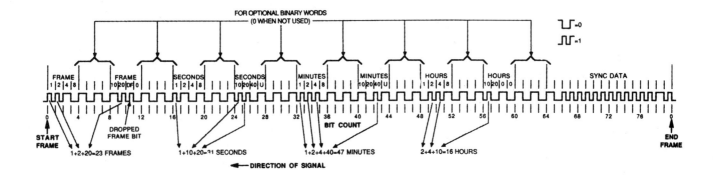

Fig. 7.4: Biphase modulation encoding.

Fig. 7.5: Biphase representation of the SMPTE/EBU time code word.

frames per second (fr/s). This monochrome rate is known as nondrop code. If this time code is read, the readout display, program length, and actual clock on the wall will all be in agreement.

This simplicity, however, was broken when the National Television Standards Committee set the frame rate for the color video signal at approximately 29.97 fr/s. This means that a time code reader set to read a monochrome rate of 30 fr/s will pick up an extra .03 frame for every passing

second when it is reading a 29.97 fr/s color program (30 - 29.97 = .03 frame/second). Over the duration of an hour, the address readout will differ from the actual clock by a total of 108 frames, or 3.6 seconds.

To correct for this discrepancy and to regain an agreement between the time code readout and the actual elapsed time, a means of frame adjustment must be introduced into the code. Since the object is to drop 108 frames over the course of an hour, the code used for color has come to be known as drop frame code. In correcting for this timing error, two frame counts for every minute of operation are omitted, with the exception of minutes 00, 10, 20, 30, 40, and 50. This has the effect of adjusting the frame count to agree with the actual elapsed program duration.

In addition to the color 29.97 drop frame code, a 29.97 nondrop frame color standard is used in video production. When this nondrop time code is used, the frame count will always advance one count per frame without any drops a condition that will result in a disagreement between the frame count and the actual "clock-on-the-wall" time over the course of the program. This has the distinct advantage of easing the time calculations that are often required within the video editing process, since no frame compensations need be taken into account for dropped frames.

Another frame rate format, which is used throughout Europe, is EBU (European Broadcast Union) time code. EBU operates by using the SMPTE 80-bit code word. However, it differs from SMPTE in that it operates at a rate of 25 frames/second. Since both monochrome and color video EBU signals run at exactly 25 frames/second, there is no need for an EBU drop frame code.

Film media use a standardized 24 frames/second format that differs from SMPTE time code. However, many newer synchronization and digital audio devices offer film sync and calculation capabilities.

SMPTE Time-Code Encoding Methods

The purpose of SMPTE time code is to synchronize, locate, and trigger audio and visual events that use analog audio, video, MIDI, and digital audio media. Each of these media is capable of storing and performing time code related tasks in a unique way (or number of ways). Because of this fact, a brief examination of the ways that time code can be handled by different system types is in order.

LTC

The first time-code application is still the most widely used encoding method. It involves the recording of SMPTE time code onto an available audio or video cue track. This method of placing time-stamped address information onto analog magnetic tape is known as longitudinal time code, or LTC. It is used to encode a biphase signal onto an analog audio or cue track as a modulated square wave signal with a bit rate of 2400 bits/second.

The recording of a perfect square wave onto a magnetic audio track is difficult, even under the best of conditions. For this reason, the SMPTE specification has set forth a standard allowable rise time of 25 ñ 5 microseconds for the recording and reproduction of code. This is equivalent to a signal bandwidth of 15 kHz, well within the range of most analog recording devices.

Variable-speed time code readers are commonly able to decode time code information at tape shuttle speed rates ranging from 1/10 to 100 times normal playspeed. This is effective for most audio applications. However, in video post-production it's often necessary to monitor a video tape at very slow or still picture speeds.

Because LTC can't be read at speeds slower than 1/10 to 1/20 of normal playspeed, a system has been adopted that allows time code to be "burned" into the video image of a copy work-tape. This process uses a special character display generator to superimpose the corresponding address numbers inside a windowed portion of the video picture (Fig. 7.6). This "window dub" allows time code to be easily seen on the screen, even at very slow or still picture shuttle speeds.

Practical Aspects of LTC

There are two fundamental aspects of LTC that can save you time and trouble when you are producing a project that involves time code. These are jam sync and time code levels. Both relate to the deterioration of longitudinal time code and recorded SMPTE levels onto tape.

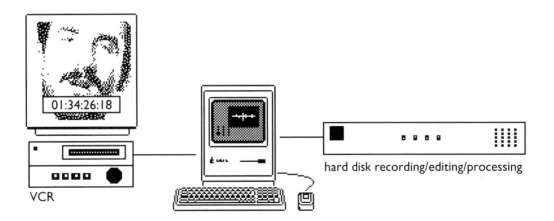

VCR

hard disk recording/editing/processing

Fig. 7.6: Example of a synchronous system that displays the video image with a "burned-in" time code window.

Longitudinal time code, as you have seen, operates by recording a series of square wave pulses onto magnetic tape. Unfortunately, this is easier said than done, since analog tape can't record square waves without creating moderate to severe waveform distortion.

Although time code readers are designed to be fairly tolerant of waveform amplitude fluctuations, the situation is severely compounded when code is dubbed (copied) by one or more generations. For this reason, a special feature known as jam sync has been incorporated into most time code synchronizers. Jam sync is the process of reading distorted code during a dub and regenerating fresh code onto the copy machine. The effect is to regenerate identical address numbers during the dubbing stage or to reconstruct defective sections of code (Fig. 7.7).

Two forms of jam sync are currently in use: one-time jam sync and continuous jam sync. In one-time jam sync, the receipt of valid time code causes the generator's output to be initialized to the first valid address number. The generator then begins to count in an ascending order on its own, in a "freewheeling" fashion. It ignores any deteriorations or discontinuities in code and produces fresh, uninterrupted address numbers.

Continuous jam sync is used in cases where the original address numbers need to remain intact

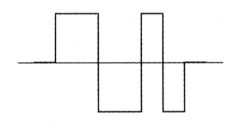

A. Reproduction of original biphase signal.

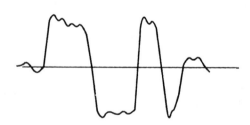

B. Reconstructed jam sync signal.

Fig. 7.7: Representation of the recorded biphase signal.

and should not be regenerated into a contiguous address count. Once the reader is activated, the generator updates the address count for each frame in accordance with the incoming address.

Crosstalk is a potential problem plaguing systems that use time code. This condition arises from the interference of high-level time code signals with adjacent audio signals or recorded tape tracks. Currently, no industry standard levels exist for the recording of time code onto magnetic tape. However, the time code levels shown in Table 7.1 have proven over time to give best results in most cases.

VITC

Another time code method used by video post-production houses is the striping of recorded videotape with VITC (Vertical Interval Time Code). VITC (pronounced "vit-c") uses the same SMPTE address and user code structure as LTC does. However, VITC is encoded onto video tape in an entirely different manner it actually encodes the time code information directly within the video signal itself.

The time-stamped signal is recorded inside an area of the signal known as the vertical blanking interval (a portion of the signal that is located outside of the visible picture scan area). Since the time code information is encoded in the video signal itself), it's possible for a video recorder to read time code at slower speeds or even still-frame. This convenience opens up an additional track on a video recorder for audio or cue information and eliminates the need for a window dub.

MIDI Time Code

For decades, the process of striping SMPTE time code onto tape has been the standard timing reference within audio and video production. With the rise of MIDI to prominence in music and audio-for-visual production, it became obvious that a similar absolute timing reference would be necessary if MIDI-based sequencers and other such programs were to maintain synchronous lock within a time-encoded production system.

Previous timing references (such as MIDI Clock and Song Position pointer) kept track of their position in a sequence as a function of the number of measures that have passed since the beginning of a song. These relative timing references had

Table 7.1 Optimum recording levels for time code.

Tape Format	Track Format	Optimum Rec Level
ATR	Edge track (highest number)	-5 VU to -10 VU
1/2" & 3/4" VCR	Audio 1 (L) track or timecode track	-5 VU to 0 VU
1" VTR	Cue track or audio 3	-5 VU to -10 VU

Note: If the VTR is equipped with AGC (automatic gain compensation), override the AGC and adjust the signal gain controls manually

their own unique set of drawbacks. However, the major problem was that the relative timing varied from one tempo to another and with changes in tempo. Since most studio-based operations are referenced to SMPTE time code (as opposed to the beats in a musical bar), studio engineers and musicians found it very tedious to convert between the two timing systems when cueing a sequenced segment or triggering a specific MIDI event.

In order for MIDI-based devices to operate in a production environment that is independent of changes in tempo or relative start times, a digital time-encoded language known as MIDI time code, or MTC, was developed. In short, MTC provides a cost-effective and easily implemented system for translating SMPTE time code into MIDI messages, which can then be distributed throughout the MIDI chain to devices or instruments that understand and execute MTC commands.

MTC doesn't replace MIDI 1.0. Rather, it is an extension in that it makes use of existing message types that either were previously undefined or were being used for other, nonconflicting purposes (such as the sample dump standard). Although MTC takes up a reasonably small percentage of MIDI's available bandwidth (about 7.68 percent at 30 frames/second), the recommended practice is to keep the MTC signal path separate from the primary MIDI performance path(s) in order to reduce the possibility of data overload or delay.

MIDI Time-Code Control Structure

The MIDI time-code format can be broken down into two parts:

- Time code
- MIDI cueing

The time code capabilities of MTC are relatively straightforward and allow both MIDI and non-MIDI devices to attain direct synchronous lock or, alternatively, to be triggered at a specific SMPTE time-code address. MIDI cueing is a format that informs MIDI devices of control-related events that are to be performed at a specific time (load, play, stop, punch in/out, reset). This communications system envisions the use of intelligent MIDI devices that are capable of preparing for a specific event in advance and then executing it at a time-encoded cue.

MIDI Time-Code Commands

MIDI time code uses three message types:

- Quarter-frame messages
- Full messages
- MIDI cueing messages

Quarter-frame messages are transmitted only while the system is running in real-time or vary-speed time and in either the forward or the reverse direction. Quarter-frame messages provide the system with its basic timing pulse. In addition, four frames are generated for every SMPTE time code field. This means that should you decide to use drop frame code (30 frames per second), the system would transmit 120 quarter-frame messages per second.

Quarter-frame messages should be thought of as groups of eight messages, which encode the SMPTE time in hours, minutes, seconds, and frames. Since eight quarter frames are needed for a complete time code message, the complete SMPTE time is updated every two frames.

Each quarter frame message contains 2 bytes. The first is "F1" (the quarter-frame common header). The second byte contains a nibble (4 bits) that represents the message number (0 through 7). The second byte also has a nibble for each of the digits of a time field (hours, minutes, seconds, or frames).

Quarter-frame messages are not sent while in the fast-forward, rewind, or locate modes, since this would unnecessarily clog or outrun the MIDI data lines. When the system is in any of these shuttle modes, a full message is used, which encodes the complete time code address within a single message.

Once a fast shuttle mode is entered, the system will generate a full message and then place itself in a "pause" mode until the time-encoded device has autolocated to its destination. After the device has resumed playing, MTC will again begin sending quarter-frame messages.

MIDI cueing messages are designed to address individual devices or programs in a system. These 13-bit messages can be used to compile a cue or edit decision list, which in turn instructs one or more devices to play, punch in, load, stop, etc., at a specific time. Each instruction within a cueing message contains a unique number, time, name, type, and space for additional information. At the present, only a small percentage of the possible 128 cueing event types have been defined.

Direct Time Lock

Direct Time Lock, also known as DTL, is a synchronization standard that allows MIDI-based sequencing programs from Mark of the Unicorn (such as Performer or Digital Performer) to be locked to SMPTE via a proprietary time-encoding protocol. Direct Time Lock relays MIDI data to and from a Macintosh computer via two message types: tape position and frame advance.

The Tape Position message is transmitted when the time code source (such as a tape machine) is started, after which the system will begin to achieve lock. This message is transmitted as a System Exclusive message and specifies the tape's SMPTE position in hours, minutes, seconds, and frames (HH:MM:SS:FF).

As its name implies, the Frame Advance message is transmitted once each frame. The first frame advance that is sent after the tape position message will correspond to the beginning of the frame specified in the Tape Position message. Successive frame advances will then correspond to successive time code frames.

After a Tape Position message has been received, the sequence will chase to that point on the tape, and MIDI playback will be readied. Once frame messages are received, the program will begin to advance in sync with the master code. If more than eight frames of time pass without a frame advance message, the program assumes that playback has stopped and will halt the sequence and wait for a new position message.

If another position message is received, the MIDI sequencer compares it to the position of its last position message. If they're the same, it will immediately continue playing. Otherwise, the MIDI sequencer will chase to the desired sequence location. If the Tape Position message isn't close to the current location, the sequencer will immediately stop and chase to the new location and begin looking for Frame Advance messages.

Enhanced Direct Time Lock

An enhanced form of Direct Time Lock, known as DTLe, has been incorporated into newer Mark of the Unicorn products (such as Performer version 3.4 and higher). DTLe is used to synchronize Performer to the MIDI Time Piece interface, via SMPTE time code.

DTLe differs from standard Direct Time Lock in that it transmits four Frame Advance messages, instead of one, for every SMPTE frame. Additionally, DTL's Tape Position (full frame) message has been expanded to include the SMPTE frame count and an identifier that establishes which device in the MIDI network is transmitting DTLe.

DTLe offers distinct advantages over its predecessor. One advantage is that it allows Performer 3.4 to establish synchronous lock with a tape machine without stopping the transport. Thus, when Performer's play button is pressed, the program will jump into sync while an audio or video machine is running. Another advantage of DTLe arises from the fact that the MIDI Time Piece transmits a Tape Position message approximately once every second, so the user is less likely to encounter such problems as dropouts or drift.

Digital Audio Synchronization

Had this chapter been written before the 1990s, it definitely would have focused on how to sync together analog machines and maybe would have mentioned a few other system types (like video and MIDI sync). However, present day coverage would be incomplete without discussing synchronization in the context of digital and random access audio systems and how they fit into modern day media production. Digital audio devices are increasingly being used in the audio and audio-for-visual

production environment. An understanding of digital sync is thus important when you are working in an environment where digital audio devices are synchronized with each other or with other video and analog media.

Need for Stable Timing Reference

Recall from the beginning of this chapter that the process of maintaining a synchronous lock between digital audio devices, or between digital and analog systems, differs from the process used to maintain relative speed between analog transports. This is due to the fact that a digital system achieves synchronous lock by adjusting its playback sample rate (and thus its speed and pitch ratio) in order to precisely match its relative playback speed to the master transport.

When a digital system is being synced to any time-encoded master source, an important consideration is the need for a source that is a stable timing reference. In other words, under normal playback conditions, the program speed of the source should vary as little as possible over time.

This need for an accurate timing source is important for several reasons. A stable source helps to maintain synchronization with other devices within a system. It also prevents the development of adverse effects on the quality of the reproduced digital signal. For example, all analog tape machines exhibit speed variations that are caused by tape slippage and transport irregularities (a fact of life known as wow and flutter). If you were to use a synchronizer to slave a disk-based recorder to a time-encoded analog source that contained tons of wow and flutter, the digital system would be required to constantly speed up and slow down to precisely match the fluctuations in the master transport, even though SMPTE sync was being used.

Quite simply, these digital fluctuations are the result of a constantly shifting sample rate and may introduce varying amounts of jitter into the digital signal's word structure. When this signal is converted back to analog, the introduced jitter could adversely affect the signal in ways ranging from a simple increase in noise to the introduction of timing errors that might cause audible glitches.

Obviously, the best possible solution would be to record the original program material by using a time-based reference that is extremely stable. Such a reference can be found in the world of video.

Black Burst

When a video signal is being copied from one machine to another, it is essential that the scanned video data (containing timing, video, and user information) be copied in perfect sync from one frame to the next. Failure to do this results in severe picture breakup or, at best, the vertical rolling of a black line over the visible picture area.

Transferring video from one machine to another is generally no problem since a video copy machine is able to synchronize its video signal directly with the playback source. However, in video post-production, it's common for a number of video transports and other sources to be routed to a single destination. Each source could be a videotape that had been recorded at another location, or machines could have been used that don't run at the same absolute time as other video recorders in the system. When you are editing between tapes in such a situation, the video frames could break up or simply not match during an edit. The result could be a very unhappy client.

This video production problem can be solved by using a single timing source known as a black burst generator. This generator produces an extremely stable timing reference (called a black burst, or house sync) that has a clock frequency of exactly 15,734.2657 Hz. The function of the black burst signal is to synchronize the SMPTE time-code frame with the video frame, so that their leading edges occur at exactly the same instant in time.

In such a system, this sync source is fed to the sync inputs of every video device within the production system (Fig. 7.8) so that their speeds are controlled by, and locked to, a single, accurate timing source. The use of black burst thus serves to resolve the issue of speed differences between the multiple video and audio transports within a system.

By resolving all video and audio devices to a single black burst reference, you are assured that relative frame transitions and speeds will be consistent and stable. This holds true even for analog machines, since their transport's inherent wow and flutter will be smoothed out as a result of being locked to this stable time base.

The following guidelines will help you obtain a stable reference code:

- If you are striping your own time code, resolve the generator timing source to black burst.

- If a VTR is selected as a master source (whether or not the videotape is in-house or from an outside source), its time base can best be ensured by resolving it to black burst.

- Whenever an analog transport is selected as the master, you can minimize timing errors by making sure that the original code was referenced to black burst. Afterwards, by resolving the analog machine to this reference, you can greatly reduce variations in wow, flutter, and skewing.

The use of black burst is not a required practice in all applications. However, as the preceding discussion shows, a stable time reference will reduce sample rate variations and timing errors when used within a multi-transport system that involves digital audio.

Synchronization Methods

Digital audio obtains its clocking source in one of two ways: from an internal source or from an external source. Whenever a digital device is recording audio as a stand-alone machine, the system's clocking source is taken from its own internal quartz crystal oscillator. However, whenever a signal is digitally copied from one device to another, the device that is doing the actual copying will derive its clock pulse from the playback machine's timing circuitry (Fig. 7.9). In this way, a stable transfer occurs with no conflict or irregularities in timing.

In theory, whenever a digital device is asked to reproduce audio that is synchronously locked to

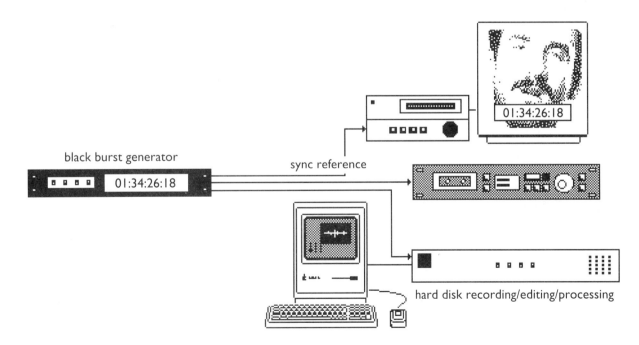

Fig. 7.8: Example of a system whose overall timing is locked to a black burst reference signal.

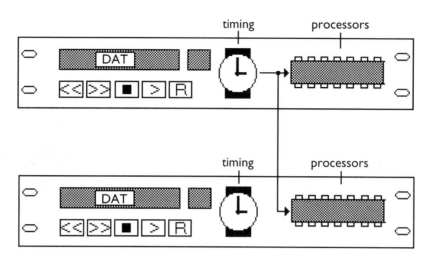

Fig. 7.9: Whenever a signal is digitally copied, the device that is doing the copying usually derives its timing from the playback machine's clock pulse

an external timing reference, its sample rate must be varied to match variations in the timing reference. In actual practice, though, digital audio systems are able to synchronize to either audio or visual program material in a number of ways, depending on the actual application at hand and the degree of timing accuracy required. These synchronization methods are:

- None
- SMPTE trigger
- Locked trigger
- Continuous

None

When no synchronization method is used, the audio signal is said to be "wild," meaning that it is not directly referenced to any time-encoded source (Fig. 7.10). Under these circumstances, the audio is generally triggered manually and its clock reference is derived solely from the device's internal timing crystal. An example might be the use of a CD player to insert a wild effect onto a video track. Just press play at the right time and POW!

SMPTE Trigger Sync

SMPTE trigger sync is a commonly used and straightforward method of achieving sync. It makes use of a playlist in order to trigger a digital audio segment to a particular SMPTE time code. However, once the event has been triggered, the digital device will play back the events in a wild fashion, deriving its timing from an internal clock reference (Fig. 7.11).

Although the audio will run wild after being triggered at the appropriate time code address, its timing will be relatively stable because it is referenced to its own internal reference clock. When syncing a short piece of audio to a stable master source (such as videotape or another digital audio device), SMPTE trigger is often the best possible choice. The reason is that the disk-based system is stable enough that the program material probably won't drift over short periods of time.

This reasoning also holds true when you are looking at the overall quality of the playback signal. The digital audio is referenced solely to its internal clock and won't vary over time in its attempts to chase the master source (a condition that could cause jitter-related problems).

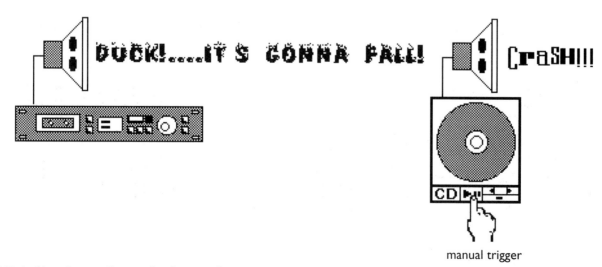

Fig. 7.10: A wild signal is manually triggered, without any reference to a time-encoded source.

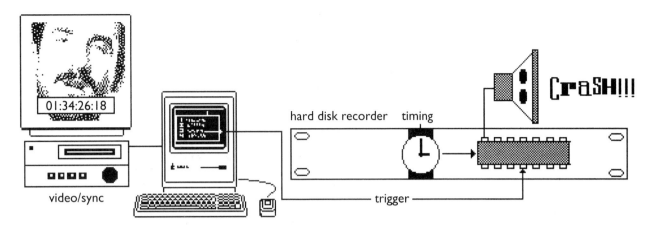

Fig. 7.11: Once a wild trigger event has occurred, the digital device will play back the event while deriving its timing from an internal clock reference.

Locked Trigger Sync

Locked trigger sync is not available to all systems and can be used only when referencing the sync timing of one digital audio device (such as a hard disk recorder) to a master reference. Synchronization using the locked trigger method is similar to SMPTE trigger in that a digital audio segment begins playback at a specific time code address (as defined by the playlist). However, instead of being referenced to its own internal clock, the system will begin to externally derive its timing clock from the digital audio master source (Fig. 7.12).

Continuous Sync

If longer segments are to be synced to a time-encoded master, or if the master is an unstable source (such as a time-encoded cassette recorder), a method known as continuous SMPTE sync should be used to prevent the audio segments from drifting out of sync.

In the continuous sync mode (Fig. 7.13), an audio segment will trigger at its appropriate time code address. Then it will begin to read and resolve its timing to incoming time code (as supplied by the master device). As you know, in order for a digital audio system to remain locked with an external time code source, it must slow down or speed up its output signal (by varying its sample

rate) so that it precisely matches the time code's speed. As a result, any variations in the master code will be followed and matched by variations in the digital output signal. An unstable master timing reference could cause the audio quality to be degraded (because of sample rate fluctuations and jitter). This can best be remedied by obtaining a stable master timing source (such as black burst) or by turning off the continuous sync function (thereby reproducing audio in a standard SMPTE trigger fashion).

All About Pull-down Sample Rates

Pull-down sample rates occur when a film soundtrack is transferred onto videotape that's being recorded in the NTSC color format. As a result of the transfer, there is a difference in frame rate of 6 frames per second. This difference is due to the fact that film runs at 24 frames/second, while the video runs at 29.97 frames/second. This discrepancy can be visually compensated for by duplicating every fourth frame of film onto the videotape (a process known as 3:2 pull-down).

Likewise, the audio tracks need to be pulled down in speed to match the picture's length and timing. Therefore, if a digital track was originally recorded at 44.1 kHz, its pull-down rate would be 44.056 kHz. Program material recorded at 48 kHz would need to be pulled down to 47.952 kHz.

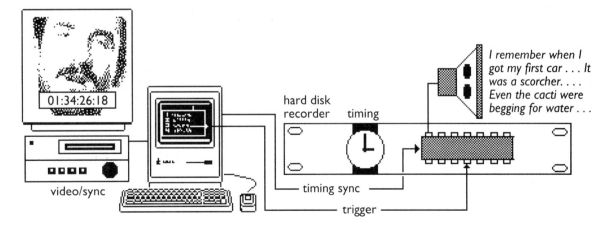

Fig. 7.12: Example of a triggered system that is locked to time code

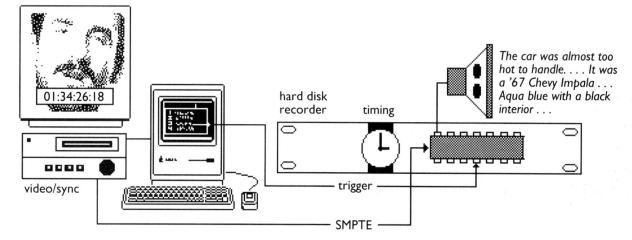

The car was almost too hot to handle. . . . It was a '67 Chevy Impala . . . Aqua blue with a black interior . . .

Fig. 7.13: Example of a system that is working in the continuous sync mode.

On a Final Note

With the increased interdependency that can exist between video tape recorders, digital and analog tape machines, MIDI hardware and software systems, hard disk recorders, and the list goes on, the subject of locking these devices together in time has become quite complex. Probably one of the best approaches towards eliminating potential sync problems is to think through your system or particular situation as thoroughly as possible before starting on a particular project. Many a time code problem has cropped up because a particular need was not anticipated in advance.

Regarding digital synchonization, this field is relatively new, and industry misconceptions and improper system designs do occasionally appear. Should you be faced with an insurmountable problem from a piece of gear, remember that the manufacturer's technical support staff is usually very helpful and can often get you out of a bind.

Chapter 8

Digital Signal Processing

Most of the processing and effects functions associated with computer-based audio are performed in the digital domain through digital signal processing, or DSP. DSP can create effects that mimic many of the standard, familiar analog tools (such as echo, reverb, and equalization). With DSP, important production and processing tasks can be performed that are difficult or impossible to achieve in the analog domain (such as real-time pitch shift and pitch/time changing tools).

Digital signal processing is accomplished by combining logic circuits, which follow basic binary computational rules. When combined in a building block fashion, these logic circuits can be used to alter the numeric values of sampled audio in a predictable way. Thousands of these logic circuits may be contained on a single integrated chip (IC).

This chapter briefly discusses how DSP works and then takes a closer look at how it can be used to alter or augment audio signals in a digital production environment.

Advantages of DSP

DSP is based on the mathematical manipulation of sampled digital audio data. Given the fact that digital audio is stored as a stream of digital words, it follows that by changing these numeric words (according to a specific mathematical formula), the nature of the data and thus the program material itself will be changed in a predictable way.

A major advantage to working with digital signal processing is that software programming can be used to configure a digital processor in order to achieve a variety of effects (such as reverb, echo and delay), as well as numerous processing functions (such as equalization, pitch shifting, and gain changing). These processors can be programmed from software to work in a wide range of configurations. Complex variables that determine how a program will ultimately perform can be applied to tailor the sound according to basic programming rules.

Once a program has been configured from either internal RAM or the system's software, complete control over a program's setup parameters can be altered and measured as discrete numbers or as percentages of a full value. Since these values are both discrete and digital, the settings can be precisely duplicated, or better yet saved to RAM or disk as a file that can be easily called up when you need it. Quite simply, few other digital devices can match a multifunction DSP system for sheer functional versatility.

Real-Time and Non real-Time DSP

The number-crunching process involved in performing DSP calculations can be performed in one of two ways: real time or non-real time.

Real-time calculations are capable of processing a signal in the here and now. In other words, real-time systems can alter, mix, or otherwise process sampled audio as it is being recorded or reproduced. In such a signal-processing environment, the signal alteration is often done while reproducing audio from disk without affecting the original soundfile data. This non-destructive editing also allows any inadvertent changes to be easily undone at a later time.

Real-time sample calculations have to be performed within a period of about 20 microseconds, so a dedicated co-processor is often used to do the dirty work (Fig. 8.1). Without it, the data load would most certainly bog down a computer's main processor and, most likely, even the audio interface's co-processor.

Non real-time signal processing, on the other hand, is used by systems that don't have or don't need a dedicated real-time processor block to perform certain or all processing tasks. Once a non

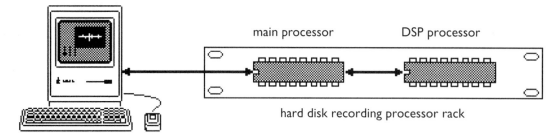

Fig. 8.1: A DSP co-processor is often used to take the load off of the main processor.

real-time data or signal processing function is invoked, the system's processor or co-processor will dedicate itself to performing the task in non-real time (which means that you have to wait while the system performs the necessary calculations).

Once the processor has finished, the final results are usually written to disk as a separate file. If this processed section is used to replace an existing nonprocessed segment (such as a faded or cross-faded area), it will often be "tagged" or mapped to marker points in the original, unprocessed sound-file areas and, upon playback, will be butt-joined with these original areas to create a single, seamless program.

As an example, suppose you have two songs that have been placed next to each other on your edit screen so that the end of one immediately jumps to the beginning of the next (Fig. 8.2A). Your goal: Create a 1-second crossfade so that the songs will seamlessly fade out of one and into the next. To accomplish this, you need to first define the region to be crossfaded (Fig. 8.2B) and then perform the crossfade. The crossfade can be written to disk as a separate, tagged file (Fig. 8.2C).

Upon playback, song A will play out until it reaches the crossfade's in-point, at which time the data will be fed from the tagged crossfade file until it reaches the end of the crossfade. Following the crossfade's out-point, the data will then be fed from the appropriate tagged point near the beginning of song B (Fig. 8.2D). The result is a seamless crossfade that leads the listener directly from song A into song B.

DSP Basics

The scope and capabilities of digital signal processing are limited only by speed, number-crunching power, and human imagination. Yet the process itself is made up of only three basic building blocks (Fig. 8.3):

- Addition
- Multiplication
- Delay

One of the best ways to understand these building blocks of digital logic is through an application. Just for fun, let's build a simple 4-in x 1-out digital mixing application that might be used to combine the output channels of a digital workstation.

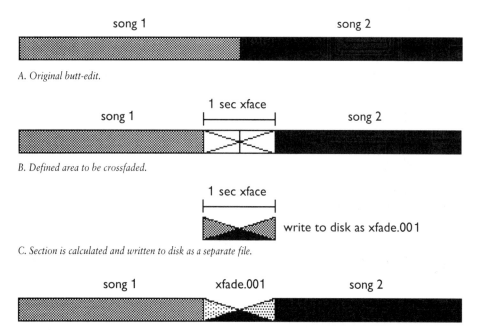

A. Original butt-edit.

B. Defined area to be crossfaded.

C. Section is calculated and written to disk as a separate file.

D. Crossfade file is tagged to the original files and is reproduced with no adverse effects.

Fig. 8.2: Example of a 1-second crossfade.

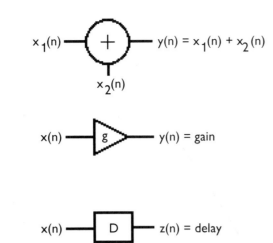

Fig. 8.3: *The DSP process is made up of only three basic building blocks: addition, multiplication (gain), and delay.*

Addition

As you might expect, a digital adder sums together the various bits at the input of the circuit in order to create a single combined result. With this straightforward building block, we can get started on our mixer by combining the four input signals into one output channel (Fig. 8.4).

Multiplication

The multiplication of sample values by a numeric coefficient allows the gain (level) of digitized audio to be changed either up or down. Whenever a sample is multiplied by a factor of 1, the result will be unity gain or no change in level. Multiplication by a factor of less than 1 will yield a reduction in gain. Likewise the multiplication by a number that is greater than 1 will result in an increase in gain.

Now that we know this, we can add gain controls to our mixer. This will give us some real control (Fig. 8.5). The addition of gain controls can be accomplished by creating digital faders that can directly supply the processor with the appropriate gain figures.

Before moving on, let's look at how multiplication can be applied to the everyday production world by calculating how the gain of a recorded soundfile can be changed over time. Examples of this applied gain change are fade-ins, fade-outs, crossfades, and changes in level.

To better understand this process, we will look at how a non-real time fade-out might be created using a hard-disk based system. Suppose you have a song that wasn't faded during a mixdown

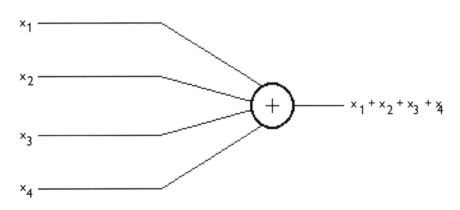

Fig. 8.4: *Inputs to our digital mixer can be summed together into a single data stream.*

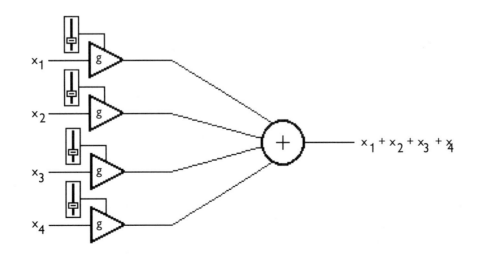

Fig. 8.5: *Gain can be added to determine the mix ratio of the combined signals.*

session but now definitely needs to be faded out over its final chorus section. The first task is to define the part of the song that needs to be faded (Fig. 8.6A), call up the fade function, and then perform the fade.

Once this task is done, it's the processor's job to continually multiply the affected samples by a diminishing coefficient. The result will be to reduce the gain over the length of the defined fade region. After the new sample has been calculated, the results will be automatically written to disk as a separate file (Fig. 8.6B). Upon playback, the fade will be tagged onto the original soundfile, ending at the appropriate point (Fig. 8.6C).

Delay

The final DSP building block deals with time, that is, the use of delay over time in order to perform a specific function or effect. In the world of DSP, delay is used in a wide variety of applications. However, this discussion will focus on two types of delay:

- Effects-related delay
- Delay at the sample level

Most modern musicians and those associated with audio production are familiar with the way that different delay ranges can accomplish a wide range of effects, and they are familiar with the use of digital delay for creating such sonic effects as doubling and echo delay. These effects (which will be discussed later in this chapter) are created from discrete delays that are 35 milliseconds or more in length (1 millisecond, or ms, equals 1 thousandth of a second).

A digital delay is accomplished by storing sampled audio directly into RAM memory. After a defined length of time (milliseconds or seconds), sampled audio can be read out from memory at a later (and thus delayed) point in time (Fig. 8.7).

As the delay time is reduced below the 10-ms range, however, a new effect begins to take hold. The effect of mixing a variable short-term delay with the original undelayed signal creates a series of peaks and dips in the signal's frequency response. This effect (known by the generic effect name of flanging) is the result of selective equalization (Fig. 8.8). Those of you who have a digital delay hanging around can check out this home-made flange effect by combining the delayed and undelayed signal and then listening for yourself.

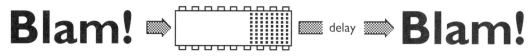

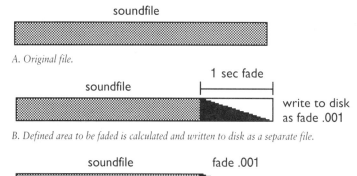

A. Original file.

B. Defined area to be faded is calculated and written to disk as a separate file.

C. Faded file is tagged to the original files and is reproduced with no audible break or adverse effect.

Fig. 8.6: Example of a 1-second fade.

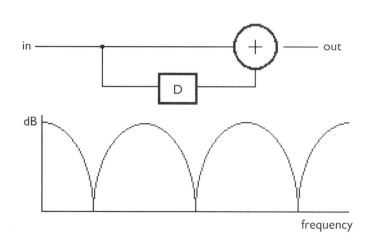

Fig. 8.7: Delay uses memory to store data, where it can be read out at a later time.

Fig. 8.8: The effect of mixing a short-term delay with the original undelayed signal creates a comb filter response, which has the generic effect name of "flanging."

By further reducing the delay times downward into the microsecond range (1 microsecond, or ms equals 1 millionth of a second), we can begin to introduce delays that affect the digitized signal at the sample level. In doing so, control over the filter characteristics can be improved to the point that selective equalization is accomplished. For example, Fig. 8.9 shows two basic equalization circuits that provide low- and high-frequency shelving characteristics, respectively, in the digital domain.

The amount of equalization to be applied (either boost or cut) depends on the multipliers that control the amount of gain to be fed from the delay modules. By adding more stages of delay and multiplication to this basic processing concept, complex stages of equalization can be assembled to create digital equalizers that are more complex and parametric in nature.

It should be pointed out that delays of such short durations are not created by using RAM delay-type circuits, which are used in creating longer delays. Rather, logic circuits known as shift registers are used. These sample level delay circuits are better suited to the task because they are simpler in design and are more cost effective.

Getting back to the digital mixer example, we can now finish our project by adding some form of equalization to the final stage. For example, Fig. 8.10 shows our project as having a very simple high-pass filter. This filter will cut out any low-end rumble that gets into our system courtesy of the air conditioner down the hall or the local transit authority.

The Real World of DSP Design

As you have seen from the preceding discussion, the basics of DSP are fairly straightforward. However, in application, these building blocks can be programmed into a processing block using some rather complex combinations and elaborate algorithms to arrive at a final result.

In addition to the complexities that can exist, there are restrictions and overhead requirements that must be used to safeguard the process from cranking out erroneous, degraded, or even disastrous results. For example, whenever a number of digital samples are mixed together using an adding circuit, the added results could easily be a large number that is beyond the system's maximum signal limit. Without proper design safeguards, a

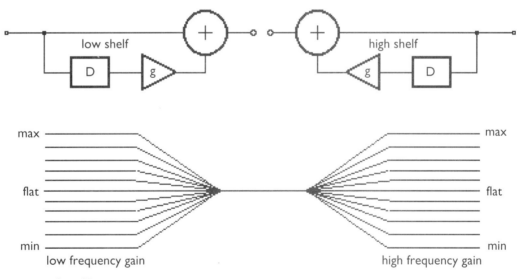

Fig. 8.9: Simple EQ circuits and possible response curves.

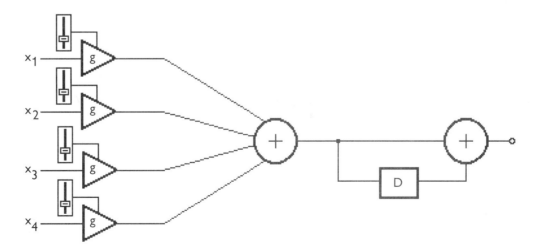

Fig. 8.10: Sample-level delays can be added to our mixer to provide equalization

condition known as bit wraparound could occur, causing the signal to output a loud POP!

Whenever signal processors are called upon to add samples together or to multiply numeric values by lengthy coefficients, it's possible for errors to accumulate or for the final results to be greater than 16-bits in wordlength. To reduce these errors to acceptable levels or to prevent the "chopping off" of potentially important least significant bit values, high-quality processors are often capable of calculating wordlength values with a resolution of up to 24- or 32-bits.

Fortunately, modern design has rid us of most of these obvious gremlins. However, the deeper you dig into DSP, the more you find that the challenges in designing a quality system are not in getting it to work, but in eliminating pesky glitches which are often the side effect of performing complex sonic functions.

DSP Functions

The remainder of this chapter will examine commonly found applications that can be found in both stand-alone and PC-based digital signal processors. These include:

- Audio delay
- Pitch-related effects
- Noise elimination
- Digital mixing
- Sample rate conversion

Audio Delay

One very common application of effects using DSP is the altering of time by introducing various forms of delay into the signal path. Creating a delay circuit is a relatively simple task to accomplish in the digital domain. In fact, the first digital audio device introduced on the market in 1971 was a digital delay.

Recall that delays in the milliseconds and seconds range rely on the use of RAM memory to store sampled audio. After a defined length of

time, the data is read out and mixed in with the original, undelayed signal. The maximum delay time that can be delivered by such a device is limited only by the sample frequency and the size of the memory block.

When program material delays of 35 to 40 ms and greater are used, the listener perceives them as a discrete delay. When mixed with the original signal, this can add depth and richness to an instrument or range of instruments. However, care needs to be taken when delay is added to an entire musical program, since the delay tends to muddy its intelligibility.

Reducing the delay time to the 15-to 35-ms range will create delays that are spaced too closely together to be perceived by the listener as discrete delays. Instead, such short delays create a "doubling" effect. When short delays are mixed in with an instrument or group of instruments, the brain is fooled into thinking that more instruments are playing than there actually are, or at least the effect will be a subjective increase in the sound's "density."

As mentioned earlier, when delays that are varied below the 15-ms range are mixed with the original undelayed signal, a "combing effect" is created. Combing is the result of equalized peaks and dips in the signal's frequency response. This rough form of digital equalization (flanging) sounds "phased" in nature, especially when the delay time is varied either manually or automatically by a low-frequency oscillator.

By combining several short-term delay modules that are slightly detuned in time, another effect known as chorusing can be achieved (Fig. 8.11). Chorusing is an effects tool often used by guitarists and other musicians to add depth, richness, and harmonic structure to their instruments.

Echo

Now that we have taken a look at single delay effects, we can add to our bag of effects tricks by successively repeating delays to create echoes. Repeated echoes are created by feeding a portion of a delayed signal's output back into itself (Fig. 8.12). By adding a multiplier stage into this loop,

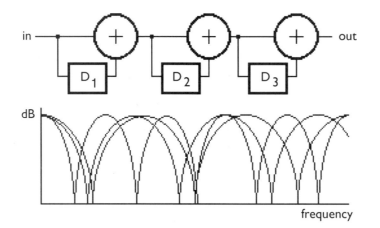

Fig. 8.11: By combining several short-term delay modules that are slightly detuned in time, an effect known as "chorusing" can be achieved.

it is possible to vary the amount of gain that is to be fed back and thus control both the level and the number of repeated echoes.

Although reverb could be placed in a separate category, reverb is actually nothing more than a series of closely spaced echoes. In nature, acoustic reverb can be broken down into three subcomponents:

- Direct signal

- Early reflections

- Reverberation

The direct signal is heard when the original sound wave travels directly from the source to the listener's position. Early reflections are the first few reflections that are reflected back to the listener from large, primary boundaries within a given space. It is generally these reflections that give the listener subconscious cues as to the perception of size and space.

The last set of reflections make up the signal's reverberation characteristic. These signals are broken down into the many random reflections that travel from boundary to boundary within the confines of a room. These reflections are so closely spaced in time that the brain is unable to discern each individual reflection and so they are perceived as a single decaying signal.

By designing a system that uses a number of delay lines, which are carefully controlled in both time and amplitude level, it is possible to create an almost infinite number of reverb characteristics. To illustrate this point, let's return to our basic building block approach to DSP and build a crude reverb processor (Fig. 8.13).

As you know, the direct signal is the first signal to arrive at the listener. Thus, it can be represented as a single data line that is added to each stage, flowing directly from the input to the output. Included in what we will call the first DSP stage are a number of individually tunable delay lines. By tuning these various modules to different times between a range of 10 ms to over a second (perceived bathroom size to Grand Canyon size), early reflections can be simulated. Following this section, one or more delay lines with echo feedback loops can be placed into our system, which is designed to repeat echoes at a very fast rate. The echoes will decay over a predetermined time.

Such a reverb unit might sound crude because its simplicity would severely limit the type and quality of sounds that it might offer. By adding more stages and placing the gain controls under microprocessor command (using various user-defined algorithms), a large library of high-quality sounds could be created.

Pitch-Related Effects

DSP functions are available that can alter the speed and pitch of an audio program. These functions, which can be designed into a stand-alone or computer-based system, involve such options as:

- Changing pitch without changing duration

- Changing duration without changing pitch

- Changing both the duration and the pitch

Before exploring the subject, you should be aware that all pitch-related processors are not created equal, since extensive DSP techniques are

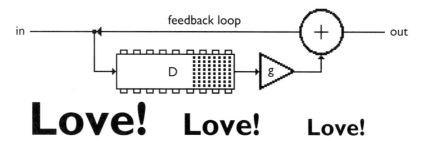

Fig. 8.12: By adding a simple feedback loop to a delay circuit, it's possible to create an echo effect.

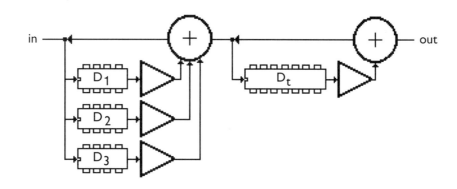

Fig. 8.13: A crude reverb processor design.

often required to perform complex tasks such as those just mentioned.

Having said this, with almost every system being unequal, the process of pitch and time shifting has a window of effectiveness. That is, it can correct or alter program material only within a limited pitchshift range. The exact range percentage will vary from system to system and with program material (voice, music, complex waveforms, etc.). In the final analysis, only your ears can judge how much distortion has been added by a particular system.

Pitch Shifting

The most common system, and the one that is the easiest to use for pitch shifting, employs complex signal-processing techniques to vary the pitch of an audio program or soundfile. This technology can take place in either real or non-real time. One of the ways that the system can operate is by writing sampled audio data into a temporary storage medium (known as a circular buffer). The audio is then resampled at either a higher or a lower rate (Fig. 8.14). Once done, a change in pitch ratio can be made by changing the rate of the newly sampled data so that it matches the original rate that existed at the buffer's input.

To keep the sample rate the same, both before and after the circular buffer, the next task is to alter the rate of the newly resampled signal so that it matches the sample rate as it existed at the device's input. The resulting change in pitch will be a ratio that exists as the difference between the internally resampled rate and the outgoing sample rate.

For example, a segment of audio can be shifted downward by sampling the data within the buffer at a higher rate than existed at the buffer's input. By reducing this newly sampled audio to the same sample rate that existed at the buffer's input, the samples are stretched out over time, thus lowering the effective pitch ratio (Fig. 8.15).

As can be seen, the effective rate has left wide gaps between each sample point. In order for the samples (both entering and leaving the pitch shifter) to be at the same rate, the system must intelligently insert samples that have been left between the gaps. Conversely, when shifting sound upward (Fig. 8.16), the signal must be internally sampled at a lower rate. After this process, the newly sampled rate is raised to match the incoming data rate, thus raising its effective pitch ratio.

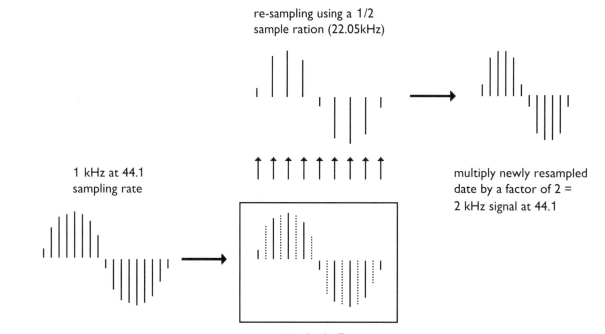

Fig. 8.14: Pitch shifting occurs by resampling data that is temporarily stored within a circular buffer at either a higher or a lower rate.

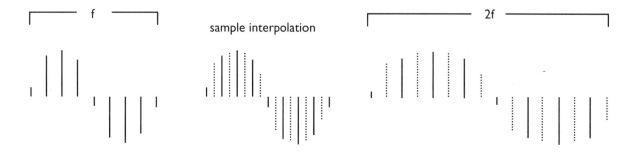

Fig. 8.15: Digital audio can be shifted downward by sampling the data within a circular buffer at a higher rate and then stretching the samples out over time in order to lower the pitch ratio.

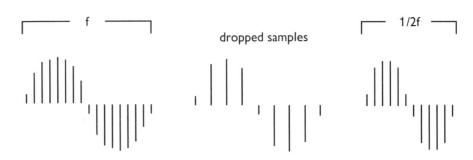

Fig. 8.16: When digital audio is shifted upward, the signal is internally sampled at a lower rate. By raising the outgoing rate, the effective pitch ratio is likewise raised.

Time Compression/Expansion

By combining variable sample rates and pitch shifting, it is possible to alter the aspects of a program's duration (varying the length of a program by raising or lowering its playback sample rate), as well as its relative pitch (shifting it either up or down). In this way a number of possible time/pitch combinations can happen:

- A program's length can be altered with a corresponding change in pitch due to sample rate change.

- A program's duration can be altered while pitch is shifted either up or down in order to maintain the same relative pitch as that of the original program material.

To illustrate how such time stretch-and-squeeze techniques might be applied, suppose that you want to stretch a 27-second public service radio spot to exactly 30 seconds. You could reduce the sample rate by the precise ratio needed for achieving a 30-second length. Then you could use pitch shifting techniques to shift the pitch by a ratio that would return the pitch to its original value.

Noise Elimination

Signal processing enhances a signal by creating an effect or altering a program. Advanced forms of signal processing can actually improve the perceived quality of previously recorded material or restore it to its original condition. Such a complex processing system is capable of reducing by various degrees the noise content of an existing recording. Noise could include such analog side effects as tape hiss, needle ticks, pops, and even certain types of distortion that were inherent in the original recording process.

This kind of DSP system can be used in a number of applications, such as restoring older program material and cleaning up material for transfer to CD. A straightforward example might include the elimination of noise from older material that is historically and/or musically important or tape noise from an analog signal that was recorded at too low a level.

Two examples of such a desktop noise eliminator for the Macintosh are the No-Noise desktop program from Sonic Solutions and the Dynamic Intelligent Noise Reduction (DINR) plug-in mod-

ule from Digidesign. Both of these programs make use of real and non-real time DSP algorithm as a noise removal system that is used to restore and clean up problematic programs from 78 rpm records, early analog material, film, etc., for remastering to compact disc.

The No-Noise system (Fig. 8-17) can be compared to an intelligent multiband expander. However, in this case, "multi" means that the audio spectrum is divided into more than 2,000 frequency bands and requires more than 53 million computations to process just 1 second of sound. Recent improvements in co-processor speeds permit complex computations such as these to be done in either real-time or non-real time.

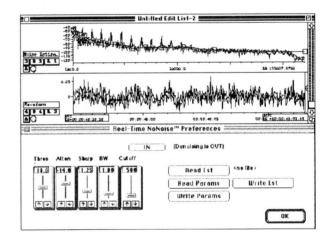

Fig. 8.17: The No-Noise desktop application (Courtesy of Sonic Solutions)

The No-Noise process often involves three stages:

- Visual analysis
- De-clicking
- De-noising

Visual Analysis

In the visual analysis stage, the soundfile is searched visually and audibly to determine the extent to which No-Noise must be applied to rid the program of noise and click pollution.

De-clicking

Once the soundfile has been checked out, No-Noise can be used to automatically remove clicks and pops. The program does not edit these noises out of the signal. Instead, it reconstructs and repairs the problem portion of a recording by performing a frequency analysis upon a segment of audio, both before and after the click. The process is then able to sample enough of the surrounding material to make a plausible guess as to the original waveform content and then proceed to paste a resynthesized segment of audio over the offender.

De-noising

After transient noises have been eliminated, the next task is to lower the background noise floor so that tape hiss, surface noise, or recurrent background noises (hum, buzzes, air-conditioner noises, and the like) are reduced or eliminated.

The noise removal aspect of No-Noise involves a set of complex computations that make intelligent estimates as to when a background noise will or will not be audible at any point in time. Specifically, the process breaks down the audio spectrum into over 2,000 frequency bands in order to predict whether louder sounds (program) will mask a softer sound (noise).

This process is performed by comparing the signal with a noise "fingerprint" known as a signature. The signature is taken from a sample of pure background noise that might exist at the beginning or end of the program, or within a momentary pause in the program.

Once the system is in action, it will search both forward and backward in time over a range of samples for each instant of music to determine what is noise and whether its removal would damage the music. If levels within one of the analyzed frequency bands fall below or equal the level of the noise signature, the processor will decide that the content is most likely noise and will digitally expand this narrow bandrange downward, thus reducing the final noise content.

Keep in mind that the process of reducing noise often provides a challenge to a DSP-based noise removal system, since each program type is different in nature and requires its own approach to cleanup. Systems such as these are not a "one mouse click does all" application. Processing variables, such as depth of reduction, audible side effects, etc., are entirely up to the user.

Digital Mixing

With the increased power, speed, and affordability that can be obtained from modern co-processing "engines," one of the more recent advances in audio technology is the occurrence of real-time mixing in the digital domain.

Ideally, one of the advantages of using a properly designed digital mixer is that no loss in quality or added noise is introduced into the signal path. Since it's possible for both the input and the output stages to be digital, the only alterations to the signal would be introduced by the signal processors themselves. However, these devices are far from perfect improper designs or extreme operating conditions (such as heavy EQ or rapid fader moves) could introduce audible distortion. There is another advantage, however, that possibly offers an even greater benefit: the ability of digital mixing systems to offer full automation over most of its control parameters.

Since the control settings for such a mixer are stored as discrete numbers, they can be easily saved as a computer file or stored in RAM. Likewise, dynamic control (continuous update of changes in fader, pan, and routing position during a mix) can be stored with equal ease. Often such static or dynamic settings can be locked to SMPTE or can be controlled remotely via MIDI messages. MIDI implementation makes possible the recording of level, panning, and other controls directly into a MIDI sequence (along with MIDI performance data). It also allows mixer settings to be varied directly from a MIDI mixer/controller system.

Digital mixing systems can be found in one of two flavors. It can exist as a stand-alone, hardware-based mixing device that includes dedicated controls, routing buttons, I/O ports, and a processor that has been specially designed for this task (Fig. 8.18). Alternatively, the mixing system can be based around the system's software of a digital audio workstation (Fig. 8.19). Such a system often displays the mixer's control plate on computer monitor and offers control over such parameters as track level, panning, auxiliary sends, and equalization.

Each type of mixing system has its own advantages and disadvantages. Perhaps the most blatant difference between the two is that a hardware mixer is designed to integrate digital audio signals from a number of possible sources, while a software system is often designed to mix the internal tracks and output destinations that exist within a digital audio workstation.

Sample Rate Conversion

In the digital domain, it is now increasingly common for audio devices to be interfaced together. The need for sample rate conversion is thus on the rise within professional settings. This process requires the use of a dedicated DSP device called a sample rate converter (Fig. 8.20). As its name suggests, it changes the rate at which a digital audio signal has been sampled to another sampling frequency. Applications for such devices include:

- The changing of a recorded sample frequency between current industry standard rates of 48 kHz (professional), 44.1 kHz (consumer), and 32 kHz (broadcast).

- The changing of a recorded sample frequency between current and older sample rates, such as the Sony F1 44.056-kHz format.

- The creating of "pull-down" rates for maintaining sync when digitally recorded audio is

Fig. 8.18: SSL's Scenaria Digital Audio/Video Production System. (Courtesy of Solid State Logic.)

transferred from film to video. For example, audio recorded at 48 kHz would need to be pulled down to 47.952 kHz for video, while 44.1 rates would be lowered to 44.056 kHz.

Sample rate conversion is carried out by stand-alone devices and certain DAWs that make use of a number of co-processors. The co-processors operate under a complex set of program algorithms in order to shift from one frequency to another without any undue side effects.

The Future of DSP

As processing engines increase in speed, power, and affordability, DSP has become integrated into all types of digital audio systems, including multi-function effects processors, digital audio workstations, hard disk recorders, and even certain tape-based digital recording systems. The future will certainly see a rise in hardware DSP systems and software algorithms that will provide new and innovative tools for adding to our processing bag of tricks.

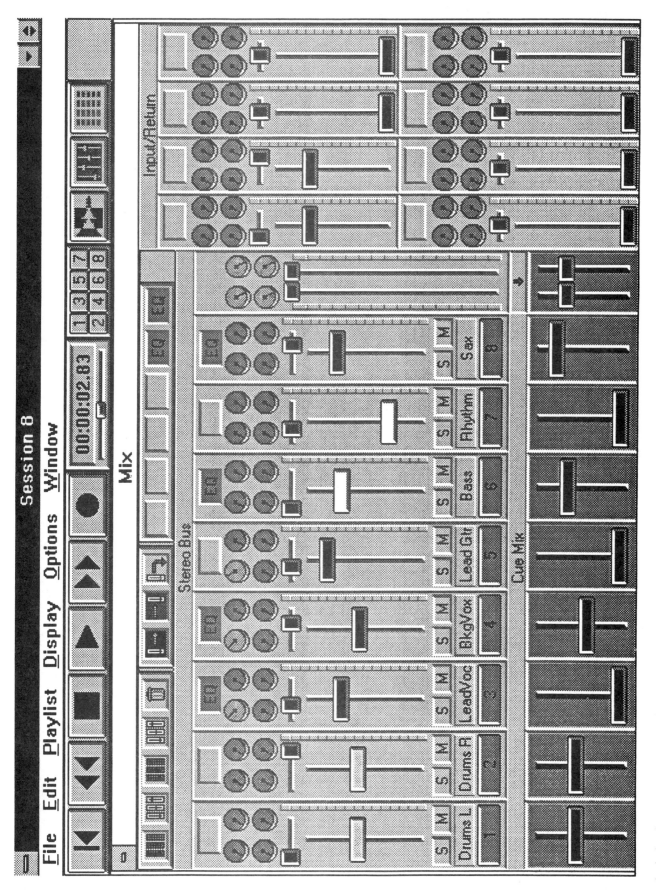

Fig. 8.19: Example of a digital mixing screen. (Courtesy of Digidesign.)

Fig. 8.20: NV 4448 digital audio sample rate converter. (Courtesy of nVision, Inc.)

Chapter 9

Random Access Audio in Multimedia Production

One of the most recent advances in personal computer technology has come with the arrival of a programming environment known as multimedia. At its maximum potential, multimedia can be thought of as a conduit that allows text, graphics, MIDI, digital audio, and even full or limited motion video to be simultaneously passed to any active program capable of responding to these media.

To briefly illustrate this kind of programming environment, suppose you were using a program designed to respond simultaneously to text, graphics, and digital audio. The program might let you read about a subject and then click on a picture icon that would show a still picture or motion graphic related to that subject. The program might also output appropriate music, speech, or sound effects.

A high degree of acceptance for this computer-based media already exists within the home, education, and business communities. As a growing enterprise, multimedia is sure to offer career opportunities to those working in the computer, visual, and audio-production industries.

This chapter will look at the various computer programming environments that allow task-related software packages to function and, at a higher level, to communicate with each other within the same computer. It will also look at how multimedia works, how it is currently affecting certain computer applications, and how it may affect the way that we deal with data in tommorow's information age.

Multimedia in Action

To better understand how multimedia might work in real-life applications (Fig. 9.1), let's look at four examples showing how multimedia could affect your life at home, at school, in the workplace, and in the world of music.

Example 1: Games

It's been a hard day at work. You want to relax, but you're still keyed up from drinking coffee all afternoon. You decide to play a game on your new multimedia computer. You choose your latest game, ArachniSaurs! After booting up the computer, you access the system's CD-ROM drive, which has the new game disk already inserted and ready to go. When the main title screen comes up, a familiar MIDI sequence begins playing from the system's internal sound generator out through the stereo system. The prehistoric spiders and other beasties begin moving around the high-resolution graphics screen. After being distracted for just a second, one of the monsters launches a sneak attack and the main hero bites one of her nine lives. At the point of her first demise, the left speaker outputs a SCREEAAAAAM!!! in true 22.050-kHz digital audio style.

When you finish the first level, the screen blanks and an ominous voice is heard. "Choose your path into the portals of doom!" A number of doors appear on the screen. Your selection of a door is followed by a theme title, graphics, and special effects related to your choice. Soon an hour or so has passed, and the stress of work is gone.

Example 2: Education

This next example finds a second grader in the school library ("Class, get your headphones out"). Johnny is brushing up on his word skills by playing a spelling game with a computer that is programmed to interact with him in various ways while he's working on the spelling lesson.

In one instance, a high-quality speech-to-text converter says the word "bicycle" and then Johnny types "bycicle." The system responds by saying "No, Johnny, that's not quite right. Try again." When Johnny spells the word right, a short "TA DA" music sequence plays, and a limited motion

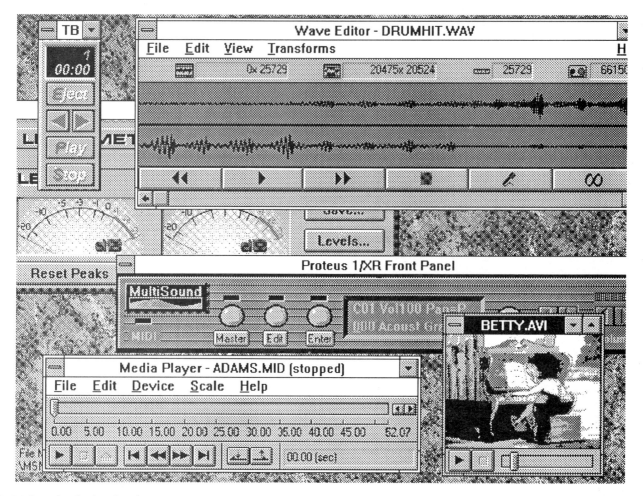

Fig. 9.1: Examples of multimedia software.

graphic appears of a kid riding a bike past a colorful background.

Next it says, "Johnny, can you spell this . . ." and a picture of a spouting whale appears. Upon spelling the word "whale" correctly, Johnny sees a full-motion video of a pod of whales and hears a digital recording of whale sounds.

The scene now switches to the local public library. You are using a multimedia encyclopedia that is stored on CD-ROM. From the glossary screen, you choose the main category "Nature," then the subcategory "Weather," and then the graphic icon titled "Thunderstorms." The screen goes black, and a series of lightning flashes appear, accompanied by the obligatory recording of lightning and thunder claps. Next, you see a series of dialog choices allowing you to choose which aspect of thunderstorms you'd like to learn about.

Textbooks also can be stored on CD-ROM. No longer limited to the typeset page, they can include text, audio, MIDI instrumentation, and screen or motion graphics. Multimedia design is strictly up to the imagination.

Example 3: Business

To take just one example of how multimedia might be integrated into the world of business, consider the creation of presentations for trade fairs, stockholders meetings, and boardroom conferences. For years, multimedia business

presentations used tape recorders, slide projectors, and VCRs to integrate sound, text, and graphics technologies.

Now, with a computerized multimedia platform, pre-programmed or interactive demonstrations that integrate these media into a single computer display system can be presented in a comparatively cost-effective manner.

For example, suppose you are a stockholder of a major corporation. Within the next year, the corporation will be releasing a new product, so it sends you a presentation on disk informing you about the new product. Upon inserting the disk and calling up the program file, you hear the corporation's music theme begin playing while a text and graphic description builds up to a dramatic unveiling of the new product. A voice says, "And now, Carrington Corporation is proud to present the new Widget Wheel!"

Following an animated stroll around the wheel, you're given a guided tour into the world of sales projections and cost estimates for the new product. Naturally, this rosy picture emphasizes the future high profits that are sure to accrue should you decide to buy more stock.

Example 4: Music Production

Business and education are not the only beneficiaries of a multimedia environment. The creative world of electronic music production can also gain extra mileage from these advances. Since this environment is capable of accessing various media at once, advances in music production are being passed onto beginners and more advanced musicians alike.

Entry-level MIDI musicians can now go out and buy multimedia hardware cards that include both a MIDI interface and music synthesis hardware in one low-cost package. Many of these packages come bundled with a beginner's sequencing package to get you started. More advanced users can also buy higher-quality hardware cards or compatible media systems to expand the number of MIDI tracks that are available and add on high-quality sample playback and cost-effective hard disk recording capabilities.

Evolution of Operating Environments

In order to gain a better understanding of the basic operating multimedia environment, we'll look briefly at the various operating system environments used by personal computing systems. These environments include:

- Single program
- Task switching
- Multitasking
- Multimedia

Single Program

A single program environment is the most basic operating environment that can be used in a personal computer. It is capable of opening and running only one program at a time. This single-task environment was the first, and only, available option to be used for many years. And it is still commonly used in both home and business program applications.

In a single program environment, the only way that data can be shared between programs is to save the resultant data from a source program to disk, quit that program, and then open a new program. For example, assume that you have just composed a letter to a business associate and that

you would like to fax the letter to that person using the new computer fax board that you just bought. In a single program environment, the only way that you could send the fax would be to save the letter in a file format that is compatible with the new board. The next step would be to close the word processor, open the fax send/receive program, import the text file into that program, and then finally send the newly encoded fax file (Fig. 9.2).

Task Switching

A computer that is operating in a task switching environment allows the user to switch between programs without having to quit one before opening the next. Although a number of programs may be available, only one application can be active at a time (Fig. 9.3). In effect, whenever an application that is compatible with this type of environment is brought to the forefront, it will automatically configure the computer's system and hardware ports for active processing. When switched to the background, it will disconnect itself from the system and port, allowing the next program to be brought to the processing forefront.

Such an environment might allow a limited block of static data to be placed into a clipboard memory so that it can be shared between foreground and background applications. However, no dynamic processing functions can be simultaneously carried out between these programs.

Multitasking

The next evolutionary step in the operating environment ladder incorporates what is known as multitasking. This type of environment allows several active programs to be run at once. To the user, it appears that each of the program applications is simultaneously active and has full control over the computer's processing functions.

In reality, however, the computer actually shares between the active applications by switching its processing attention from one program to the next in a sequential fashion (Fig. 9.4). It does this switching at such a high rate of speed that each program appears to be running in a seamless, independent manner. For example, in such an environment, you could be importing a file to disk

Fig. 9.2: When working in a single program environment, you must quit one program before opening the next.

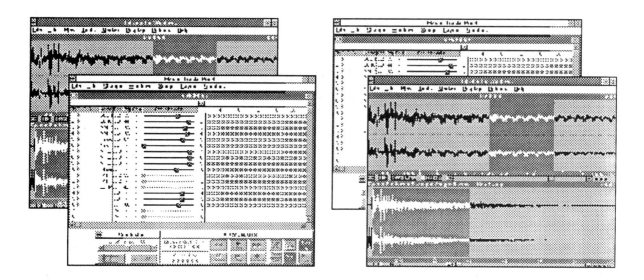

Fig. 9.3: Programs can easily be switched from the inactive background to the active foreground in a task-switching environment.

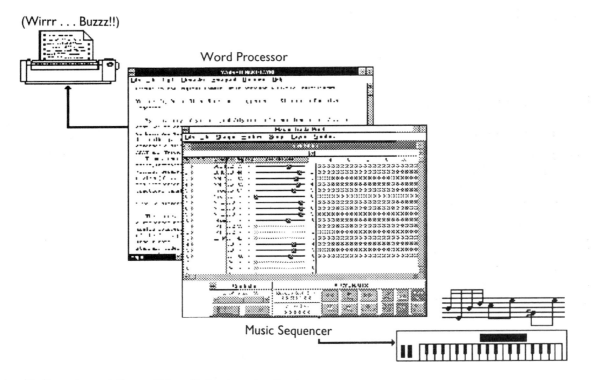

Fig. 9.4: A multitasking environment allows multiple applications to remain active at once.

over a modem port while at the same time you were writing a document and/or viewing a graphics file.

Unfortunately, there is a minor trade-off in processing speed whenever multiple applications are open. Because the computer's processor is quickly switching from one program to the next, the amount of processing time that the computer can devote to each will be equally divided (and thus reduced) by the number of applications that are open at any one time.

As an example, if you have three programs open, the processing speed of each program will be proportionately reduced. If the program is graphic in nature, the screen may take longer to redraw or an animation may move at a slower pace. A task-related program may simply take longer to come

up with its final results. One answer to this dilemma is to upgrade your computer's processing speed so that it is fast enough that the lag created by opening multiple applications is still tolerable.

Data Sharing

The next stage in system evolution is the development of an application environment that is capable of sharing data directly between open programs in real time. In such an environment, certain elements of the data being processed can be made instantly accessible to other compatible programs. These programs can then likewise process or update the information accordingly (Fig. 9.5). This form of data distribution is known as inter-application communication (IAC).

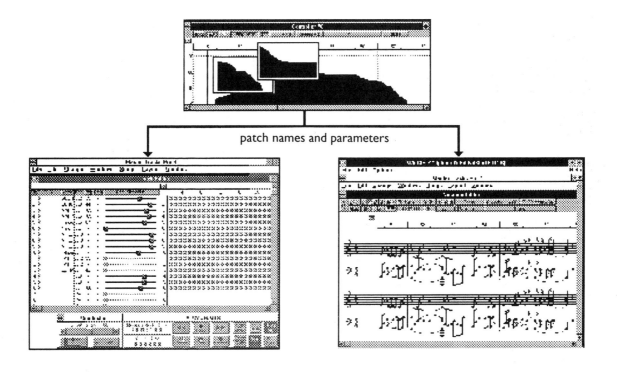

Fig. 9.5: Inter-application communication allows data to be instantly accessible to all compatible programs.

The Multimedia Environment

The newest and highest program environment on the evolutionary ladder is multimedia. This environment, by definition, operates on a multitasking platform to offer simultaneous and interactive access to graphics, text, MIDI, sound generation, and digital audio (Fig. 9.6) on a PC.

The heart of a multimedia system is a computer system that meets a certain minimum number of processing and hardware requirements. These include (but are not limited to):

- A CPU processing speed that is fast enough to allow a number of simultaneous operations to be carried out without a significant compromise in speed or performance.

- Sufficient RAM to process a number of applications in a multitasking environment.

- Compatible graphics capabilities.

- Hardware sound card(s) (including sound generation and digital audio and MIDI capabilities).

- CD-ROM drive (optional).

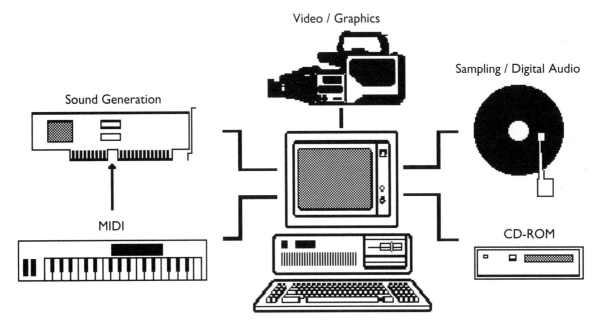

Fig. 9.6: Example of a multimedia environment.

Graphics

The graphic images that are displayed on a computer screen are created from a vertical and horizontal matrix of dots known as pixels. These pixels are composed of various shades of red, green, and blue phosphors. The pixels can be mixed in various combinations to create almost any imaginable color.

Just as digital audio amplitudes can be represented by a digital word with a width of n bits, individual pixels can be represented by a similar encoding process. For example, a black and white image can be encoded using a series of single-bit words (0 = white, 1 = black). Four bits can represent 16 colors; eight bits can produce 256. A 24-bit word can yield a whopping 16.7 million individual colors.

A collection of pixels combined to create a screen display is called a bitmap. As an example, the graphic resolution of a VGA screen (commonly used in an IBM/Windows environment) is 640 x 480 pixels. The intensity and color values for each pixel in an overall bitmap must be stored within a special high-speed RAM memory known as a video buffer, after which time they can be displayed on the monitor.

Multimedia graphics can be displayed and manipulated in a number of ways. With paint programs, you can create or import two-dimensional bitmap drawings, which can then be imported into documents or displayed on a screen to illustrate a point. For example, many of the figures in this book were created with the help of a paint program.

Object-oriented CAD (computer-assisted design) programs take basic paint techniques a step farther by allowing you to create three-dimensional images. The first step in this process is to create objects using a series of wire frame models that provide coordinates for the precise dimensional relationship, shape, and size of objects that appear on the screen (Fig. 9.7, left).

Once the coordinates have been established, you can instruct the computer to rotate each 3-D image on the screen in any direction. By giving to each surface attributes such as color, and light intensity/shading, you can render the objects into a final form that looks amazingly realistic (Fig. 9.7, right).

By playing back a series of either two- or three-dimensional images in a sequential fashion, you can create animated motion on the screen. For example, a graphics application might allow a series of 2-D paint images of a company logo to be stepped through in a short sequence, creating the illusion of limited motion. On a larger and more involved scale, a computer could be used to render complex, three-dimensional images at higher frame rates, creating the illusion of full-motion film or video special effects.

Desktop Digital Video

Digital video (or DTV) has become an important part of the multimedia environment in that it provides us with a way of viewing full-motion video images on our computer screens (Fig. 9.8).

By sampling a video image and placing it within an on-screen window, DTV can achieve frame rates that can vary from 12 frames-per-second (fr/s) for animation to roughly 30 fr/s for high-quality video images. Don't be fooled by these seemingly slow rates (when compared to the sampling rates that are used in audio). Fact is, that when you multiply the number of graphic pixels that are needed to create a single frame by the number of

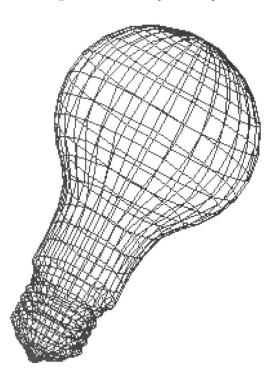

Fig. 9.7: Image from an object-oriented drawing program.

Fig. 9.8: Example of a digital video window.

frames that pass in a second, we would quickly come up with a density of stored digital data that can far surpass the storage requirements of digital audio.

The two most recent standards to be adopted for widespread DTV use are QuickTime (which was primarily designed for the Macintosh) and Video for Windows from MicroSoft (for the IBM-Windows PC). Both of these and other video standards rely upon data compression to reduce the heavy storage and data throughput requirements that even a small DTV window can draw.

In application, DTV can add immensely to multimedia's entertainment and instructional value and through the use of various levels of synchronization can be locked to other media sources (such as digital audio and MIDI) for professional desktop multimedia and audio-for-video production and post-production.

MIDI

MIDI is an important implementation within multimedia because it allows sound effects and or music to be generated without the high data overhead that is required by digital audio. High quality digital audio can take up to 10 megabytes per stereo minute for disk storage. A simple or even complex MIDI sequence, on the other hand, might accomplish a similar effect with only a few kilobytes of stored data and very little processing overhead.

Fully equipped MIDI systems can easily be accessed by professional sequencing and other types of software that can communicate MIDI data in a multimedia environment. However, it is also possible for MIDI performance data to be routed from an applications program to a single sound-generating chip. For example, entry-level sound cards will often use a single FM synthesis chip that is capable of outputting a range of simultaneous sounds that include musical instruments, percussion, and sound effects.

Algorithmic programs written for these chips can synthesize human speech for the purpose of reading text directly from the computer's screen or text file. High-end hardware cards might include a quality synthesizer or sample playback chip. Examples of such cards include Digidesign's MacProteus (Mac) and Turtle Beach Softworks' MultiSound card (IBM/Windows Multimedia), both of which use E-mu's Proteus chip (a 32-voice, high-quality sample playback system).

General MIDI

Since its inception, MIDI has been a standardized language for relaying performance and control-related data. However, the basic instrument sounds that are reproduced by almost any electronic music setup will invariably change from one setup to the next (and often even within the setup whenever patch settings are changed). In one setup, MIDI data that is being transmitted over channel 5 might trigger an upright bass sound, while another setup might have channel 5 set to trigger an entirely different device that might output a "Zaxxon spacegun from hell."

This lack of conformity has brought about a single set of standardized MIDI patch settings that have come to be known as General MIDI. This standardized series of sound settings has been defined so that common and popular instrument sounds are mapped to various program change numbers. For example, calling up General MIDI patch #1 will always call up an acoustic grand piano, while #59 will always call up a tuba. When you are playing a game or using an interactive program, the General MIDI sound patch you hear should be the same sound you would always hear.

Table 9.1: General MIDI sound set groupings.

Program #	Instrument Group
1–8	Piano
9–16	Chromatic Percussion
17–24	Organ
25–32	Guitar
33–40	Bass
41–48	Strings
49–56	Ensemble
57–64	Brass
65–72	Reed
73–80	Pipe
81–88	Synth Lead
89–96	Synth Pad
97–104	Synth Effects
105–112	Ethnic
113–120	Percussive
121–128	Sound Effects

Note: Channel 10 is reserved for general percussion sounds.

Digital Audio

Digital audio is obviously an important aspect of multimedia production. Certain personal computers have 8-bit, and even 16-bit, converters built-in for sampling and reproducing digital audio. However, facilities for high-quality digital audio will usually involve the addition of a dedicated hardware card.

Digital audio can be used in multimedia for a number of computer-related applications. These include:

- Music and sound effects to add realism to games that support multimedia sound ("ZAP! Ha Ha, you missed me!").

- Music and sound effects to alert you to typical computer prompts. For example, when an application error occurs, the speakers might output ("SCREEECH. . . .Wipe out!").

- Output audio relating to CD-ROM applications, multimedia presentations, and multimedia interactive software.

Multimedia can also be used by imaginative software companies to integrate various media together in a way that was not thought possible on entry-level computing systems. For years, costly Macintosh-based systems have been required to simultaneously output digital audio and MIDI. However, with the introduction of a multimedia approach to programming, less expensive digital audio/MIDI software packages can accomplish similar results using hardware that is affordable for even the beginner or enthusiast.

Bit and Sample Rate Specifications

Professional and consumer digital audio equipment operates at sample rates of 44.1 and 48 kHz, with a resolution of 16 bits or greater. In contrast, hardware for computer multimedia systems often works at varying sample rates and with varying bit widths (depending on audio quality, disk space requirements, and the sample rate capabilities of the installed hardware systems).

In a game, for example, a short sound effect that originally was stored on floppy disk might have a sample rate of only 11.025 kHz, with only an 8-bit width. A short orchestral passage that is encoded on a "Music Education" CD-ROM disc might be sampled at 22.050 kHz using a 16-bit word structure. High-quality sampled audio or sounds on CD-ROM that can be played on a regular CD player (CD-audio) would be recorded at 44.1 kHz (16-bits).

Table 9.2 lists the various sample rates and file size requirements that are required to store one minute of digital audio data for a specified sample rate and bit width.

Table 9.2: File size requirements required to store one minute of digital audio data.

Sample Rate	Bit Width	File Size Per Minute
11 kHz	8-bit, mono	660KB/minute
11 kHz	8-bit, stereo	1.3MB/minute
11 kHz	16-bit, mono	1.3MB/minute
11 kHz	16-bit, stereo	2.6MB/minute
22 kHz	8-bit, mono	1.3MB/minute
22 kHz	8-bit, stereo	2.6MB/minute
22 kHz	16-bit, mono	2.6MB/minute
22 kHz	16-bit, stereo	5.3MB/minute
44.1 kHz	8-bit, mono	2.6MB/minute
44.1 kHz	8-bit, stereo	5.3MB/minute
44.1 kHz	16-bit, mono	5.3MB/minute
44.1 kHz	16-bit, stereo	10.5MB/minute

Multimedia systems can deal with sampled digital audio in one of two ways:

- A samplefile can be loaded into, and reproduced directly from, RAM.

- A soundfile can be recorded to, and reproduced directly from, hard disk.

Sample Playback

Certain program applications require that digitized audio be loaded into RAM before it can be processed and reproduced. This method of dealing with multimedia audio is not widely used because of the amount of RAM space taken up by even a small samplefile. There are two advantages to this type of data storage. The first is the very short access time that is required to output an effect. The second is the ability to calculate limited DSP effects directly within RAM (such as adding an echo effect, reversing the waveform, changing levels, etc.), without the need for extensive dedicated processing hardware.

Hard Disk Recording

More commonly, digital audio is transferred directly to, and reproduced from, hard disk. This is true for the storage of both short and longer soundfile data, since there is usually only a minor trade-off in access time and the limitations of placing all but the shortest samplefile into RAM would place a burden on valuable memory real estate.

In a standardized multimedia environment, stored digital audio is routed directly through a single system-wide sound driver to processing hardware for D/A conversion. This stored data can reside on hard disk, CD-ROM, or other fast-access, high density medium. It can be stored in various sample rate and bit-width formats, depending on the fidelity required by the program application and the capabilities of the D/A hardware.

Multimedia Sound Hardware

Anticipating the development of multimedia, newer high-powered computer systems have incorporated digital audio and MIDI capabilities into their design. For example, certain Macintosh, Commodore, and Atari computers offer microphone and line-level in and out signals for recording 8-bit digital audio directly to and from hard disk at various sample rates (generally up to 22 kHz). More highly powered PCs have begun to offer internal digital I/O ports that are capable of processing at rates up to 48 kHz, with up to 16-bit resolution.

With internal sound hardware such as this, you need only add the necessary software for recording, editing, and playing back audio or MIDI data from either a standard or a multimedia platform. Computers that are not equipped with high-res internal audio capabilities can generally be "souped up" by adding on a quality digital audio, MIDI, and/or sound-generating hardware card.

Although multimedia is certainly alive and well on many computer fronts (such as HyperCard for the Macintosh), one of the fastest growing markets in multimedia has come into existence with the release of Microsoft's Windows Multimedia environment. Since most IBM- compatible PCs are not equipped with internal digital audio and MIDI interface ports, the design and manufacture of external hardware cards for these systems has quickly become a strong growth industry.

An example of such a hardware card is the Sound Blaster Pro from Creative Labs, Inc. The Sound Blaster Pro features 8-bit D/A and A/D conversion at sample rates between 4 kHz and 44.1 kHz, allowing hard disk recording and samplefile playback from disk. MIDI is fully implemented, and sound generation is carried out from a built-in set of FM synthesis chips that can provide up to 22 polyphonic voices. MIDI is fully implemented (16 channels). There are provisions for a joystick game port, direct CD-ROM interface

with internal connector for CD-audio, 4 watt/channel power output amplifier, and hardware automatic gain control (AGC) for limiting the dynamic range of the microphone input channel.

The software that comes bundled with Sound Blaster Pro includes a hard disk editing program, SBTalker (an ASCII text-to-speech program), CD Music Player (an application for controlling and playing CD-audio discs from the CD-ROM drive), MIDI sequencing program, and MMPlay Presentation (a multimedia graphics, audio, MIDI-scripted animation program).

Another such hardware card is the MultiSound Sound Card for Windows Multimedia from Turtle Beach Softworks (Fig. 9.9). This full-sized AT-style card offers high-quality ROM sample generation, a MIDI interface, and digital audio hard disk recording/playback capabilities for the IBM running under Windows.

Sound generation occurs through the card's use of the 32-voice Proteus XR/1 16-bit sample performance chip (E-mu Systems, Inc.), which is loaded with both the industry-famous Proteus XR/1's samples and the sound patch data, as well as a specially programmed set of General MIDI patches for multimedia MIDI applications.

Sixteen-bit hard disk recording at 44.1-kHz, 22.050-kHz, and 11.025-kHz sample rates is also possible through the use of an entry-level editing program (included) or an advanced editing program (optional) having additional DSP edit functions. Both hard disk and sample playback data are encoded on disk using the standard Wave (.WAV) format. Full MIDI implementation is designed into the card, though you can piggyback your existing MIDI interface alongside of the MultiSound's MIDI ports (thus giving your system 32-channel, or higher, MIDI capabilities).

Besides its basic hardware functions, the MultiSound comes with a number of systems-related applications (Fig. 9.10):

- The Proteus Front Panel is a functional copy of the standard Proteus front panel layout. These controls give direct access to all of the same MIDI and parameter controls that are found on the module. One exception is the Preset button that lets you access either Proteus, General MIDI, or user-programmable patch presets.

- The MIDI Patch Bay provides MIDI patch routing access between the Proteus, MIDI interface, and the Windows operating environment. In short, it lets you route data to and from different hardware/software applications on the system.

- The Record Prep prepares incoming analog levels for recording to hard disk. The most striking feature is the stereo VU meter section. Each meter has two moving needles. One is calibrated to VU ballistics, and the other registers peak hold levels.

Fig. 9.9: Turtle Beach's MultiSound Sound Card for Windows Multimedia. (Courtesy of Turtle Beach Softworks.)

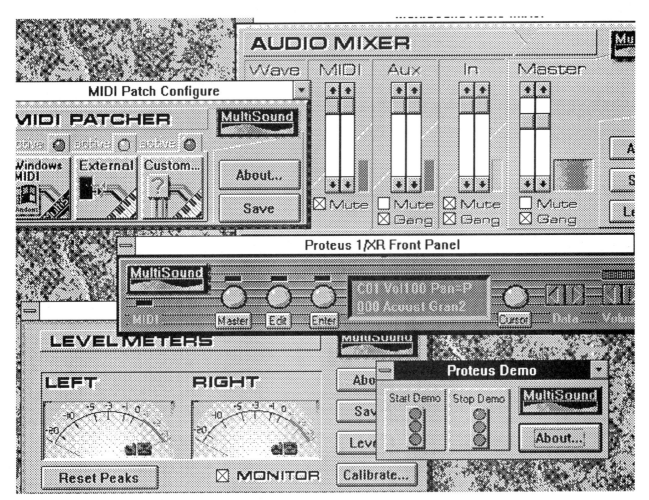

Fig. 9.10: Application programs that are bundled with the MultiSound hardware card. (Courtesy of Turtle Beach Softworks.)

- The Output Volume Mixer lets you mix the MIDI, digital audio, auxiliary, and input signals so that they can be simultaneously routed through the MultiSound card. This on-screen mixer lets you combine and alter these levels in real time, while offering independent channel muting, L/R channel balance, or ganged stereo level changes.

CD-ROM and CD-I

Whenever video, animated graphics, and sampled audio are involved, the data density is often so high that storage of media and program data on floppy disks is nearly useless. Although a hard disk is capable of storing relatively high data densities, it is generally plagued with the problem of being nonremovable. Optical media thus becomes the most practical solution to this dilemma, since it is an extremely high-density media, it's removable, and it can be easily duplicated for mass distribution.

Currently, the most common means of distributing high density program and multimedia-related data in a read-only format makes use of two compact disc media:

- CD ROM

- CD-I

CD-ROM

The CD-ROM (Compact Disc Read Only Memory) format was developed to extend the digital audio CD format so that any form of data could be optically encoded onto this universally recognized media.

When used in conjunction with a personal computer, this read only medium can store up to 680 megabytes of data relating to computer programs, database information, text, MIDI, graphics, animation, and video data. In recent times, the CD-ROM has become popularly accepted as an entirely new publishing medium, when used either as a multimedia or as a data storage media.

Unlike its brother, the CD-audio disc, the CD-ROM is not tied to any particular data format. This means that it is strictly up to the programming manufacturers to specify what is contained within the disc. For example, CD-ROM could easily store general text data, as well as consumer information relating to east coast pharmaceutical sales for the year 1992, or a database of telephone numbers for major U.S. cities. A single disc might contain all the necessary programs, graphics, MIDI, and audio effects that are needed to play a particular game or piece of learning software.

CD-ROM drives are now quite affordable, and software that was once manufactured only in limited numbers has become less expensive as the market for this medium has increased. Such drives can be installed directly into the computer's drive bay, or external stand-alone models can be purchased. Most CD-ROM drives are also capable of playing CD audio discs and include software for controlling playback functions directly from a computer applications program.

It's worth mentioning a new phenomenon that involves using the CD medium to produce and distribute prerecorded media for the multimedia platform. This is similar to the use of CD-audio discs to produce and distribute music and sound effects libraries, or CD-ROM to dis-tribute prerecorded and factory-edited samplefiles that can be loaded directly into a sampler or sample edit program and then played from a MIDI keyboard.

This medium can be used to encode data in such forms as clipart graphics, MIDI sequences, and digital audio soundfiles. An example of this type of disc is MusicBytes from Prosonus. MusicBytes is a license-free CD-ROM for Windows Multimedia compatible systems. It contains preedited music clips (in lengths of 60, 30, 15, and 5 seconds), sound effects (recorded in both 11.025-kHz and 22.050-kHz Wave formats), music and effects in the CD-audio format (playable on any CD player), and sequenced standard MIDI file music clips (General MIDI format). In addition, a search database program is included for searching, auditioning, copying, and cataloging the various media files that exist on disc.

CD-I

Another medium that offers tremendous potential as a publishing format for multimedia information is CD-I (Compact Disc Interactive). Although it is an extension of the CD-ROM (which is not tied to any particular data format), CD-I includes a set of rigidly defined format standards for encoding text, graphics, MIDI, digital audio, and video information.

CD-I specifications define how the various media are to be encoded onto disc, how the files are to be logically laid out on disc, and what the various grades of resolution are for each media type. They also define precise hardware specifications for reading CD-I discs and decoding the various multimedia information.

Before discussing the various formats, it's important to realize that this strict standardization means that CD-I hardware can be designed to work independently of a personal computer. In fact, one of the primary motivations behind the standard is to create an interactive educational and home entertainment environment that would be affordably priced. It is hoped that most homes would be equipped with a CD-I system by the end of the century, just as most homes now have a television and CD-audio player.

Although many CD-I hardware systems are capable of exporting data to certain personal computers, these systems are primarily designed to integrate into various media devices that already exist in most homes. For example, the graphics output port can be a composite video signal that can be plugged directly into any standard television, in either NTSC (North American) or PAL/SECAM (European) formats. Stereo analog audio outputs are, of course, provided for plugging the system into the home stereo, and a single MIDI output port is also generally provided. Once these ports have been connected, you need only place a CD-I disc title into the player and you're off in multimedia land.

Just as the demand for CD-I systems is expected to drive hardware prices down, so is the demand for CD-I discs expected to lower their prices. Titles could include games, music, graphics, and educational software.

CD-I Formats

The CD-I specification defines a number of resolution levels for graphics, audio, and other media. Such levels make it possible for very large amounts of data to be efficiently packed onto a disc, using the most memory efficient means to convey the information. Here are brief descriptions of these resolution levels as they relate to graphics and digital audio:

- Graphics. CD-I is capable of painting still or animated graphics onto a video monitor as a high-res "natural picture," as well as at two lower-resolution graphics levels. Three levels of video resolution are also supported: normal, double, and high resolution, each of which operates at various pixel encoding resolutions and data densities.

- Audio. The CD-I specification defines four levels of digital audio resolution, as shown in Table 9.3. A programmer can encode any of these levels onto disc according to the fidelity

and data storage requirements. The first of these levels is the CD-audio mode. The inclusion of this 16 bit/PCM standard means that portions of a CD-I disc can also be encoded with high-quality audio. It also ensures that regular CD audio discs containing music can be played on any CD-I player.

- The three remaining audio formats (known as Hi-Fi music mode, Mid-Fi music mode, and Speech mode) make use of a data encoding system known as Adaptive Delta Pulse Code Modulation (ADPCM). This encoding scheme is more memory efficient than the more commonly used PCM encoding method. When this scheme is combined with lower sampling rates at 4- or 8-bit resolution, it is possible to pack large amounts of audio data onto a disc with varying levels of fidelity.

Table 9.3 Audio formats defined by the CD-I Specification.

Mode	Encoding	Sample Rate/Bits	Channels
CD-Audio	PCM (stereo)	44.1 kHz/16-bit	1
Hi-Fi	ADPCM (stereo/mono)	37.8 kHz/8-bit	2/4
Mid-Fi	ADPCM (stereo/mono)	37.8 kHz/4-bit	4/8
Speech	ADPCM (stereo/mono)	18.9 kHz/4-bit	8/16

Chapter 10

Random Access Audio Within Music Production

During the 1990s, the music industry has seen and embraced many changes that have occurred in both technology and production styles as a result of random access technology. The industry has advanced from using digital technology as a simple tool for creating delays or for triggering short drum samples, all the way to using full-blown integrated digital audio workstations and powerful hard disk systems whose memory and available features have increased and whose price has decreased.

The music industry has been the driving force behind the many advances in random access technology. These advances have been instrumental in bringing a high-quality production environment into the home and project studio. This same technology that has given new tools to the professional studio community has also required that it change its marketing strategies to grow along with these independent home and project facilities.

With the introduction of hard disk production and editing, more powerful and integrated sample technology, and digital signal processing, the music industry received new tools and toys to play with. At its best, this technology has freed the artist to achieve and manipulate sounds in an environment that promotes creative freedom and individual expression.

The Tapeless Studio

"The tapeless studio?" What does that mean? This buzz term is surrounded by as much controversy as that other buzz word "the digital audio workstation." Why are these terms so controversial and hard to define?

One answer is that these terms usually don't bring a single device to mind. More often than not they refer to hardware and software systems that revolve around that ever-present central processing unit, the personal computer. The problem that individuals and their industries have with defining

these systems has everything to do with their greatest overall strengths. These are:

- Both the tapeless studio and the digital audio workstation are a collection of integrated software and hardware systems that work together to perform a task or a range of integrated production tasks.

- The tasks are just as modular as the system's concept is. This means that one individual's system might be designed to edit only recorded audio tracks, while another person's system might be designed to integrate the worlds of MIDI and digital audio production. One system might be basic in concept, and another might make extensive use of multiple channels, multitrack tape, automated outboard effects, and mixing gear . . . the list goes on.

Integration

In the world of analog technology, each device carries out a single, dedicated function. As an example, a tape recorder is a tape recorder, and a spring reverb unit is just that. Even an electronic organ like a Hammond B3 or a Farfisa is an organ with certain characteristic sounds and nothing else. Although each device is designed with one purpose in mind, when combined with other devices they are able to work together to accomplish a single goal: recording produced music for records and/or commercial airplay.

With the advent of digital and computer-based technology, the shift has begun away from systems comprising a collection of dedicated and independent devices towards a series of subsystems that are connected to a central data processing and distribution point the computer (Fig. 10.1). Instead of being independent in their functions, these hardware and software subsystems are able to communicate and to be controlled in a system-wide fashion.

Fig. 10.1: In a computer-based system, the computer often acts as a central processor and distribution center. (Courtesy of Opcode Systems, Inc.)

As an example, let's build a professional tape-less facility and put it through its paces (Fig. 10.2). For starters, let's choose a fast, high-powered PC processing hub and load it with plenty of memory, such as a Macintosh Quadra with 16Mb of internal RAM, an 80Mb hard drive for holding program data, a CD-ROM drive for holding sample data, and an erasable-optical drive that can store up to 2 hours of audio on a single, removable disc.

To this we can add professional sequencing software, MIDI interface, sample editing software, a 4-channel hard disk recording system, outboard signal processing effects, a MIDI remote controller, and lots of MIDI instruments (including samplers, sample playback synths, and drum machines).

A Hypothetical Demo Project

A lot of production power lurks under the hood of such a production system, so let's make use of this horsepower to finish a hypothetical demo project a TV commercial that was promised to a New York agency by the end of the month. We begin our quest in Los Angeles by laying out the sequenced MIDI tracks in sync to the time-encoded video picture. This is done by laying down a series of rhythm tracks at exactly 114 bpm (beats per minute) to provide the basic foundation.

Over this foundation, a lot of time is spent laying down keyboard melody and harmony parts. Finding just the right bass sound proves a problem, but that is finally solved by locating a sample

in one of our CD-ROM libraries of an upright bass. "Punchiness" needs to be added to the sample, so we decide to first load the sample into the digital audio editing software. Here, we can EQ the sound to our liking and even compress it digitally.

Once that is done, the sound is dumped from the editing program into a sampler (via SCSI). The final bass sound is then beefed up by layering another bass patch from one of the synths over the sampled bass.

After a day or so, we add other sampled instruments to the sequence (along with a basic string arrangement). We also add more rhythm tracks to the original, repolished tracks. This basically completes the sequence. Now's the time to bring in Tony (the west coast producer) and get his thoughts on the matter. After his input and a few changes, the music tracks are basically ready to go and the voice talent can come in and read the voice scripting.

Since our facility has a small recording booth, we don't have to go elsewhere to record the voice talent. We can record her voice track directly to the removable-optical disc, which will (along with the sequenced music) be in sync with the video picture. With a video playback monitor in both rooms, the talent can record her lines while viewing the picture. The session goes very well. And since the recording medium is random access, it is a simple matter to record and save various dialog takes onto the disc.

Fig. 10.2: An example of an SSL Scenaria professional tapeless production system. (Courtesy of Solid State Logic and Mixed Nuts, NYC.)

Once the session is finished, we can review the alternate takes that were recorded on several of the channels and select the best ones. On the third line, we decide that the first part of the sentence isn't strong enough, although its ending is perfect. This is not a problem, since the beginning on take 2 is good and can be cut and pasted into the good take on the final version.

The completed processes bring the work in our tapeless studio nearly to a close. The rest of the project needs to be finished in a professional recording studio. However, we do have a final task. We need to rent a digital multitrack tape machine for a day so that we can transfer the sequenced and voice tracks to the tape. In this way, we won't be using up valuable studio time for doing transfers.

Remember the basic string arrangement in our sequence? It was created so that it could be printed out as a score and a small string ensemble could be brought into the studio and recorded onto the final master tape. Once the score is printed, the final tapes are taken into the studio and transferred, the strings added, and the final results mixed and sent off to New York with a few days to spare.

This music biz fantasy is only one possible production scenario. The same system that was used to create a straight ahead TV commercial might be used to edit 40 car horns for transfer to a sampler. These samples can then be sequenced along with a few other rhythm and harmonic-structured instruments to create a modern gamalan (Javanese gong and bell) orchestra, complete with automated mixing and wild and crazy effects that change settings under automated MIDI commands. It could also be used to edit and assemble the mixdown of a recording into an entirely new composition or dance piece. Heck, the computer could even be used as a plain ol' word processor for writing letters.

A More Modest System

Now that we've tried an expensive, top-of-the-line system, let's see what we can do using a cost-effective random access system (Fig. 10.3). In a system like this, we might simply have an IBM-compatible operating under a multimedia program such as Windows 3.1 or higher, a 200Mb hard disk, a high quality multimedia hardware card, a sequencing program, and a few outboard MIDI instruments and digital effects devices.

Most multimedia hardware cards have digital audio capabilities, a MIDI interface, and multi-timbral (multiple voice) sound generators. Thus, almost all the hardware features needed for basic music production are already included. Let's assume that our system is loaded with a high-quality multimedia hardware card, which includes both hardware and software applications for hard-disk recording, a MIDI interface, and a sample playback chip.

Since this system is operating in a multimedia environment, all of these media are available to the system at once. Thus, when working with a sequencing package that is able to synchronize or trigger digital audio soundfiles, it is possible for a low-cost system to play back recorded soundfiles at the same time that both internal and external MIDI instruments are responding to sequenced MIDI data. Obviously, there will be sacrifices in control when using such a low-cost system over a more expensive system. However, recent advances in multimedia technology have minimized the sacrifices in basic sound quality.

With such a system, you can create a sequence using many (if not all) of the approaches that were used in the high cost system. Once the sequence has been refined, it is potentially a simple matter to play back the sequence, while at the same time recording a vocal or acoustic instrument track directly to hard disk. Using a triggered soundfile approach, you can then edit various sections of the soundfile down into smaller sections (verse, chorus, solo, etc.).

Once edited, these short pieces can be played back directly from hard disk while being triggered from the sequencer or directly from time code using either SMPTE or MTC. Mixing could also be accomplished by using MIDI controller messages to automate the sequence levels. The digital audio tracks could be mixed either manually or from a MIDI-based mixer. In addition, effects patches could easily be automated directly from within the MIDI sequence.

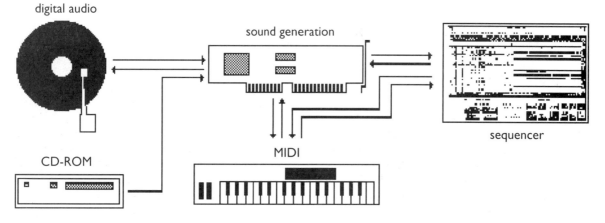

Fig. 10.3: Audio production that is based around a multimedia hardware card.

Soundfile Management

Unlike the tape recorder, which is a linear memory storage device, random-access audio systems store data as "sound chunks." These chunks can be moved, copied, looped, shortened, and processed so that they creatively blend into a production.

The content of these audio chunks is strictly up to you and your creative talents. The discussion here will focus on how and where they can be placed into a project. Recall from Chapter 5 that there are basically four ways in which a soundfile or defined region can be manipulated in a random access editing environment:

- Graphic editing
- Playlist editing
- Disk-based mix editing
- Object-oriented editing

Let's review these systems to see how they hold up when they're used to record, edit, and synchronize a few simple lead vocal verses to a MIDI sequence.

Graphic Editing

In the graphic editing method, soundfile data is graphically displayed and output as a continuous stream of sound data that flows from the beginning to the end of an edited soundfile. In essence, this method works best when there's no break in the resultant soundfile output (as in a final edited song). This edit style is nearly ideal for editing a project or pieces of a finished mix into a continuous, edited recording.

Playlist Editing

A far better edit method for this application would be a playlist editing system. A playlist is a sequential listing of defined regions that can be reproduced either in a sequential fashion (with one region immediately following the other) or at a particular event time.

This system is well suited to the task of triggering soundfile events (such as recorded vocal verses) at a series of specific time-code address points. Thus, it would be a simple matter to define just the audio data that is contained in each verse, name each one (Verse1, Verse2, etc.), and then trigger them at the appropriate times in the MIDI sequence.

Disk-Based Mix Editing

The disk-based editor (sometimes known as a layer editor) is similar to a playlist system. However, instead of displaying these regions in a vertical list fashion, the named regions are represented as a series of horizontal bars that are stacked on top of each other in a vertical array. Should one or more of these bars overlap in the vertical stack, the sample values that exist in the overlapped regions will be digitally mixed together

and stored to disk in a way that offers a pseudo-multichannel editing environment.

Since vocal verses don't overlap in this instance, a disk-based mix system would work just as effectively as a playlist edit system, assuming that each region could be triggered to time code. However, if time-code triggering isn't possible, overall playback sync can be locked to time code and each event could be slipped in time to match the verse trigger times.

Object-Oriented Editing

Object-oriented editing is an on-screen style popular with many newer DAW and hard disk systems. This method relies on the definition and naming of a region, which can thereafter exist as a graphically defined block or "object." These objects have the advantages of both graphic and playlist editing technology in that you can easily view defined regions on the screen and you also can slip their trigger times to match other event start times. This edit style is ideally suited to triggering independent regions within a multichannel production environment.

Obviously, when a recorded track or a series of audio events is being played back in sync with either a MIDI sequence, multitrack master, or video tape, it's of primary importance that the absolute timing reference be stable. Otherwise, the audio will drift in relation to the master source. Chapter 7 discussed the two types of sync that can be used when triggering soundfile data from an external timing source, and we will quickly review them here:

- Triggered sync
- Continuous sync

Triggered sync refers to the firing of an event at a particular point within a production. The soundfile can be triggered via time code or other programming means. However, once the event has been triggered, it will derive its playback timing reference from its own internal processors. In other words, once the soundfile has begun playing back, absolute synchronization with the master source could be lost because of possible cumulative timing errors and drift.

When you are working in this mode, the best way to avoid timing problems is to keep each event reasonably short. The reason for this is simple: shorter events have less time to drift out of sync.

If soundfile timing errors can't be tolerated within a production, a feature known as continuous sync is offered by high-end systems. This mode allows a system to trigger a soundfile internally at a particular event time. However, once the soundfile has begun, the system's timing reference will be derived from the master timing source. In this way, any drift in time between the master and the soundfile will be compensated for, thus eliminating any inherent timing errors between the two.

Tape in the Tapeless Studio

With current technology, up to four channels of digital audio can be simultaneously transferred, with few problems, to and from a hard or optical disk. Although random access systems are available in channel configurations of 8, 16, 24, and even higher, production and project studio owners have to ask themselves if the added hardware, software, and research and development costs are really worth it.

When working in an audio-for-visual medium where you often need to move dialog, ambience, and sound effects tracks in time to fit a picture, such a multichannel system might be cost effective. However, within music production, such time slip manipulations are not nearly as important as simply capturing the sounds onto a stable, cost-effective recording medium like multitrack tape.

A hard disk recording system or DAW makes it possible for recorded tracks to be easily cut, copied, processed, and assembled into a final form directly from hard disk. When all you need are additional tracks, a multitrack tape machine can be integrated into a computer-based system, thus bringing its own strengths into the partnership.

The simplest and most traditional way to integrate a multitrack machine into a workstation environment is through the use of time code. In such a setting, the multitrack is often designated as the master machine, while all digital audio and MIDI events follow in a slave configuration (Fig. 10.4). Most professional MIDI interface devices are able to both generate and read standard longitudinal time code as well as MIDI time code.

Recently, the integration of the multitrack recorder into the world of random access audio has undergone a quantum leap with the introduction of the affordable multitrack digital audio tape

recorder. One such recorder, the ADAT from the Alesis Corporation (Fig. 10.5), can store eight tracks of digital audio onto standard S VHS (video cassette) tape. Through a rather ingenious design, a proprietary synchronization scheme allows up to 16 ADATs to be locked together, offering a total of up to 128 tracks!

Although you might not need this many tracks, there are other features unique to this and other digital multitrack machines. These include the ability to transfer audio data to hard disk for editing, combining, and/or processing originally recorded tracks and the ability to "fly" these edited tracks back to an open track on the recorder in sync.

Another innovation that is helping to integrate multitrack and video recorders into the digital audio workstation environment is the development of MIDI machine control (MMC). This protocol is a recent extension of the MIDI 1.0 spec, which provides for the transmission of transport-related commands via MIDI. At the time of this writing, MMC is not fully implemented into both software and hardware systems. But my crystal ball says that in the future many of you will have a MIDI jack on the back of your digital, and even an analog, multitrack recorder that will allow these devices to be controlled from computer-related hardware and software.

A digital audio workstation/multitrack recorder combination that is MMC-ready might be able to maintain control over the multitrack's transport functions directly from the hard disk or sequencing software. For example, assume you have a sequence that needs to have backing solos transferred from a sampler. You program the samples to trigger at three SMPTE time addresses that fall at the end of each chorus.

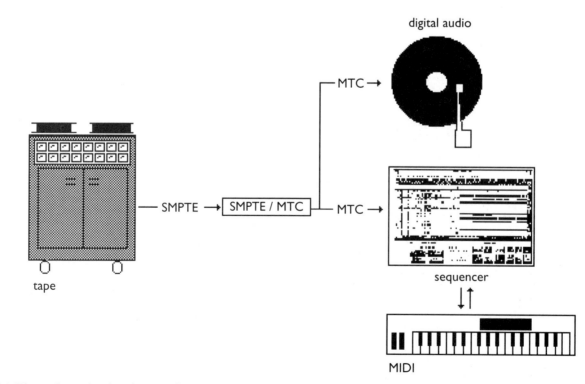

Fig. 10.4: When working with multitrack tape, random access systems will generally maintain sync by following the recorder's time code track.

Fig. 10.5: The ADAT digital multitrack recording system. (Courtesy of Alesis Corp.)

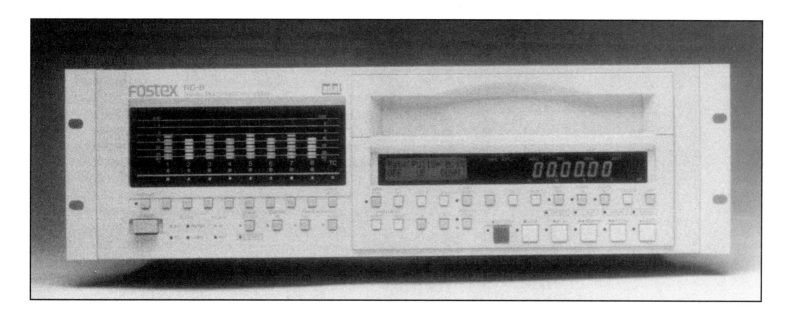

Fig. 10.6: *The RD-8 digital multitrack recorder. (Courtesy of Fostex America.)*

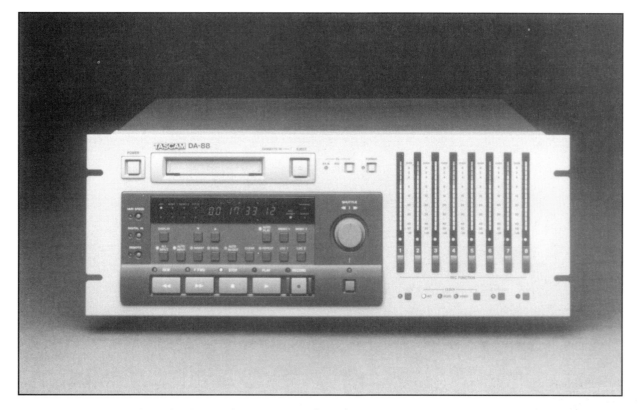

Fig. 10.7: The DA-88 digital multitrack recorder. (Courtesy of Tascam, TEAC Professional Division.)

Now that you have MMC, your next step might be to program the sequencer to place the multitrack into record on track 14 just before the sample's trigger time and then to drop out after each solo. Once done, you need only sit back and watch the system do its job under full automation. Heck, you might even be able to tell the system to chase to the next punch point so that you don't have to listen to the verses that fall between them.

MIDI Controlled Effects

A well-known fact about today's music production is that it relies heavily on signal-processing technology. With this technology, sounds can be augmented in a way that lets you re-create a natural room ambience or creatively layer effects in ways that are personal and unique. Such digital signal processors are often capable of being configured to perform a wide range of effects and dynamic signal control functions:

Auto panning	Fading
Chorusing	Flanging
Compression	Gating
De-essing	Limiting
Delay	Pitch change
Echo	Reverb
Expansion	

For many years, digital effects devices have implemented MIDI in varying degrees into their basic control and editing structure. This simple fact makes it possible for these devices to be directly integrated into a DAW or MIDI system in two possible ways:

- Direct control over program and possibly control parameters (such as delay time, depth, rate, filtering, etc.) from either a MIDI remote controller device or a computer editor/librarian program.

- Automated control over these effects and their parameters

Effects Automation Within MIDI Production

One of the simplest and most common ways to automate an effects device within a MIDI sequence or live performance is to use program change commands. Most MIDI-equipped effects devices allow effects patch data (indicating effects type and parameter information) to be named and stored in a register bank. This is similar to the same way that a characteristic sound patch can be stored into, and recalled from, an instrument's memory register. By embedding a MIDI program change command that matches a particular effects device patch within a sequence, the desired effects patch number can be called up by the device, either at the beginning of a song or at any time within it.

As an example, suppose you want to mix down a 30-second radio commercial that's being made for the Crash-O-Rama stock car races at the Behemoth dome next Saturday. The voice tracks are recorded on hard disk, while a sequence is being transmitted in sync to four electronic instruments over eight MIDI channels.

The effects need to be larger than life and are rather complex. The best way to handle this is to program the effects so that they change automatically at various times within the spot (Fig. 10.8). By assigning patch numbers to the specific effects settings needed in the commercial, you can program the sequence to transmit corresponding program changes and thus automate the scene changes on cue.

Effects Editing via MIDI

In addition to editing real-time program changes, you can often edit effects parameters (such as reverb time, delay times, EQ, and chorus depth) through the use of Systems Exclusive (Sys-Ex) messages. Sys-Ex is a protocol for communicating customized MIDI messages between MIDI devices. Control over these messages can be carried out in real-time through the use of either an external hardware-based MIDI controller or a software based one.

Computer-based editing software, known as a patch editor, is also able to edit effects parameters. This is accomplished by using a program that displays numeric values or graphics that directly represent the device's control parameter settings. Once the desired effect or effects have been edited, these settings can be named and placed into the effect device's patch bank.

After a device's bank of preset locations has been filled, a patch editor or librarian program allows patch bank data to be transmitted to the host computer by way of a system exclusive MIDI data dump. In this way, any number of effects patch banks can be stored, recalled, and loaded back into the device at any time.

Mixing in a Tapeless World

The number of physical inputs, outputs, and effects commonly encountered in most modern random access and MIDI-based facilities has increased greatly. This has caused a parallel increase in the demand on mixing requirements, both in the areas of hardware design and software programming.

Although most traditional console and mixer devices haven't changed much in recent history, electronic music production has constantly placed new demands on them. For example, a drum machine with six outputs and a sampler with eight outputs might dominate an average-sized mixer, leaving room for little else.

In such a case, a system might easily outgrow its capabilities, leaving you with the unpleasant choice of either upgrading, getting an additional mixer, or dealing with the one you have as best you can. Caveat emptor (let the buyer beware) when buying a console or mixer. It is always wise to anticipate your future growth needs.

The following sections detail a few of the mixing options that are available to those who are, or wish to be, in the MIDI and random access workaday world.

Hardware Mixers

The most popular way to handle the increased number of inputs and effects requirements is to use an outboard line mixer. These rack-mountable, high-quality devices often provide 16 or 24 line-level inputs, two or more auxiliary effects sends, and either two- or four-output channel busses. Some designs offer special "mult" inputs that allow multiple mixers to be piggybacked on one another without using additional line-level input strips.

A number of high-quality, affordable console designs are also available that are fitted with up to 32-channels, 4 or 8 auxiliary sends and 8 output channel busses. An excellent example of this type of console is the Mackie 28.8 (Fig. 10.9).

MIDI-Based Mixing

As a performance- and control-related language, MIDI is capable of transmitting both dynamic and controller information to electronic instruments that can respond to these messages (which in today's production environment is just about all of them). The artist thus has dynamic and expressive control over such parameters as velocity (individual note volume), main volume (a particular voice's output volume), and pan position (Fig. 10.10). This is accomplished by transmitting a scaled velocity or controller messages that range in value from 0 to 127.

Since these messages can be transmitted to individual instruments and/or voices within a MIDI sequence, it is possible to creatively mix a composition in the MIDI domain. Of course, the greatest benefits of MIDI-based mixing are total level settings recall, full automation, and the ability to save your mix along with the performance data.

To take better advantage of mix-related controller messages, MIDI-based programs are beginning to integrate controls such as volume faders, pan knobs, and MIDI mute buttons into their software (Fig. 10.11). These controls can be

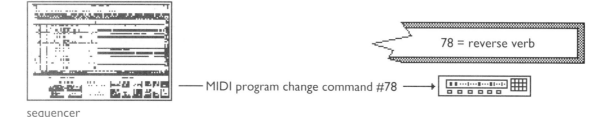

sequencer
——— MIDI program change command #78 ———➤
78 = reverse verb

Fig. 10.8: Patch settings can be easily transmitted to either MIDI instruments or MIDI-equipped effects devices via program change commands.

Fig. 10.9: Mackie 24.8 mixer. (Courtesy of Mackie Designs Inc.)

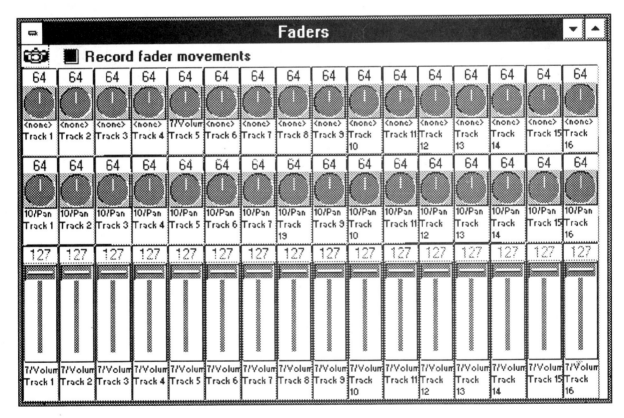

Fig. 10.10: Control over MIDI *velocity settings within Cakewalk Pro for Windows. (Courtesy of Twelve Tone Systems.)*

"pasted" onto a screen and assigned to a specific channel and controller in a way that best fits the application at hand. For example, a program might let you place a set of fader controls within the same screen as the main sequencer page. You could then record or change levels, pan positions, or other related controls in real-time.

Hardware Controllers

Sequencing and other controller programs have come a long way towards allowing easy access to on-screen mix controls. Nevertheless, much of the time you still have to go through a number of screen pages to tweak a particular volume control, pan pot, or other control parameter. As a solution

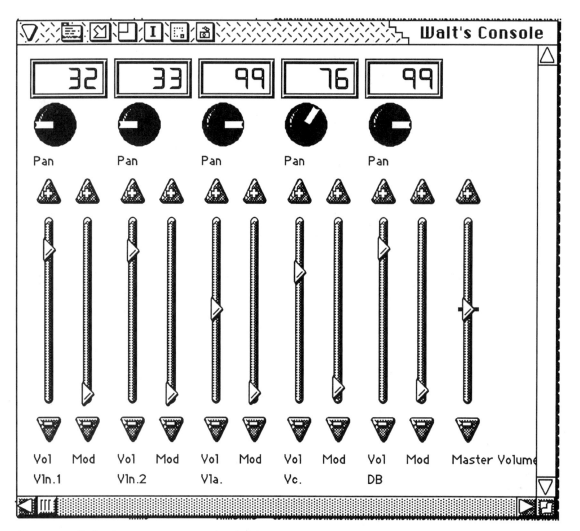

Fig. 10.11: Performer's controller-based automation. (Courtesy of Mark of the Unicorn, Inc.)

to this virtual reality dilemma, the MIDI remote controller (Fig. 10.12) was designed so that the user could simply grab and move a data slider or rotary knob in real-time.

Such a device could be easily programmed to affect continuous controller data over a number of MIDI channels or groups of channels. Controllers such as these are often equipped with either 8- or 16-data sliders, momentary buttons (for muting channels and other single-event controls), and rotary data knobs.

In recent years, a growing number of mixers have integrated MIDI into their control structure. A few have even been exclusively designed to be remotely controlled via MIDI controller messages. Mixers that are capable of responding to MIDI can be either analog or digital in nature. The degree to which a mixer can be automated will vary from one design to another (Fig. 10.13).

Typically, most medium-range recording consoles for the project studio allow their inputs to respond to MIDI mute messages. This allows inputs to be muted under automated sequence control. Others also offer some degree of level control, while a few offer an even greater range of automated control.

Other design variations allow mixer settings to be simply captured as an overall "snapshot." The settings can be saved as a patch number and recalled from MIDI through the use of the program change command.

Computer-Based Mixing Systems

Another important piece that fits into the MIDI-based mixing puzzle is the emergence of computer-based digital mixers. These mixers often exist in the software domain as the part of the digital audio workstation that takes care of signal routing and mixing functions. These systems don't pretend to be the answer to all your mixing needs. Rather, they are meant to operate in conjunction with other MIDI and hardware mixers to provide a powerful environment for mixing and automating audio that has been recorded onto hard disk.

Instead of using analog methods to change or route these signal levels, the signals are usually processed in the digital domain by using high-speed DSP processors to calculate the relative gain changes in real-time. In addition to this interesting fact, these mix functions are able to route digital signals to an internal computer application (such as an internal reverb processor or digital delay module), or they can often route digitally converted analog signals to an external destination (such as an external effects device or headphone cue amplifier).

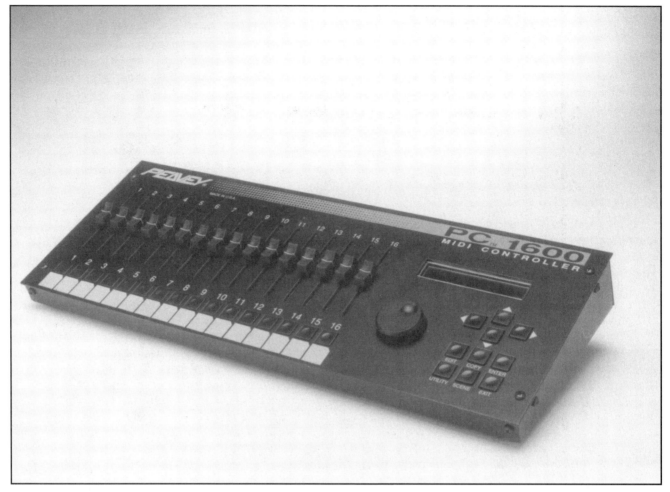

Fig. 10.12: Peavey's PC-1600 M<small>IDI</small> controller. (Courtesy of Peavey Electronics Corp.)

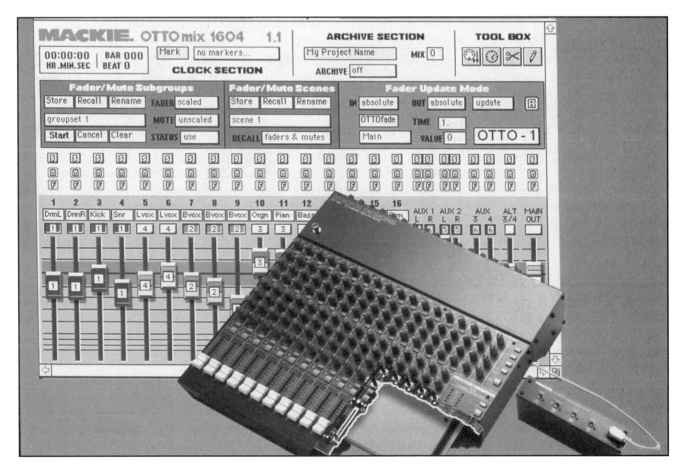

Fig. 10.13: OTTO M<small>IDI</small> automation for the Mackie 1604 mixer. (Courtesy of Mackie Designs.)

One well-known example of such a digital mixing application is integrated into Digidesign's ProTools system. This comprehensive, real-time mixing system allows any number of internal digital audio sources (such as output channels, internal effects returns, etc.) to be assigned to an input module. Each channel strip offers such provisions as channel fader, metering, solo/mute, panning, record status indicator, and two independent effects sends that can be digitally routed to a source or converted to analog for distribution.

Music Printing Programs

In recent years, the field of transcribing musical scores onto paper has been directly affected both by the personal computer and by MIDI (Fig. 10.14). This rather cumbersome process has been speeded up and improved through the introduction of new generations of computer software (known as music printing or computer scoring programs). This kind of software allows musical notation data to be automatically entered into a score directly from a MIDI sequence or real-time MIDI input; or it can be edited manually on-screen by the user.

Such software programs allow the artist to change and configure a score by using standard computer cut, copy, and paste techniques. These programs are also capable of reading the score and converting it back into MIDI data, which can then be transmitted to the various connected instruments and modules. Once you're happy with the outcome, you can easily print a hard copy printout of the sequenced song or score.

There are many examples of how music printing programs are used in the music industry. When outside musicians are contracted for, music printing programs can be invaluable for printing vocal lead sheets or instrumental parts. Musical passage or published songs can be notated for legal copyright purposes. Modern orchestrators for commercials, film, studio projects, and even symphonic scoring often compose on their own MIDI system.

Once done, the final scores can be printed with little added time and effort. Besides saving time and money on transcription services, composing directly to MIDI makes it possible for the composer to hear the score before a session or performance without having to spend a fortune on union musicians.

Hard Disk Recording in the Professional Music Studio

The personal or "home" studio is now considered by many as a cost-effective and powerfully creative alternative to the high-costs of working in a professional recording facility. It provides an affordable, integrated computer-based production system that is capable of simultaneously communicating digital audio and MIDI in a systemwide fashion. Realizing this, many progressive studios have turned this lemon situation into lemonade by offering their services in a way that augments what can be produced at home or in a project facility.

For example, even though the demo on a featured song might sound great with a sampled piano, the benefits that might be gained by replacing the sequenced tracks with a 9-foot acoustic grand in a professional studio are fairly evident. Should a song call for a 35-piece gospel choir, few facilities can substitute for a recording studio that's under the technical direction of a qualified engineer.

Last, but not least. Although many personal facilities are equipped with high-quality mixing and signal-processing systems and are generally placed in a quality monitoring environment, a professional mixing room can offer distinct advantages. A professional studio's wide range of top-notch mixing and effects tools and its monitoring environment can help to ensure that what you hear in the studio is what will be heard on the radio.

PENTAGRAM

by Homer G. Lambrecht

© 1990 Homer G. Lambrecht

Fig. 10.14: Example of a score that has been notated using Finale. (Courtesy of Coda Music Software.)

In the final analysis, personal and professional facilities each bring their own strengths to a production. You must decide which is best for your project's needs.

From a purely technical standpoint, random access audio is as deeply entrenched in the recording studio as it is in most other aspects of audio production. As will be evident, the ways in which random access audio is applied will often change to best suit a sound medium that primarily deals with the art and business of acoustic recording.

Music Tracking

At this writing, digital and analog tape is still the medium of choice for recording multitrack audio. However, this does not mean that multitrack recording to disk isn't possible or even done on a regular basis. It's just a simple truth that random-access multitrack recording currently takes a backseat to its tape-based predecessor.

The reasons for this are twofold. First, the storage requirements that are needed to store continuous multichannel data can add up very quickly. As I write this, high-capacity, erasable optical disks are only just becoming feasible as a fast-access, removable storage medium. Until this time, hard disk was the only viable medium. This meant having to back up and load multiple hard drives for each and every session. Even with this provision, memory real-estate limited your recording time.

The second aspect that reduces the need for multichannel random access is the fact that acoustic music recording is often linear in nature. It doesn't have to be, but it often is. For example, an acoustic drum set could easily take up six channels on a machine and could play during an entire performance. A situation like this could quickly eat away at a system's storage memory. A digital or analog recorder could care less about such a memory consideration.

In the end, the multitrack recorder and the multichannel hard disk recorder each have their own advantages and can be mixed and matched in a production environment at will.

Sample Triggering

It's common knowledge that drum machines and sampled percussion sounds can provide an easy way to achieve high quality performance and rhythm sounds in the studio. However, sample technology can be applied to music production in another way. This involves the use of samplefile triggering.

The term trigger refers to a sample's ability to be accessed and reproduced from RAM through the use of an event start switch. The switch can be initiated manually (by pressing a button, hitting a trigger pad, or playing on a MIDI performance keyboard), or it can be "fired" under time-code automation or as a sequenced MIDI event.

The following sections outline only a few of the ways that samplefile triggering can be applied to music technology, both in the studio and on stage.

Sample Fly-Ins

In addition to being used for performance sampling, samples are commonly used in the music and sound production environment for a fly-in. A fly-in (a term originally taken from the phrase "on-the-fly") refers to the placement of a sampled vocal or instrumental phrase at one or more points within an existing composition.

This is best explained by example. Assume that you are doing a Hip Hop dance remix of a tune that did well on the dance music circuit. Armed with a copy of the original multitrack master, the producer decides that he wants to lift a vocal phrase from one of the group's other hits and fly it into this remix. Fortunately, one of the group's members sampled that sound off the original master and can get a DAT copy to you this afternoon.

After loading the sample back into a sampler, you lock a sequencer up to the master tape and program the trigger times into it at the appropriate measures (Fig. 10.15). Then you need only place an open track on the multitrack into record and let the sequencer trigger the sounds at just the right times.

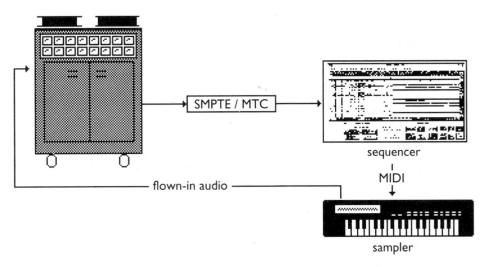

Fig. 10.15: Example of how an audio track might be flown onto multitrack tape.

This flown-in segment could just as well have been a sampled set of background vocals, a guitar riff, a number of vocal samples for flying in the lead vocals . . . you name it. The only thing you need to guard against with this approach is the possibility of overusing a sample and wearing out its welcome.

There are also several ways that samples can be flown in. They can be loaded into a sampler and triggered manually from a music keyboard or a MIDI sequencer. Certain samplers are able to trigger internal samples at defined time-code times, making it possible to trigger directly from the code recorded on the master tape. Alternatively, the samples can be transferred onto hard disk and triggered directly from disk, according to event times that are encoded into a playlist.

Sample Replacement

Another way that sample technology can apply to the day-to-day workings of studio production is through sample replacement. This application makes it possible for recorded sounds that are recurring in nature to be replaced by a sampled sound. "Recurring," in this case, refers to (but isn't limited to) percussion sounds. This process can replace one sound with another, particularly sounds that were poorly recorded or have a lot of leakage from other tracks.

As an example, let's return to the Hip Hop dance remix. The producer wants to replace the kick and snare drums that have been recorded onto tape with some killer sounds that are one of

his trademarks. To keep the original human feel of the acoustic kick and snare tracks, you simply replace them by using the recorded signal to trigger the two samples (Fig. 10.16).

By plugging the tape track outputs directly into two of the sampler's trigger inputs, you begin to hear the new samples . . . not bad. The only problem is that there's a noticeable lag in the trigger times of both samples. Even though the trigger inputs are supposed to be really fast, there's still a delay between what comes off tape and the sample trigger times. Still, no problem.

When you are working with an analog multi-track recorder, you can place the kick and snare tracks into the sync mode. Placing these tracks into "sync" causes the trigger signals to be reproduced off the record head. The outputs are thus being played back in advance of the other signals that are playing back off the reproduce head. The next step is to introduce a digital delay into both lines and then use this signal to drive the trigger inputs (Fig. 10.17). By delaying both tracks, it's a simple matter to alter the trigger times so that both samples are brought back in sync with the rest of the recorded tracks.

As you can see, this process is relatively simple when you're using an analog machine. However, if the tape was recorded using a digital machine, you don't really have this luxury, since these recorders don't have a sync head. In this situation, the best that you can hope for is to trigger the samples by using a triggering device that has a very fast response time and doesn't introduce appreciable lag times.

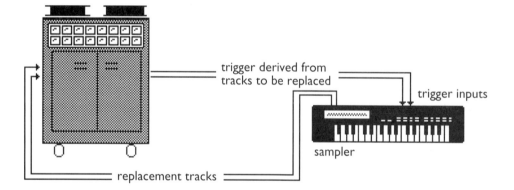

Fig. 10.16: Example of how a sampler might be used to replace existing tracks on a multitrack tape.

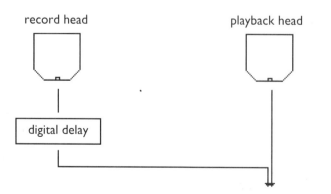

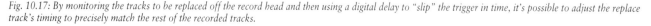

Fig. 10.17: By monitoring the tracks to be replaced off the record head and then using a digital delay to "slip" the trigger in time, it's possible to adjust the replace track's timing to precisely match the rest of the recorded tracks.

Live Triggered Sound

Triggered sample technology is also very much alive and well in live performance (both in the studio and on stage). Besides the traditional keyboard performance sampler, triggered samples are used to generate or augment existing acoustic sounds.

One obvious example is the use of electronic trigger pads that are placed alongside acoustic drums to fire percussive or other expressive sounds. In addition to using electronic playing pads, it's also possible to use the signal output of a microphone or contact pickup to trigger a recorded sample. Both of these methods will generally function by generating a voltage signal that, in turn, is used to fire the trigger's detection circuit.

A number of multiple-input trigger devices are available on the market. They detect the individual trigger inputs and generate a programmable MIDI note event. This feature has also been designed into a few drum machine designs, including the Alesis D4.

An acquaintance of mine who is an ethnic foot percussionist has devised an ingenious application of sample triggering. She has brought triggered events into her life by designing a portable stage that has an array of trigger sensors built into its dancing surface. These sensors not only trigger complex samples but also trigger lights that are designed into the stage. Her show often involves a variety of live musicians, and the live performance can be sequenced and looped on the-fly, allowing her to interact with complex rhythms that were danced just seconds before.

Random Access Editing

Random access audio has many novel uses in home, project, and professional facilities during the production phase. However, its use as a post-production editing tool is its biggest strength.

The editing of a mixed song or series of compositions into a final product can take many forms. Modern-day editors are capable of gain and fade changes, accurate digital equalization, pitch changes, time changes, and full edit capabilities.

On the applications front, hard disk edit technology can be used to alter and assemble a song or project in numerous ways. For example, at least one world-class symphony orchestra records compositions as a series of short passages and uses a hard disk editor to check for continuity, after which the passages are assembled into the finished product during a final edit session.

Formatting individual songs into a final "album" project is a particular strength that is shared by playlist editors. These editors have plenty of hard disk space (a 600Mb/1-hour disk is usually sufficient for most projects). This process is simply done by loading the final song masters onto the hard disk in any order. By defining and naming each song as a region, you can easily arrange each song into the order of the finished release. Of course, you'll have to record silence and define a few regions (1 sec, 3 sec, etc.) so that they can be placed between the songs.

Once done, you can audition the song transitions to see how they work out. If you want to change the order, simply move the song position in the playlist and check the new results.

Here are two points that could improve your final results. Even though you placed a defined length of silence between each song, you can easily cut out portions of the silence to adjust the "feel" of the transition timing. Also, those systems that are capable of changing the gain of a soundfile (particularly real-time gain changes) can be used to adjust any discrepancies in gain that might exist between songs a valuable tool that shouldn't be overlooked.

Compact Disc Recording Systems

Until recently, if an audio program needed to be recorded onto compact disc, the entire process of cutting a CD master and then fabricating the discs had to be undertaken. This process is often too labor-intensive and expensive to be an option if you want a limited number of discs. It is also time intensive, taking weeks or even months. So what are your options if you want just a few discs or a single disc . . . and you want it now?

Fortunately, the development of write-once optical disk technology has made it possible for digital data to be optically encoded onto such a disc in the CD format. The result is a recordable audio media called CD-Write Once, often better known as Compact Disc Recordable, or CD-R. The words "compact disc" refer to the fact that program material that has been recorded onto a disc will play back on any standard CD player.

With the advent of CD recording technology, it's now a simple matter for fully compatible CDs to be recorded on site in limited quantities. These discs can be used in various ways:

- To create a "test pressing" of a recorded project that could be taken home by a producer, musician, record executive, etc., and played back on a number of systems and in different environments.

- To record music segments or "stings" that could be easily played back on a CD player at the beginning or end of a radio or TV program (or during it).

- To record broadcast commercials, promotional spots, station logos, and IDs.

- To create programmable sound effects, music, and speech for theme parks, museums, sales displays, and industrial displays.

- As a backup archive for an audio project, sound effects, etc.

- To create your own personal sound effects or sample library.

CD recorders work basically by encoding digital audio data onto a disc in a way that conforms to the "Orange Book" (CD-R) standard. Audio data encoded onto disc according to this standard doesn't need to be recorded all in one sitting but can be added as the user sees fit.

The short-term drawback to this method is that such a disc cannot be played back on standard CD players. This is due to the fact that a table of contents (TOC) file hasn't yet been encoded onto the disc. A TOC is a basic lookup table that is encoded at the beginning of each disc. It includes information pertaining to subcode data, index numbering, timing information, emphasis, copy prohibit data, etc.

Once all the audio data has been recorded onto the disc, it can be prepared or programmed to include a TOC file. This process makes the disc conform to "Red Book" (CD-audio) standards, ideally meaning that it can be played on any commercial CD player.

The way in which the audio and TOC data are written to disc and programmed by the user will vary between systems. However, the user and programming interface can be broken down into three blurry categories:

- Self-contained system

- Integrated system

- Stand-alone system

In a self-contained system (Fig. 10.18), the optical drive, processing circuits, and control systems are designed into a single package. These devices are usually straightforward in their disc preparation procedures and can receive track and index information from an external source (such as a DAT recorder or digital audio workstation).

In an integrated system design, the optical drive and processing system are contained in their own hardware housings. However, the programming and control environment is entirely in the software domain.

Often these disc preparation/control systems are designed to work in conjunction with a DAW or hard disk editing program. Selections can be manipulated and assembled in a random access fashion, either through the use of on-screen markers (indicating the beginning of an index, etc.) or by placing defined regions into a sequential playlist.

An example of such a software-based CD maker is Masterlist CD from Digidesign (Fig. 10.19). This system allows CD masters that are encoded with complete PQ subcodes to be created on a Macintosh using Digidesign's ProTools or SoundTools audio interface and editing software and can be directly transferred to any number of affordable SCSI controlled CD recorders (or 8mm Exabyte tape drive in the DDP format).

The finished Red-Book compatible master can then be accepted at the duplication plant for direct transfer to a glass master, thus eliminating the need for 1610/1630 transfers and separate PQ code entries by those who may be less familiar with a project than you are.

Finally, the term "stand-alone system" loosely denotes a professional package, such as Digidesign's Masterlist CD, that contains all of the necessary hardware and programming systems for cutting a compact disc. The major difference is the fact that the software (which often makes use of an internal processor) is not integrated into another computer-based audio environment. Instead, the TOC programming must be independently entered into the system before any audio can be recorded onto disc.

Fig. 10.18: The Marantz CDR610 Compact Disc Recorder and remote control. (Courtesy of Marantz Professional Products/Superscope Technologies, Inc.)

Chapter 11

Hard Disk Recording Within Audio-for-Visual Production

In recent years, there has been a great increase in the use of random-access audio systems within all phases of TV and film post-production. This is true not only for the creative process of music scoring and sound effects production, but also for the actual assembly, re-recording and mixing of dialog, effects, and background presence tracks into a finished soundtrack.

This chapter examines how random access systems have affected audio production for the visual media. It also looks at a number of practical applications that have been changed by this technology.

Advantages of Random Access Audio

The extensive use of random access audio (Fig. 11.1) in the TV and film media is attributable to such key factors as:

- Increased production speed
- Simplified access to cataloged soundfile data
- Time-slip capabilities
- Time compression and expansion

Increased Production Speed

The increased production speed that random-access audio systems offer is obviously due to their random access nature. For example, when traditional tape-based systems are used, complex synchronizers are needed to maintain total control over all transport and sync functions. This almost always means that the tape-based audio recorder has to physically "chase" a master video or film transport when shuttling in the forward and rewind directions and then nudge into sync when playing back and recording.

Although you don't lose a lot of time during the actual chase and sync process, an extra 30 seconds here and a minute there can easily add up over the course of a session. By contrast, a disk-based system can generally achieve synchronous lock in less than a few seconds. You simply rewind the videotape, press the play button, and before you know it, you're locked up.

Simplified Access to Cataloged Soundfile Data

Access to soundfile data can be fast and easy. If you have a large enough hard drive, or if you have removable opticals or multiple drives, you can have instantaneous on-line access to dialog, background, and effects soundfiles.

For example, suppose you need the sound of frogs croaking. After searching several nature-sound CD libraries for lakeside frogs, you find the effect you want on track 21 of a certain disc. Now you need only transfer a copy of these sounds to the main production disk, edit it if necessary, and you're in business.

Time-Slip Capabilities

One of the greatest advantages that comes with combining random access audio with visual media production is the ability to slip audio events in time. Time slipping refers to the movement in time of a visually related sound effect or dialog with respect to the picture.

For example, suppose you are working on a TV commercial spot for a haunted house. You decide to add a sound effect to accent the closing of a coffin. First, you need the sound. Since it doesn't seem to exist on any of your effects CDs, you improvise by pitching the sound of a door-slam way down and then adding some reverb. Perfect! Second, you need to place the effect. If you were

Fig. 11.1: A hard disk recording system in an audio-for-visual production setting. (Courtesy of OSC.)

working with multitrack tape, you'd have to place it by either manually or automatically triggering the effect at the appropriate event time. If your timing was off, you'd have to re-record the effect until you got it just right.

However, since you are using a disk-based system, all you have to do is record the effect as a soundfile (and possibly define it as a region) and then instruct the system to play the effect at a specified SMPTE event time. If the effect is placed too early or too late, you can easily slip it in time by entering a new SMPTE start time (Fig. 11.2).

Random access soundfile data can be synchronously placed into a program in a number of ways. Predictably, the two most common methods are:

- Soundfile/samplefile triggering

- Continuous sync

Sounds that are short in duration (such as sound effects, a series of successive sounds, background sounds, or incidental off screen dialog) can be programmed to trigger at a specific time-code address. Once triggered, the digital timing reference will be taken from the hard disk recorder or sampling system.

Sounds that require absolute timing accuracy (such as on-screen dialog and important background sounds) will most often be played back in a continuous sync manner. This means that once a sound is triggered, its timing reference will be

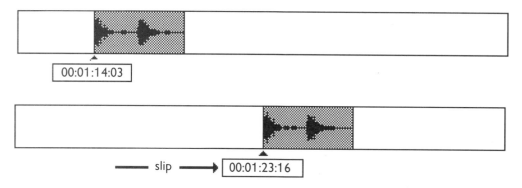

Fig. 11.2: A region's trigger time can be slipped forward or backward.

derived from a master timing source (such as house sync or time code as it exists on the master videotape).

Time Compression and Expansion

Another DSP tool that is well suited to random access audio-for-visual production is time compression and expansion. As you saw in Chapter 8, by combining both sample rate and pitch shift technology, it's possible to alter a program's duration and pitch.

By varying both pitch and duration in relative proportions, you can change a program's length without affecting its pitch. For example, a hardware- or software-based system might allow a dialog track to be slowed down along with a video track, while maintaining its original pitch. You can also use these systems to "stretch" or "squeeze" a program or effect to fit a desired length. For example, a 28-second background music track could be easily processed to precisely fit into a 30-second time span.

Digital Video

With the significant increases in available hard disk or disc space and increases in processing speed has come the ability to record, display and manipulate digital video images directly on your computer's screen. Such a handy little feature can give us capabilities that certainly aren't limited to but include:

- The ability to put together your own little multimedia video extravaganza

- Allows a professional audio-for-film or -video production engineer to assemble effects or mix a visual score to picture without the need for an additional video deck or monitor.

- Allows for a film or video production to be edited to time code in a random access fashion without the need for additional hardware.

As this last option indicates, the elimination of extraneous video hardware is often a plus, but the real advantage to desktop digital video is the fact that it is random access in nature. This means that any scene or frame can be called up without the associated delays of slow video tape wind and the time required for audio to sync up to a video track is virtually instantaneous. Of course, all of this adds up to a tremendous savings in time.

It also bears mentioning, that although digital video eats up disk memory at a rate that far surpasses digital audio's memory requirements, recent advances in video compression schemes have brought disk space requirements to a level that can be afforded by both the professional audio post-production facility and serious desktop professional.

Phases in Audio-for-Visual Post-production

The following sections briefly detail the more important aspects of audio-for-visual post-production. By no means does every project involve all of these phases. There is a wide variety of phases, depending on the project's complexity and budget. This discussion presents an overview of how the audio for a project having a medium-to-large budget might be assembled and produced in a partial or fully random access environment.

Spotting

Often, the first step in audio post-production involves searching for and arranging in logical order the numerous dialog or effects cues that were recorded at the time of the original shoot. This process, known as spotting, often includes the search for and logging of additional sound cues that didn't exist on the original source recordings but that need to be placed into the program at a later time. In short, spotting is the process of planning out the various elements that go into the creation of a video or film soundtrack.

During this preparatory process, an effects editor reviews videotape dubs of the original video or film footage. These dubs include a visible window that indicates the original time-code address locations, which can be read at any forward or reverse shuttle speed, including still-frame. By viewing a staggering amount of footage, the editor is able to locate the desired dialog, background, and effects takes, as well as to create a detailed log that precisely notes their SMPTE in-and-out location points.

The final result of this phase is a written edit decision list (EDL) that can be used within the next phase (laydown) to assemble the various source and effects sounds into an edited master tape or disk-based playlist.

Laydown

Once a project has been spotted, the next phase is transferring the synchronized source audio tracks from the original field tapes or videotapes to a multitrack tape recorder or hard disk-based system. This process, known as the laydown phase, can be transferred either in a computer-assisted on-line fashion or manually.

At this point, the process of transferring audio to a tape-based or a random access system will begin to differ. When transferring audio from the original source tapes to a multitrack tape recorder, a basic time-code "map" must be built from the edit decision list.

This map provides detailed time code and offset instructions for copying the source tapes onto the multitrack tape in a synchronous and sequential order. Once the transfer process has been carried out, the resulting sound edits will be in perfect sync with the final edited videotape or film print.

The transfer process can be complicated and lengthy, and there is little room for timing errors, since any discrepancy will be physically recorded onto the tape and must be re-recorded.

In contrast, the process of transferring synchronous audio onto a disk-based system can be much easier because the data isn't physically recorded onto a fixed medium. During a random-access laydown session, the original source data can be recorded to disk without requiring a complicated synchronization system.

You need only transfer the original source audio onto disk, along with its original or regenerated time-code address information. Once transferred, you can enter the edit decision list into the system as a time-encoded playlist. The playlist would be used to trigger each soundfile at the appropriate times in synchronous lock with incoming time code (Fig. 11.3).

Of course, a major advantage to laying down source audio, sound effects, and background presence in a random access environment is the ability to slip or offset individual events in time with almost no fuss. With such a system, it's also a simple matter to replace original dialog with rebuilt tracks or to add effects or presence tracks at a later time without having to worry about the physical constraints of tape.

Automatic Dialog Replacement

Whenever a video or film project has been shot on location, some of the original dialog or presence tracks (background sounds in a scene) will be less than ideal. For example, suppose that during a complex oil well explosion scene costing mega bucks, the hero runs into the camera shot and delivers an emotional line. Unfortunately, just at that moment, an off-camera gas canister misfires, rendering the line unusable.

What can be done? The scene was much too expensive to reshoot. Fortunately, there is a solution. The dialog track can be re-recorded back at the studio during a process that is known as automatic dialog replacement (ADR), or looping.

The term "looping" refers to the practice of continually repeating short segments of film or video. These loops are synchronously locked to a recording medium (such as mag film, tape recorder, or more recently a hard disk recorder) in a way that lets the actor see and hear the dialog that is to be replaced. Using this process, the actor can work to match the tone and inflections of the original dialog.

Once the performance has been mastered, the engineer switches off the original audio (allowing the artist to better concentrate and to reduce the possibility of leakage onto the replaced track). The

Fig. 11.3: In certain systems, edit decision lists can be directly entered into the system in order to speed up the post-production process. (Courtesy of Solid State Logic.)

rebuilt audio is recorded onto the fresh tracks for later resynchronization to the final edited film (Fig. 11.4). This process is continued until all required tracks have been properly rebuilt.

In the past, synchronized magnetic tape or multitrack tape recorders were used to record replaced dialog. However, the most flexible medium is by far the hard disk recorder. When locked to a video recorder that's been programmed to continuously loop between specific time-encoded address points, it's possible for a hard disk recorder to quickly sync to the video source and record and save various dialog takes to disk as a soundfile.

Since these dialog tracks are recorded onto a random access medium, you can quickly review alternate takes and then edit the best parts of several takes into a single performance.

Digital Audio Research has designed a unique approach to ADR into its SoundStation family of random access systems. This approach involves a DSP process called WORDFIT. It helps a sound editor "hit the mark" on the first pass by electronically comparing the newly recorded replacement track with the original location sound recording. The replacement track is digitally sampled and time-compressed or expanded in a way that maintains proper pitch while fitting the articulation of the replacement track to the movement of the actor's lips as they appear on the screen.

According to the manufacturer, this DSP process is accurate to within one hundredth of a second. Elements that were previously out of sync by as much as a second or more can now be precisely synchronized.

Sound Effects

In the same way that strong visual effects now play an important role in modern video and film production, sound effects, or SFX, can also have a profound supportive impact upon a visual medium. For example, where would the morally derailed TV show "Pee Wee's Playhouse" have been without its seemingly endless stream of funky sound effects? And, when a member of Star Trek's crew beams down to a planet, would this effect have the same impact without the obligatory "shimmering" sound?

Sound effects come in all shapes and sizes, and many people have devoted their lives to collecting these sounds so that they can be used in increasingly creative ways. The following sections briefly detail many of the ways that these effects can be achieved or commercially purchased.

Live Sound Effects

When a film or video is being shot on location, the most effective sound effect that can be captured onto tape is sometimes the original on- or off-camera effect. In this situation, the goal of the sound recordist is to capture the original synchronous sound onto tape as cleanly as possible.

In the post-production phase, the sound can be transferred to a multitrack recorder at the appropriate time or triggered from a sampler or hard disk recorder. If the effect is just too good to pass up, you might want to save it to DAT tape or onto a personal sound-effects archive disk.

Foley

In the early 1940s, a sound mixer named George Foley designed a process by which on-camera background sounds that had been lost through the ADR process could be replaced with relative ease.

This process, now known as Foley, is accomplished through much the same process as ADR, in that the picture and existing field tracks are repeatedly looped until the "Foley artist" has a basic feel for the effect. Once ready, the performed effect can be recorded onto a synchronous storage medium for layback into the sound track during the mixdown phase.

Replacing on- or off-camera sounds can call for any number of Foley props that can be used in innumerable situations. One of the mainstay props of a studio that regularly does Foley is the Foley stage.

Basically, this stage is a variable-surface floor that might include hardwood, gravel, cement, and other types of areas needed to reproduce the various footstep sounds commonly encountered in a film or video. Beyond these surfaces, the sky's the limit for the range of ingenious props that are used to replace flawed or nonexistent original effects.

time-encoded video dub

hard disk recorder

Fig. 11.4: Graphic mockup of an ADR session.

At this point you might ask, "Why use a live recorded effect when there are countless prerecorded sound effect tracks to choose from?" This question has been the subject of many a debate. Basically there are three points of view. One camp says go ahead and use prerecorded effects samples, while another says that the vast number of unique situations and nuances needed to properly recreate an effect requires the skills of a live effects artist. A middle ground view might make use of both, depending on the situation (and budget).

Certain prerecorded effects might work just fine, while others might fail miserably. For example, the varied inflections occurring in just a few footsteps or in a series of door knocks can be quite surprising. Repeated monotone samples can sometimes be more noticeable than no effect at all. That's not to say that creative manipulation of prerecorded samples can't save your day. Necessity is truly the mother of creative invention.

CD Effects/Music Library

In addition to originally recorded effects or background sounds (often referred to as presence), another popular source is the sound effects and music library (Fig. 11.5).

The sound effects library is designed to offer an array of easily accessible music tracks, sound effects, and presence tracks on compact disc. A huge variety of SFX libraries are currently available for use with broadcast and audio production, although they often vary in their degree of comprehensiveness. Some SFX libraries focus on specific types or categories of sounds. For example, libraries might be placed into such categories as animal sounds, comedy music and effects, 5-15-30 second music stings for commercial radio and TV, nature sounds, etc.

Triggering Methods

In random access production, one can find more than one way to accomplish an audio-related task. Sound effects triggering is no exception.

The degree of involvement and triggering methods will often depend on the complexity and the general demands of the task at hand. In addition to triggering an effects soundfile directly from hard disk, other approaches involve triggering sounds from CD or from a sampling device.

Triggering from a CD

One of the simplest and most straightforward ways to create an effect is by triggering a sound directly from CD. Since these effects are already stored onto CD and are indexed for easy access, you can simply play the effect at the appropriate time. For background sounds and other effects that don't require precise timing, you can trigger the sound manually by taking the machine out of pause at the right time.

Whenever precise timing is required, professional CD players with external triggering can be used. The external triggering is done by using a synchronizer or other device that can read SMPTE or MIDI time code. The device then outputs a trigger voltage at a programmed event time (Fig. 11.6).

Multiple disc systems are able to place the database cataloging, access, and triggering of comprehensive sound effects and/or music libraries under automated computer control. These automated library and sound organizers are generally designed to revolve around CD "jukebox" systems, which are capable of holding 60 or more discs at a time.

When placed under software control, these jukebox systems are capable of accessing titles according to classification, length, musical style, effect type, etc. This feature makes it much easier to access effects that are loaded into the system. For example, during a spotting session for a cartoon soundtrack, you could easily request to listen to all "boing" or "twangy" spring sounds. Once you found the right one from your comedy sounds disc, you could enter it into an events playlist for direct time-code triggering during the mixdown phase, or you could load the effect directly onto hard disk.

Triggering from a Sample

If a large number of fast-paced effects cues are called for during a passage, sample triggering is a good choice. It's a fairly straightforward task to load the effects into a sampler and then map the effects across the keys of a MIDI keyboard. By connecting a sequencer that has been synchronized to picture, you can then build up the effects scene by using standard MIDI or events list techniques.

Processed Effects

In a connected digital audio environment, a number of DSP tools are at your disposal for processing or otherwise changing an effect to match what the visual image calls for. For example, suppose that a particular scene in a film calls for the sound of an old western windmill that's slowly turning in the wind. Of course, the best sound for the situation might have been a field recording of the windmill itself. However, this didn't happen since the recordist was afraid of heights and wasn't about to climb the mill's scaffolds to get a reasonably clean sound.

By default, the task falls to you, the sound editor. You don't have a recording of a mill, but you do have a CD effects disc that includes a recording of a squeaky hand crank. By pitching the sample of the hand crank down about an octave, you are able to resample and loop a few crank revolutions in such a way that the sound fits into the picture in perfect sync.

The moral to this little story is simply that sampled sounds can be creatively processed and don't have to be used as is. By pitch shifting, reversing, time compressing, or even resynthesizing these sounds, you might be personally rewarded with effects cues that range from being totally unobtrusive to wonderfully strange and unnatural.

Fig. 11.5: *The Hollywood Edge family of CD libraries. (Courtesy of The Hollywood Edge.)*

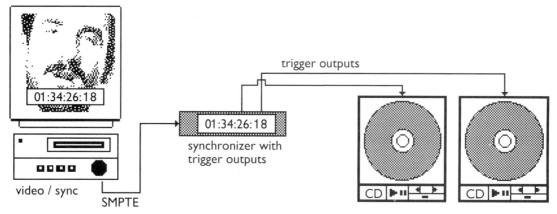

Fig. 11.6: *Professional CD systems can be slaved to time code in order to accurately trigger effects and music.*

Chapter 12

Hard Disk Recording Within the Broadcast Industry

In recent years, the broadcast industry has shown a strong interest in random-access audio systems and has begun to integrate these systems into many of its production networks. The main reason for this can be summed up in the phrase "time is money" an expression that's long been a driving force behind media production.

Digital quality and the ability to access audio data with little or no lag time is of tremendous benefit in both the preproduction and the on-the-air programming phases. However, for station owners and accountants, it's the automation benefits of random access programming that make their eyes light up.

Benefits of Hard Disk Recording

On the preproduction side, hard disk recording offers the same advantages to broadcast as it does to other media. For example, a hard disk recorder or multichannel workstation could be an instrumental tool for editing and producing in-house commercials, dialog tracks, news programs and segments, station IDs, etc.

Let's take the example of a news segment. Suppose you are editing an interview that took place between a national personality and the Emir of Kuwait. During this interview, translations were not made while the questions and answers were being given but instead were made between responses. Since the final program is to time out at 15 minutes, you have ahead a big editing job.

Using a tape recorder and a trusty razor blade, you could expect to be editing for the better part of an afternoon. Using a computer-based hard disk editor, you can reduce the same session to only slightly over an hour. In addition to increased speed, this type of non-destructive editing has

another advantage over tape: you can correct a bad edit more easily or make changes in the program at a later time.

On the down side, all is not sweetness and light when working in a tapeless environment. All too often, simple carelessness, hardware incompatibilities, and software problems result in lost data and major headaches. When in doubt, and even when you're not, always have a backup of your data, either on tape or on disk.

The Role of the Compact Disc in Broadcast Production

In addition to revolutionizing the music and consumer audio industries, the CD has been widely accepted by the broadcast industries ever since its inception in 1982. The all-too-familiar clicks and pops of records were gone from the CD, and "disc" jockeys could easily cue up a song by simply entering its index number and pressing play at the right time.

Automation

Besides the advantage in quality, a major advantage of the CD is automation. The automation of on-the-air programming from CD can take several forms, ranging from simple operator assistance to full program automation. To one degree or another, the basic concept behind each of these approaches is events triggering.

As an example, an operator-assisted system might consist of two professional CD players both operated from a single control panel (Fig. 12.1). By programming the controller, you could cue up a CD on transport #2 so that 2 seconds after transport #1 finishes playing a song the second one will trigger and begin playing a new song. In essence, this example makes use of a short, simple playlist that contains triggering instructions:

1. end of song on transport #1
2. wait 2 seconds
3. trigger transport #2

In the not-so-distant past, a radio station's automation system often made use of two or more reel-to-reel tape machines that played back program material at slow tape speeds. Of course, these slow speeds resulted in poor quality, lots of noise, and wow and flutter problems. A current random access system, by contrast, can completely eliminate these problems by providing an environment that can control and trigger compact discs and other soundfile storage media according to a preprogrammed on-the-air playlist.

A key component to such an automation system, that can store and handle up to 200 compact discs at one time, is known as a CD jukebox. When placed under computer control (Fig. 12.2), a CD jukebox can be automated to search, load, and trigger sound effects and/or on-the-air programming according to a sequential or time-encoded playlist.

Another side benefit to an automation system is that audio material no longer has to be recorded to tape in real time. Instead of merely copying the audio to tape, only the disc and index information have to be entered into the playlist. The speed and flexibility of being able to search for a particular

artist or title, songs in the current top billboard rating, a musical category, a certain time period, and other related information from a computer database can substantially reduce the time needed to assemble a program's playlist.

The Cart Machine

In its original form, the analog cart machine is a simple tape-based machine that can record and/or play back short audio segments. These segments are made up of advertisement commercials, station identifications, public service spots, and other station-related program material. The term cart refers to the fact that each segment is recorded onto tape that has been loaded into a special cartridge. Once recorded, these "carts" can be labeled and organized for easy access.

Of course, in recent times the venerable analog cart has had competition from random-access digital counterparts: the hard disk recorder and the recordable CD.

The Hard Disk Recorder as a Cart Machine

Because a hard disk is easily recorded, edited, and accessed, it is often useful as a random-access replacement for the cart machine. The lack of removability one of the greatest objections to using a hard disk in this application has been recently solved by the introduction of optical drives that are recordable and have fast-access times.

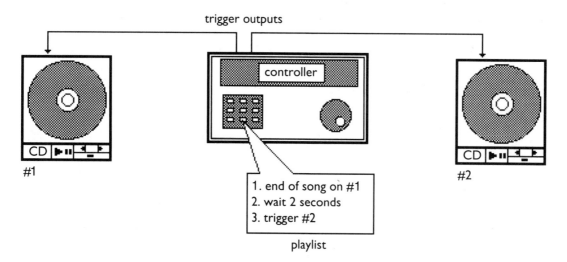

Fig. 12.1: *Example of a professional CD playback system in a semi-automated environment.*

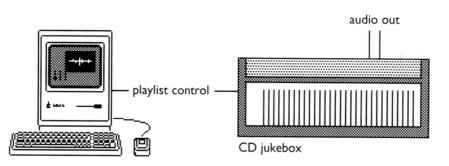

Fig. 12.2: *A computer can be used to fully automate CD jukebox systems.*

Removable drives can offer up to an hour of CD-quality programming, which is generally enough to record the most commonly used station IDs, stings, and maybe even commercial spots. (A sting is a short effect that usually accentuates an event or dialog; for example, applause or a short Bart Simpson quip.) If all of the necessary sound-files can't be recorded onto a single disk, a second drive could be added to provide automated on-line access. Otherwise, the optical discs can simply be swapped at the appropriate times.

Again, the obvious advantages of loading program soundfiles onto disk are the easy access and the system automation. Musical and effects stings can be fired much faster and more spontaneously when triggered from disk. As an example, some software programs let the user trigger sound cues directly from a computer keyboard. Firing a "You Won A Zillion Dollars!" sound cue might be as simple as clicking a mouse or pressing a single function key (Fig. 12.3).

In an automated system, these hard disk sound-files could easily be programmed into the on-the-air playlist and triggered at the appropriate times between CD song titles.

The CD Cart Recorder as a Cart Machine

In addition to being stored on hard or optical disk, soundfile data can be recorded and played back onto CD in a pseudo-cart form by using a CD recording system. This is useful when a station needs to record and play back in-house program information. With a CD recorder, a station could "burn" any number of CDs, each of which might contain station IDs, commercials, or stings. Probably the greatest advantage to this approach is the ability to locate a particular soundfile by its index number and play back this sound cue from any standard CD player.

Recall from Chapter 10 that CD recorders produce CDs according to two standards:

- The Orange Book standard
- The Red Book standard

The Orange Book standard allows soundfile data to be recorded onto a CD. However, since no table of contents (TOC) has been encoded onto the disc, it can't be played back on any CD player and usually not even on other CD recording systems. The advantage to this standard is that additional material can be recorded onto the disc at a later time.

After all the information that you need has been recorded onto a recordable CD, you can program and encode a TOC at the header of the disc. Once that is done, the disc conforms to the Red Book standard and will play back on any CD player.

As of this writing, Denon America has created one exception to this basic rule by creating a compatible CD recorder and a CD player. This system allows discs that have been recorded according to the Orange Book standard to be played on their own CD cart players. An obvious advantage is that more information can be recorded onto a disc (up to 63 minutes worth). And, at a later time, a TOC can still be generated by the CD cart recorder so that the disc can be played on any standard CD recorder.

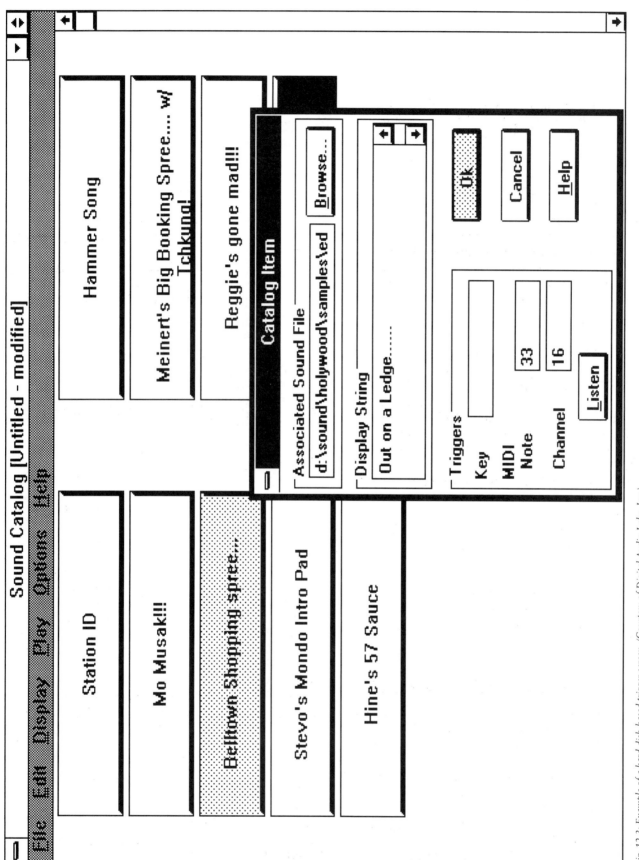

Fig. 12.3: Example of a hard-disk-based trigger screen. (Courtesy of Digital Audio Labs, Inc.)

Bibliography

The following books, brochures, manuals, and magazine articles provided valuable source material for this book and are recommended to anyone desiring more information about topics related to hard disk recording and random access audio.

Books

Huber, D. Audio Production Techniques for Video. Boston/London: Focal Press, 1991.

Huber, D. The MIDI Manual. Carmel, Indiana: Howard W. Sams & Company, 1990.

Huber, D. Random Access Audio: An Introduction. Menlo Park, California: Digidesign Inc., 1990.

Huber, D. and Robert Runstein. Modern Recording Techniques. 3d ed. Carmel, Indiana: Howard W. Sams & Company, 1989.

Pohlmann, K. Principles of Digital Audio. 2nd ed. Carmel, Indiana: Howard W. Sams & Company, 1991.

Rumsey, F. Tapeless Sound Recording. London, England & Boston: Focal Press, 1990.

Watkinson, J. The Art of Digital Audio. Revised reprint. London, England & Boston: Focal Press, 1989.

Brochures and Manuals

DN-7700r CD Cart Recorder. Preliminary product information. Denon America, Inc., 1992.

"Line Conditioners." Sales brochure. Tripp Lite, 1990.

"Motorola DSP Motorola's 16-, 24-, and 32-Bit Digital Signal Processing Families." Sales brochure. Motorola Inc., 1991.

"Post Pro SD." Brochure. New England Digital Corporation, 1990.

Pro Tools Operations Manual. Digidesign, 1991.

"SampleCell 16-Bit Stereo Sample Playback Card for the Macintosh II." Digidesign brochure. Digidesign, 1991.

"S1100 MIDI Stereo Digital Sampler," Akai professional brochure. Akai, 1990.

"S1100EX 16-Voice Polyphonic Expansion Unit."

Akai professional brochure. Akai, 1991.

Sound Designer II Operations Manual. Digidesign, 1989.

Soundstation II product brochure. Digital Audio Research, 1987.

Video Slave Driver Operations Manual. Digidesign, 1991.

Magazine Articles

Berger, J. "Multimedia." Electronic Musican (November 1991).

Davies, R. "Musical Multitasking." Electronic Musician (April 1990).

Huber, D. "The FCN-1 Format Converter." Electronic Musician (August 1992).

Huber, D. "Micro Technology Unlimited: Review." Electronic Musician (February 1992).

Huber, D . "The Sonic Solution." Studio Sound (April 1990).

Katz, B. "The D-10 Pro Story." Digital Domain 1990.

Huber, D . "Everything You Always Wanted to Know About Jitter but Were Afraid to Ask." The FCN-1 User's Guide, rev III (July 1991).

Metzger, N. and N. Freundlich. "Erasable Optical Disks." Popular Science (May 1987).

Miller, M. "Synchronization Survival Guide." Mix (October 1991).

Mountain, T. "The Integrity of Digital Copying: A Scientific Approach." Mix (October 1991).

Orazio, M. "Some of Digital Audio's Dilemmas." TV Technology (April 1990).

Redmond, N. "MIDI Manager for the Macintosh." Electronic Musician (May 1990).

Rumsey, F. "Digital Audio Synchronization." Studio Sound (March 1991).

Rumsey, F. "Megabytes per Minute." Studio Sound (October 1991).

Rumsey, F . "The Truth About SCMS." Studio Sound (May 1991).

"The SMDI Protocol." Sidebar article. Electronic Musician (May 1992).

Streicher, Ron. "DAT in the Real World Part One." Recording Engineer/Producer (April 1991).

Trubitt, D. (Rudy). "Multimedia Sound." Electronic Musician (May 1990).

Index

M

Macintoshes
  Audio IFF soundfile format, 92, 156
  building random-access audio systems around, 48
  digital video standard, 145
  SND Resource soundfile format, 91
MacProteus card, 145
MADI (Multichannel Audio Digital Interface)
format, 108–109
magnetic disks, 42
magneto-optical disk (MOD), 44–46
mapping
  MIDI, 35
  samplers, 67–68
Mark of the Unicorn products, locking to SMPTE, 119
markers, 77
master control transports, 113
MDT (Multiband Dynamics Tool), 156
memory
  linear-access, 8–10
  random-access (RAM), 8–11, 38
  read-only (ROM), 37–38
  storage
    disk-based, 40–47
    solid-state, 37–38
messages
  All Notes Off, 33
  Channel Pressure (After Touch), 29–30
  Control Change, 30–32
  Frame Advance, 119–120
  full, 119
  Local Control, 33
  MIDI, 25–27
    Channel Mode, 33–34
    channel voice, 28–32
    cueing, 119
    System, 34, 71, 160
  Mono Mode On, 33–34
  MTC quarter-frame, 34
  Note Off, 29
  Note On, 28
  Omni Mode Off, 33
  Omni Mode On, 33
  Pitch Bend Change, 32
  Poly Mode On, 34
  Polyphonic Key Pressure, 29
  Program Change, 30
  quarter-frame, 119
  Reset All Controllers, 33
  Song Position Pointer (SPP), 34
  Song Select, 34
  Tape Position, 119
  Tune Request, 34
Micro Technology Unlimited Microsound
two-channel system, 92–93
MicroSoft Video for Windows, 145
MicroSound two-channel digital recording system, 92–93
Mid-Fi music mode, 150
MIDI (musical instrument digital interface), 25, 52, 55
  automating digital effects, 159–160
  channels, 27–28
  controlling digital effects, 159
  editing digital effects, 160
  filtering, 34–35
  General, 145–146
  in multimedia environments, 145–146
  machine control (MMC) protocol, 156
  mapping, 35
  messages, 25–27

    Channel Mode, 33–34
    channel voice, 28–32
    cueing, 119
    System, 34, 71, 160
  Patch Bay program, 147
  remote controllers, 162
  SDS (sample dump standard), 70, 71
  time code (MTC), 15, 118–119
  triggering drum machines, 63–64
MIDI-based mixing, 160–161
miking, guidelines for, 73
mixers
  computer-based digital, 162–164
  hardware, 160
  MIDI, 160–161
mixing, 160
  digital, 160
  MIDI-based, 160–162
MMC (MIDI machine control) protocol, 156
MOD (magneto-optical disk), 44–46
modes
  CD-audio, 150
  Hi-Fi music, 150
  jog, 78
  Mid-Fi music, 150
  shuttle, 150
  Speech, 150
modular systems, 51
modulation, 23
Mono Mode On messages, 33–34
monophonic sampling devices, 60
Mountain, Dr. Toby, 104
MSB bit, 27
MTC (MIDI-time code) standard, 15
  quarter-frame messages, 34
Multiband Dynamics Tool (MDT), 156
Multichannel Audio Digital Interface (MADI) format,
108–109
multichannel
  digital audio workstations (DAWs), 96
  hard disk recorders, 93–94
    versus multitrack recorders, 93–94, 165
    virtual tracks, 94
multimedia, 16, 139
  business, 140
  education, 139–140
  environment, 48
    desktop digital video, 144–145
    digital audio, 146–149
    graphics, 144
    hardware and software requirements, 143
    MIDI, 145–146
  games, 139
  music production, 140–141
  storing
    in CD-I (Compact Disc-Interactive), 149–150
    in CD-ROM (Compact Disc-Read Only Memory),
148–149
multiplication with DSP (digital signal
processing), 127–128
MultiSound
  card, 145
  Sound Card for Windows Multimedia, 147
multitasking, 91, 141–142
multitimbral instruments, 28
multitrack
  digital audio tape recorders, 156
  recording versus multichannel hard disk
recording, 93–94, 165
  tape in tapeless studios, 156–160